Michael H...

FLORENCE

A HISTORY OF FLORENTINE HOMOSEXUALITY

COVER: PIAZZA DELLA SIGNORIA BY GIUSEPPE ZOCCHI

© 2018

Dante wrote: ''In Florence homosexuality was widespread, so much so the world said 'florenzen', when they referred to sodomy.''

1

Photo of me taken in Paris, my life there related in my autobiography *Michael Hone: His World, His Loves.* My other books include: *Cellini* [a fully-revised 2018 edition], *Caravaggio* [a fully-revised 2018 edition], *Cesare Borgia, Renaissance Murders, TROY, Greek Homosexuality, ARGO, Alcibiades the Schoolboy, RENT BOYS, Buckingham, Homoerotic Art (in full color), Sailors and Homosexuality, The Essence of Being Gay, John (Jack) Nicholson, THE SACRED BAND, German Homosexuality, Gay Genius, SPARTA, Charles XII of Sweden, Mediterranean Homosexual Pleasure, CAPRI, Boarding School Homosexuality, American Homosexual Giants, HUSTLERS* and *Christ has his John, I have my George: The History of British Homosexuality.* I live in the South of France.

DEDICATION

This book is dedicated to Cicero whose wisdom I would like to pass on to the reader: ''The art of life is to deal with problems as they arise, rather than destroy one's spirit by worrying about them too far in advance.''

CONTENTS

PART I

BEGINNINGS

CHAPTER ONE

CHAPTER TWO

CHAPTER THREE

CHAPTER FOUR

PART II

FLORENTINE ARTISTS
[PART ONE]

PART I

BEGINNINGS

CHAPTER ONE

ETRUSCANS AND EARLY FLORENCE

Etruscans settled into Tuscany which was then, as today, the most beautiful part of Italy, sun blessed, its soil rich, its valleys and undulating hills verdant. Etruscan men and women took elaborate care of their bodies, shaven hairless, the men proud to show themselves naked, as did the woman, if not as often. Nights spent in drinking and lascivious discourse ended in intercourse where husbands shared their wives and took advantage of the wives of others, where youths and boys were especially sexually prized, and the resultant children were brought up without the slightest care of who fathered them. Vice did not exist among the Etruscans, just pleasure. Most historians believe the seven kings who founded Rome were of Etruscan origin, settlers who came from the ''north'', perhaps the Balkans, perhaps Asia Minor. Etruscans were noted experts in metalwork, pottery and consummate merchants. Their first settlements were in Tuscany, in the towns of Etruria and Fiesole, both of which have their importance in our story.

The Etruscans went on to rule Rome, which grew into an empire while Florence remained small and unimportant, and even during the life of Julius Caesar it was little more than a Roman stopover, with Roman baths, temples, a theater and a Forum. An aqueduct connected the town to the springs of Monte Morello and the first wells were dug, the water soil-filtered from the nearby Arno River. A colosseum was later added, a model-sized version of Rome's own. With the fall of Rome came increased barbarian invasions, Ostrogoths, Visigoths, Huns, Vandals and Lombards, who gave their name to a neighboring region, Lombardy. The population of the city descended from 10,000 in 100 A.D. to 1,000 in 500 A.D.

Tuscany and Lombardy today, thanks to Google Maps

In 754 Pope Stephen II traveled to Paris where he anointed Pepin the Short, King of the Franks--from whom France took its name--in exchange for his help against the Lombards. The Lombards were obliged to surrender their lands to the pope, lands that became known as the Papal States. In 800 Charlemagne, Pepin's son, was crowned in Rome and the Holy Roman Empire came into existence. By then Christianity, which had been holding on by a thread, had gained enough followers--among them Florentines--to make its hold unbreakable, largely due to its promise of eternal life and its mystical ceremonies that accompanied all the major events of a believer's life, birth, marriage and death. It was a huge consolation to the sick, to those who had lost a loved one, and it promised that sinners, even rapists and murders, would eventually dine with Christ. It was while attending church that Galeazzo Maria Sforza was stabbed to death, as was Lorenzo de' Medici's brother Giuliano, his belief in God so strong that he entered the cathedral without his usual chainmail armor, events covered later.

Florence was a vassal of the Holy Roman Empire. By 1100 it was already recognized as the pearl of Tuscany, and thanks largely to its importance as a trade route, the population increased from 1,000 in the sixth century to 20,000 in the eleventh. The town was enclosed by walls in 1078 and rich and noble families built towers that spotted the horizon, over a hundred in the early 1100s, towers that looked down on the hovels of the poor, towers like the surviving Torre dei Donati.

The Torre dei Donati and an idea of what the ancient skyline of Florence resembled.

The earliest documented proof of the existence of the Ponte Vecchio dated from 996. It was destroyed by fire and floods, today's version completed in 1345. It was joined by the Ponte alla Carraia in 1220, the Ponte alle Grazie in 1227 and the Ponte Santa Trinita in 1252. The city was ruled by an oligarchy of noble families, each with its own army that attacked neighboring towns in an effort to gain primacy. The armies consisted of nobles on horseback, at the head of the people armed with what they could afford, some with pointed sticks, others pitchforks. The feudal nobles were at the boot of the Holy Roman Emperor, but because the emperors rarely sent troops into Italy, the people formed communes that over time assumed power, eventually forcing the nobles to pledge obedience to them, at times at religious ceremonies.

Ponte Vecchio and Ponte Santa Trinita

Just as the towers of earlier times waged war for primacy, so now Florence imposed itself on neighboring towns, any invented pretext serving to give the impression of legitimacy. The power of Florence was mightily increased when Holy Roman Emperor Frederick I entered Italy in 1154 to impose his own weight on the growing power of the communes, attempting to bolster, at the same time, the lessening powers of the nobles, his supporters. He won a victory over Milan but was forced to give way to forces sent against him by Pope Alexander III whom Frederick wished to replace with someone more docile. He ended up kissing the pope's feet and knees. The loss of royal influence boosted the charge of adrenaline in Florentines who obtained the submission of Pisa and Lucca, about which we'll learn more later in the life of Lorenzo de' Medici.

By 1170 the population of Florence reached 30,000 and new protective walls replaced the former ones. But Florentine union, until then ideal, was severely fractured when Frederick's grandson, Frederick II, reentered Italy with the same intention as his grandfather, the imposition of Holy Roman Empire authority. Frederick had even greater reason for imposing his will in that he'd been excommunicated, twice, by Pope Gregory IX, and deposed as emperor by Pope Gregory X. But now Frederick was able to force Florentines to accept one of his bastard sons as Podestà [chief magistrate]. The seismic division of Florentines occurred when the noble segment of Florence, wishing to regain their former powers, backed Frederick. They formed a party known as Ghibellines, the mortal enemies of the popes' supporters, the party of the Guelphs. The word vendetta is Italian, and although the Italians didn't invent the concept of revenge, no other people perfected it as did they. The Ghibellines and the Guelphs donned differing clothing, the easier to recognize and perpetuate Capulet/Montague-style reprisals. Italian girls had always been locked away in Brinks-like protection that boys had always set siege to, none more than the Ghibellines/Guelphs, and any Ghibelline who could insert himself between the legs of a Guelph girl, or any Ghibelline would could do likewise, was a hero paraded through the streets on the shoulders of his comrades, no one as proud as the boy's father, no one a mournful as the boy's mother when his murdered body, splattered in blood and dust, was abandoned on the family doorstep.

While the emperor's son was Podestà of Florence, the imperial-backing Ghibelline showed their power by destroying 36 Florentine Guelph towers, one of which just missed crushing the Baptistery, its fall deflected by the miraculous intervention of John the Baptist, affirmed bystanders. Another miracle of sorts occurred when Frederick II suddenly died and his son fled from Florence. Papal Guelphs returned and the skyline of Florence lost an equal number of Ghibelline towers. The papal Guelphs flexed their muscles by attacking Ghibelline Siena, 70,000 men age 15 and over against a far smaller force, but the Sienese were fighting for their homes, and the fact that they were accompanied by German mercenaries gave them a startling victory, 10,000 Florentines and their allies killed, 20,000 more locked away in Sienese prisons. The Ghibellines then went on to Florence where 90 Guelph towers bit the dust.

The Baptistery

The Ghibellines called for reconciliation among Florentines, rejected by the French pope Clement IV who obliged French King Louis IX to invade Tuscany. Florence was retaken, as was Siena, both now Guelph. The number of Ghibelline towers pulled down is unknown, probably because there were so few left to tumble.

SIENA was ghibelline, therefore enemy of Florence

Dante was a Guelph supporter. In his *Divine Comedy* he has two groups of penitents, those who had been guilty of same-sex lust and those guilty of opposite-sex lust, who met together and, in effect, rubbed noses like the eskimoses, before going on to complete their purification. Startlingly new for the age, he treated both sexualities as equals, and both are sinful only when done in excess, to be compared with something mildly sinful like gluttony.

Dante by Botticelli.

In the late 1200s the population reach 45,000, far more than London. Trade was in augmentation and banking was on the rise, thanks to loans to the kings of France and the popes [who rarely repaid them, but their prestige inspired a multitude of investors], as well as the stability of the money, gold florins, lire, soldi and denari. Tanned goods, wool in exotic colors, grain, oil, livestock, timber and wines were Florentine exports. Boys were educated and could read, write and do sums from age 7, apprenticed at age 13, and should a lad have insufficient enthusiasm, ''beat him like a dog, as if he were your own'', wrote Lapo Mazzei, a quote brought to us by Christopher Hibbert in his *Florence*, 1993. The city had become so solid that it could now allow the return of exiled Ghibellines.

Fires were common in Florence, the wooden hovels burned to the ground and gradually replaced in stone. The chief precaution against conflagrations were sacks put aside to carry away one's valuables, and ropes to lower victims to the ground. Plagues were current, as water supplies were polluted; rubbish thrown into the streets, along with chamber pots emptied from windows; and nearly any spot proved convenient to squat and relieve oneself. Historian Villani claimed that the ''pestilence'' of 1340 took 15,000 lives in Florence alone [killing 450 million worldwide], while in some localities entire towns ceased to exist. Laborers saw huge increases in their wages, but the additional costs depressed the economy. The population nonetheless reached 100,000 in 1338, more boys than girls, but boyhood mishaps, wars, feuds and vendettas between clans and families rapidly put girls in the majority.

The homes of the rich had fresh water from their own wells and a satisfactory drainage system for sinks and latrines. Women had dresses sewn with pearls and jewels, with long trains and wide sleeves, the breasts padded or exposed to a maximum. Men wore ankle-length gowns with hoods, the hoods replaced in the 1500s with caps or hats. Men had swinging money pouches at their waists, and pockets made their first appearance. Youths wore short tunics with hose up to the groin, the groin covered by codpieces.

Short tunics, hose to the groin, codpieces held in place by ribbons.

The ground floor of houses served as shops and storerooms, a floor added to the height as families enlarged. Meals consisted of meat--pork, sheep, goats and calves--some vegetables and sauces, those of the wealthy so rich they produced gout, a major cause of suffering, and even death, especially among the Medici. Only the wealthy could retire behind the stone walls of their palaces to escape the street noise of bartering, hawking, animated conversation and announcements made by town criers.

The streets were crowded with people, shopping, selling and banking, women were carried in litters and men weaved their ways between whores who were obliged to wear gloves and tiny bells in their hair, while in early Athens prostitutes of both sexes went naked so customers could see the exact nature of the merchandise, making deceit improbable (1).

Hats, hose and shoe wear.

CHAPTER TWO

COSIMO DE' MEDICIS

It is alongside Lorenzo de' Medici that we will make our entry into Florentine society, beginning with his grandfather, Cosimo, the greatest of all the Medici.

The bright light of the period, the Florentine Cosimo de' Medici, grandfather of the future Lorenzo *Il Magnifico,* was the star of the Renaissance. The story of Cosimo begins to the north of Florence, in the city-state of Milan, ruled by Duke Filippo Maria Visconti, a hugely ugly and hugely fat recluse who kept to his fortress away from the sight of those--ambassadors, kings, emperors and the like--who might judge his physical hideousness. He had a dream, that of becoming lord over as much of the land surrounding Milan as militarily possible, a dream that led him to attack the Romagne, home of tiny fiefdoms such as Forlì, Imola and Faenza. He also attacked the Florence of Cosimo de' Medici. But before the attack, let's picture this incredible excuse for a human being. He was paranoiac to the extreme, switching bedrooms as many as three times a night to avoid assassination. He murdered his older brother Gian Maria Visconti, a ruler of incredible cruelty who dressed his dogs to devour whomever he sicced them on. When he found his wife lacking in enthusiasm to be covered by his walrus-like blubber, Filippo Maria accused her of having an affair with a young page and had both beheaded. He did have time to father an illegitimate daughter, Bianca.

The attack of Filippo Maria on Florence pushed Cosimo to hire a mercenary, the extraordinary Francesco Sforza. Cosimo wanted Francesco to destroy the power of Milan but Francesco Sforza hesitated before entering the city-state as he had plans to marry Bianca and take over Milan without having to wage war. His plan worked, he married the beauty, but as Filippo Maria had not formally named him as his successor, Milan declared itself a republic on Filippo Maria's death, a mere hiccup for Sforza who garrisoned the town and had himself declared duke. But Sforza's contacts with Cosomo had been so humane and intellectually stimulating that Milan and Florence became friends. Cosimo backed Sforza financially to such an extent that Cosimo's palace became, literally, the Bank of Milan.

After the fall of Rome the lights went out over Europe. New Christians like Charlemagne were proud of their ignorance, declaring that they were above grammar. Charlemagne gave a choice to conquered peoples, either they convert or they would fall to the sword. During just one morning 4,500 were beheaded when they hesitated. In Constantinople the first emperor to convert, Constantine, watched helpless while 3,000 Christians died under the sword of other Christians over the interpretation of the new faith, and during the Fourth Crusade the city itself was sacked and the inhabitants massacred when the crusaders failed to receive the monies the new emperor promised them. People converted easily thanks to the guarantee of an afterlife, but went on with everyday violence in which thousands died in drunken brawls, sexual disputes and sports such as tournaments. Fear of disease and plague, invasion and famine, lightning and floods, dark forests of boars, bears and wolves, all combined to unite families in backward villages, where incest and a limited gene pool assured mental deficiency. Hunched over, afraid of every storm, medieval men lived out their existence is pure anonymity. There were no clocks, not even calendars among them, and even the century in which they lived was both unknown and of no importance. The Great Schism--a pope in Rome and one in Avignon--was unknown to the peasants who passed their days in perpetual toil, seeking out the church at the time of baptisms, marriages and deaths, alongside priests as ignorant as they. Illiterate, pockmarked, gullible, superstitious, for them there were no changes anywhere simply because they were unaware of all. They didn't even have surnames, because none was needed. Only later, when the ancient world was rediscovered, did the individual begin to emerge from the formless masses. Then they would take names in order to distinguish one from the other--the smithy became Smith, the tailor Taylor. Anonymity: nothing is known of the twenty-three generations it took to build the cathedral of Canterbury. But finally names emerged from the mist, those of da Vinci, Michelangelo, Botticelli, all thanks to the rediscovery of the ancient texts, a rediscovery and a rebirth: a Renaissance.

In Florence Cosimo de' Medici helped found humanism with his friend Niccolò Niccoli. Cosimo offered Niccoli the funds necessary to send him far and wide, even to the Holy Land, in search of the ancient manuscripts that would bring the words of the likes of Plato into the very living rooms and libraries of the Medici, hundreds and hundreds of volumes. Each discovery that Cosimo made, each old text he unearthed, was like Howard Carter peering into the tomb of Tutankhamen. Cosimo employed forty-five copyists to spread the liberating concepts of the ancients, assisted by Niccoli who wore a Roman toga to the embarrassment of his entourage. Greek studies became a part of Florentine university instruction and artists like Donatello and Brunelleschi built their art along classical lines.

Cosimo de' Medici

The Renaissance was Florence, and Florence was the Renaissance. Why this should be so is unknown; perhaps the other great sites of the times, Naples and Milan, were too despotic, perhaps Venice too stable; Rome was out of the running because, until the intervention of Julius II [the Warrior Pope), it was Hicksville, dirty, smelly and soiled by papal hangers-on and other such bovines. Traditionally, Florentine merchants vied with each other in their support of the arts. Lorenzo Ghiberti was commissioned to build the doors of the Baptistery of San Giovanni, a task that took twenty years. Philippo Brunelleschi somehow capped the Cathedral of Santa Maria del Fiore with a towering roof--the enigma being how the walls of the cathedral can bear the tons of weight--that is still the city's major landmark. Donatello's art seduced Cosimo--as his body did many a Florentine male--who put up with his every caprice. When a merchant refused a bronze head that Donatello had spent a month producing, arguing that a month's labor wasn't worth so much, Donatello sent it hurling from the heights of a tower where it had been taken to capture the best light, all the while protesting that he was an artist, not some laborer paid monthly wages.

It took the Dark Ages to make sodomy a crime, whereas in ancient Rome male-male sex had been simply an alternative means to pleasure. Amusingly, the exception to the Dark Ages prohibition of same-sex sex didn't apply to *boys* in Italy, boys could literally do anything they wanted with a male friend, which simply fell under the category of ''kids will be kids''. It was sexuality; it was in no way *homo*sexuality.

It was known that Cosimo's grandson, the great *Il Magnifico* himself, had a marked preference for boy buttocks. The preference was illegal but so prevalent that it was rarely prosecuted. But *rarely* prosecuted still meant that thousands of cases were brought before the courts, which shows the prevalence of the phenomena. A man could be castrated for having sex with a boy; boys 14 to 18 had to pay a fine of 100 lire; boys under 14 paid 50 lire. Foreigners could be legally beaten by whoever caught them *in flagrante delicto*, and if found guilty by a tribunal they could be burned at the stake. In reality no one was much bothered unless he raped a young boy or had sex with children. Consensual sex was more or less admitted; it was the coercive variety that was prosecuted.

Every boy wanted to marry a virgin. So boys who tried to seduce girls could find themselves in mortal danger as families were set on protecting their capital, their virgin girls, girls who served to form the alliances so necessary during the Renaissance. A girl deflowered was no longer an asset. To the contrary, she exposed her family to the open ridicule of the nobility. On the other hand it was accepted that boys needed physical release. The least harmful means of such release was between themselves, a measure that was silently but totally acknowledged.

Naturally, boys could pay for sex in whorehouses or on the street, especially around the old market called the Mercato Vecchio. Alleys at night often saw girls lined up against walls while the boys humped them through the drop-fronts of their skin-tight trousers, drop fronts attached by ribbons that could be rapidly untied.

Cosimo the great humanist died, but not before fathering Piero who in turn fathered the great Lorenzo *Il Magnifico*. The image of Cosimo that I love best is reported by an ambassador who, when he visited him, found him in bed between his two sons, Piero and Giovanni, one old man and two others middle-aged, all three suffering from gout. Much has been said about Lorenzo's ugliness, a nose so flattened it deformed his voice and destroyed his sense of smell. Piero sent his wife Lucrezia to Rome to find a wife for their son. The choice fell on Clarice Orsini, beautiful but scoffed at by Lorenzo's friends behind his back as she was not known for her intelligence. The match was a step up for Lorenzo because the Orsini were nobles well entrenched in the church, many of whom had been cardinals, and there had even been one Orsini pope.

Il Magnifico

Piero, too ill to do so himself, had Lorenzo organize a tournament in celebration of his betrothal, a contest between combatants on horses, armed with lances, aimed at unseating each other. It was said to have cost 8,000 florins while Clarice's dowry had been a modest 2,000 in comparison. There were banners and pennants and Lorenzo himself wore a cloak of white silk lined with scarlet and rode a white charger. Italy throughout the ages, as much today as then, is known for its *jeunesse dorée*. Lorenzo had the best education possible, thanks to his grandfather Cosimo who allowed him to participate in the meetings of the Platonic Academy he had founded. His mother was versed in the arts and Lorenzo spent his life collecting the finest manuscripts, paintings, sculptures, coins and jewels--although far fewer than Cosimo. He loved riding and hunting with falcons, giving full voice to dirty songs that amused his comrades as much as himself. He was not drawn to banking but he had the gift of appointing the right men to do the job in his place. He could be a brilliant conversationalist, an ardent churchgoer, and still slum the nights away in taverns and bordellos, ending the evening in the early hours by serenading the virgin sweetheart of one of his friends--after they had all fulfilled the lustful yearnings of their young flesh. He wrote poems, one of which warned of the ephemeral nature of youth, exhorting himself to make the most of what he had--and he had plenty. Again, then as today, Italians have always been among the most sensual people on earth, and who could represent the beauty of the era better than the painter Botticelli whose *Primavera* is among the most gorgeous works of the human hand.

At that time in Florence there existed special letterboxes that citizens used to denounce other citizens. It was in this way that Botticelli, 1445-1510, came to the attention of the authorities. He was accused of ''keeping a boy.'' An investigation took place but as ironclad proof was unavailable the charges were dropped. As he was now well known and visibly had only a few more years to live [six, as it would turn out], the Office of the Night responsible for such cases turned a blind eye. His reputation didn't seem to have suffered as afterwards he was appointed to decide where Michelangelo's *David* would be placed in Florence, housed to protect it from the elements or, as Michelangelo wished, outside in view of all in the splendid Piazza della Signoria. It was decided to put it outside, but the original was later replaced by a copy so that the original could be protected inside.

Botticelli self-portrait from his *Adoration of the Magi.*

The incomparable beauty of Botticelli's art and of Botticelli himself are attested in his *Adoration of the Magi* self-portrait. He later turned towards the cretin Savonarola and burned part of his gorgeous *oeuvre* that he deemed too erotic, to our eternal loss [if in fact he did so, which is doubted by some]. The great Guicciardini in his marvelous *Storie fiorentini* tells us more about Savonarola: ''There were no more games in public, and even at home they were played in an atmosphere of fear. The taverns, which had been the meeting places for all the rowdy youth who enjoy every vice, were all closed up. Sodomy was ended and women abandoned showy and lascivious clothing, and young men resolved to live in a saintly and civilized way. They went to church regularly, wore their hair short and cast stones and cursed dishonest men, card players and women who dressed lewdly. They went to the carnival and collected all the dice, cards, paintings and corrupt books, and burned them publicly in the Piazza della Signoria. Savonarola brought help to men who abandoned pomp and vanities, and restricted themselves to the simplicity of a religious and Christian life.''

Botticelli came into the world as Alessandro di Mariano di Vanni Filipepi, in Florence, but was called Sandro. Botticelli means ''little wine barrels'' and was applied to his flabby brother, although for some reason the name spread to the whole family. As with Verrocchio and many other artists, he too began as an apprentice goldsmith. At age 17 he was admitted into the workshop of Filippo Lippi who taught him perspective and techniques in fresco, as well as the beauty of pale colors in contrast to the brighter palate that Botticelli favored. Under the protection of Lorenzo *Il Magnifico* and Medici patronage in general, he became famous and rich, and has enriched our lives and knowledge by producing paintings of Lorenzo, Giuliano, Cosimo, Piero and Giovanni de' Medici. Then Savonarola entered the stage and a part of Botticelli's works went up in smoke [again, supposedly, as the art historian Vasari doesn't say a word about the bonfire], followed by Savonarola himself, burned at the stake.

Botticelli's *Primavera.*

Incredibly, he went into an artistic eclipse due to the eminence of Michelangelo, da Vinci and Raphael, but reason won out and today he is firmly in the firmament of Renaissance geniuses. He did little painting after Savonarola's bonfire of the vanities, most of which were on the lines of ascetic religious themes. It's true that the bonfire occurred in 1497 and his great triumphs years earlier, *Primavera* in 1482 and the *Birth of Venus* in 1486. At his death he was poor and unaccompanied to his final resting place.

Detail from Botticelli's *Mary with Child and Angels.*

Francesco Sforza died, leaving Milan to his son Galeazzo Maria Sforza. Galeazzo Maria Sforza was a psychopath who didn't hesitate to tear off a man's limbs with his own hands or rape a woman, noble or not. His sexual appetite was hard to appease but once his lust fulfilled, the woman was handed to his entourage for their needs. He detested poachers, strangling one to death on a rabbit pushed down his throat and another was nailed inside a coffin and then buried alive. A priest who predicted Galeazzo would have a short life was starved to death. Galeazzo was finally brought down by three conspirators, one of whom was a very young man named Girolamo Olgiati who, thanks to Galeazzo's library to which the duke gave him access, was able to read the lives of Brutus and Cassius and how they tried to bring republicanism back to Rome through the assassination of Caesar [a perfect example of how the ancient texts formed the Renaissance mind]. That was his ideal for Milan. A second conspirator, known only as Lampugnano, had obscure motives concerning land deals. The third conspirator was Carlo Visconti whose sister had been dishonored by the duke, a motive of importance today but at the time everyone was throwing his daughter or wife at Galeazzo in the hope of gaining profit. They met in church. Who struck first is in question, but the version I prefer has Visconti [the boy whose sister was raped] on his knees as if requesting a favor as the duke walked down the nave. When Galeazzo paused to listen to him, Visconti plunged his dagger into the duke's genitals. The other men followed suit. Galeazzo, at age 32, was dead before he hit the marble flooring. The three assassins, certain of public support, did not bother to hide. Instead of thanking them, the citizens of Milan killed Lampugnano instantly and then dragged his body through the streets; the other two were caught later by Galeazzo's guard and their genitals were cut off and stuffed into their mouths before they were disemboweled, decapitated and quartered [the limbs torn from the body by a horse attached to each]. As he was dying one of the three is reported to have shouted out, ''Death is perhaps terrible, but honor and glory are eternal!'' Which may be true as I'm retelling the story *500 years* after the event.

CHAPTER THREE

THE PAZZI PLOT TO KILL *IL MAGNIFICO*
1478

Pope Sixtus IV had met the twenty-year-old Lorenzo de' Medici and had found Lorenzo to be a darling boy, the reason he asked Lorenzo, as the head of the Medici banking system, for a loan of 40,000 florins in order to buy Imola. Sixtus wanted Imola as a gift to his son Girolamo Riario, whom the pope passed off as one of his numerous nephews. Because the pope already owed 10,000 florins to the Medici bank, Lorenzo hesitated, a hesitation that would cost him dearly. The pope, apoplectic, turned to the Pazzi, bankers who immediately agreed. The Pazzi were an old family with money that went way back. The manager of the Rome branch of the Pazzi bank, Francesco de' Pazzi, hated Lorenzo whom he found arrogant and far too rich for a parvenu. He hatched a plan to assassinate both Lorenzo and his brother Giuliano. For this he turned to Girolamo Riario, now lord of Imola, and Francesco Salviati, an enemy of the Medici, whom Lorenzo had forbidden to cross Florentine territory. Salviati wanted to get to Pisa where Sixtus had named him archbishop and Lorenzo's refusal to let him pass deprived him of huge sums of money. The conspirators went to get Sixtus' permission ''to take care of Lorenzo'' which the pope gave, although piously adding that he wanted no bloodshed. The conspirators then went to see Jacopo de' Pazzi, the head of the clan, who refused his consent until he was told that the pope himself had blessed the endeavor.

Sixtus IV by Botticelli

On the day of the planned murders, Easter Sunday, Francesco de' Pazzi went to the Medici palace in search of

Giuliano who said he wouldn't be going to church because he felt ill. Giuliano was an exception among the Medici for several reasons. Although older than Lorenzo, he was never offered a position of real power by his brother. He was far handsomer than the younger Lorenzo and liked to think of himself as a woman killer, which made his entourage laugh because he lacked his brother's charm, meaning that his bed was often empty whereas Lorenzo's never lacked for company. In addition, the youths laughed behind his back because when he did find someone, far from being the heartless enslaver of women's hearts he said he was, he would fall head over heels in love, love that invariably ended with *his* heart broken. Francesco de' Pazzi was accompanied to Lorenzo's palace to fetch Giuliano by Bernardo Baroncelli, a banker and friend of both Francesco and the Medici. They persuaded Giuliano to go to church, giving him a friendly manly hug when he consented--in order to find out if he was wearing armor under his cloak.

In the cathedral Giuliano was separated from Lorenzo by a few yards. Sometime during the High Mass, thanks to a predecided signal, Baroncelli struck Giuliano with his dagger that pierced his brain. Francesco followed with more blows, twenty all together, instantly killing Giuliano. Nearby two priests attached Lorenzo, one of whom nicked his neck with a dagger, but Lorenzo whipped off his cloak and held it up as protection, his sword already in his hand. As friends came to Lorenzo's aid, the attackers fled. One friend risked his life by sucking the blood oozing from Lorenzo's wound, afraid the dagger had been poisoned. Lorenzo ran to his palace, perhaps believing that his brother, whom he had not seen fall, had already returned there.

Giuliano de' Medici

    The second act of the drama took place at the Palazzo della Signoria, the Florentine Town Hall, a wonderful crenellated tower that overlooks the Piazza della Signoria and the God-inspired statue of Michelangelo's *David*. Here Salviati, the man Lorenzo had forbidden to cross Florentine land so that he could take up his position as archbishop of Pisa, led a pack of thirty mercenaries. Due to the archbishop's renown, he was allowed to enter the Palazzo della Signoria but due to his incredible nervousness the guards felt that something was terribly amiss. The archbishop was separated from his men who were invited into a nearby chamber that one the guards immediately locked. Government officials sounded the alarm, bells that tolled in emergencies, the ringing of which automatically set in motion the ringing of other bells in other churches surrounding Florence, until the entire countryside knew that something was wrong and, in response, sent armed men to the Piazza della Signoria. The moment the guards at the Palazzo found out what had happened, they killed the thirty followers of Salviati, throwing them from the windows of the crenellated tower. Francesco was found at his palace, badly wounded by a knife blow he had inflicted on himself while stabbing Giuliano. He was taken naked to the Palazzo and hung by the neck from an upper window. Archbishop Salviati himself was flung from the same window, in full vestments. Eerily, he sank his teeth into Francesco, perhaps in revenge for getting him into such a mess, perhaps to ease the noose around his neck, perhaps due to an involuntary convulsion.

Palazzo della Signoria

The fifty-seven-year-old Jacopo ran for his life into the country where he was recognized by peasants, arrested, sent to a dungeon and tortured. He was then taken to the Palazzo della Signoria from whose tower he too was hurled, dressed only in his drawers. His body was cut down and pulled through the streets of Florence by boys beating it with sticks before being nailed to the door of his palace against which they banged his head, yelling out ''Open up, the master is back!'' Other deaths followed, more than a hundred in all as plotters and believed plotters were hounded down.

Da Vinci drawing of Bernardo Baroncelli

Sixtus, sick with rage that an archbishop had been hung by the neck in his ceremonial robes, excommunicated all of Florence when the citizens refused to turn over Lorenzo to a papal court. The pope declared war on the city-state and turned to Lorenzo's dear friend, King Ferrante of Naples, for troops which the king provided. The pope named Montefeltro, Duke of Urbino, to head the forces. Now old, the duke proved far less valorous than in times gone by. In the meantime, excommunication had put Florence in the position of a leper, cold-shouldered by its neighbors. Bands of armed youths descended on the city, robbing and raping and depriving it of food. Last rites couldn't be given and the dead couldn't be buried. Lorenzo, seeing that something extraordinary had to be done, took a ship from Pisa to Naples to appeal directly to Ferrante, a courageous move as Ferrante was a psychopath as liable to cut off his head as to kiss him. Before leaving Florence Lorenzo had mortgaged his castles and palaces to raise money, money he now spent like water on making gifts to the Neapolitans, on lavish festivals and on charities. It's said, though, that although he laughed at the side of Ferrante during the day, he was in despair at night. Finally Ferrante, faced with French desires to conquer Naples on the one hand and, on the other hand, confronted with Turkish ships that were approaching, freed the young man. Also thanks to the Turks, Sixtus decided that he needed Florence at his side in his attempt to mount a crusade against them. He lifted the excommunication.

Lorenzo *Il Magnifico*

CHAPTER FOUR

FERRANTE
LORENZO *IL MAGNIFICO* DE' MEDICI
THE ORGINS OF POPE ALEXANDER VI

The study of the fascinating life of Ferrante King of Naples affords us the occasion to glimpse into the behind-the-scenes of Renaissance murderers and sociopaths, as well as covering his family history and, along the way, the origins of the worst-of-the-worst, the Borgia.

The Medici revenge against the Pazzi and others who had tried to assassinate Lorenzo de' Medici was so severe--especially Cardinal Salviati being hung from the window of the Palazzo della Signoria--that all of Florence was excommunicated. The pope then requested that Ferrante of Naples attack Florence. Lorenzo's father Piero had already attempted to shore up his relations with King Ferrante by sending Lorenza, superb from the heights of his seventeen years. Lorenzo did more than anticipated, charming the king out of his socks with his youthful candor, intelligence, sparkle and spunk.

So Lorenzo returned to Naples to persuade Ferrante that he had more to gain by his remaining friends with Florence. Certainly Ferrante had him visit his famous museum where he placed the dried cadavers of his enemies, pickled in herbs and dressed in what they wore when alive. When Ferrante suspected someone of plotting against him, he took him to visit his museum as a deterrent. Before their demise Ferrante locked his prisoners in cages and let them go insane before starving them to death.

Ferrante, Ferdinand I, King of Naples

The story of Ferrante is the story of three charismas, Lorenzo's as we've seen, capable of charming the birds from the trees, that of Ferrante's father Alfonso, and that of the first Borgia of importance, Alonso.

Alonso Borgia's ancestors had been Spanish condottieri who had chased Muslims from Valencia, taking over a good part of their lands for themselves. Entering the university at age fourteen, Alonso left with two doctorates in law. Due to his expertise in canon law, he was chosen as a member of a council set up to bring an end to the Great Schism which had seen popes in both Rome and in Avignon. Rome had two families of great and competing importance, the Orsini and the Colonna, and it was a Colonna who became Pope Martin V, although there had been a holdout, an insignificant Spaniard who was proclaimed, by the vote of three cardinals, Clement VIII. Alfonso V of Aragon was the only person to recognize him.

In 1417 King Alfonso V of Aragon, a kingdom that had absorbed Alonso's birthplace of Valencia, invited Alonso to meet with him. Alfonso was just 21 and King of Sicily, Corsica and Sardinia as well as Aragon. His sights were now set on conquering Naples ever since Queen Joanna, of disputed sanity, invited him to protect the city that was under the threat of French siege. As an enticement she decreed that he would succeed her.

At the time Naples was a kingdom that included the whole of the south of Italy. It was a world power. It would bring Alfonso wealth and perhaps be the first building block in Alfonso's domination over the entire peninsula, from Milan to Calabria. Naples was by far the largest city, with over 100,000 people, compared to Rome's 35,000, and its origin went all the way back to the Greeks who founded Neopolis. Some Neapolitans felt they were lucky to have been chosen as the capital of the empire Alfonso envisioned, but most had seen so any dukes, lords, kings and tyrants over the centuries that they were totally indifferent now.

Alfonso had heard of Alonso Borgia and liked him enough during their first interview to make him his secretary, with the assignment of getting Martin V's accord to his intervention in Naples. As Naples was considered to be under the jurisdiction of the church, as were the Papal States, the pope's assent was vital. Alfonso believed that Martin, tired of the feuds engendered by the Great Schism, feuds during which Spain had played a key role, would welcome him with open arms. In addition, Martin, a Colonna, was having problems as usual with the Orsini, and Alfonso felt Martin would be happy to have the virile Alfonso's backing.

The opposite occurred. Convinced by the power of France, Martin threw his support behind them. Two years of war followed, during which the French, having killed Alfonso's brother Pedro in battle, blew his body through a cannon into the Aragon lines. In retaliation Alfonso went to Marseille and burned the city to the ground. Tired of all the fuss, Joanna went over to her former enemies and declared France her legal heir. In point of fact, Joanna was a crazy nymphomaniac who offered her kingdom to any male willing to impregnate her.

Alfonso and Alonso Borgia, both highly intelligent, realized that the only solution to the problem would be through very fine negotiations. Alonso was assigned to contact Martin and together they worked out a compromise. King Alfonso would drop the Spanish Clement VIII and accept Martin as the one and only legitimate pope, and Martin would recognize King Alfonso's right to Naples. Clement VIII was offered the bishopric of Palma Mallorca. In thanks for his good offices, Alonso Borgia was given the bishopric of his native Valencia, an extremely rich diocese he accepted after first taking the necessary steps to become a priest.

Eventually his grandson Cesare Borgia would become Duke of Valencia.

The war for Naples continued between Aragon and France with Alfonso himself falling into the hands of Filippo Maria Visconti [more concerning Filippo Maria Visconti later]. Visconti was a condottiere fighting for the French and should normally have turned Alfonso over to them, but like Lorenzo, Alfonso was so charming that he ended up fascinating the sadistic tyrant, persuading him that it would be better for Milan to have the less powerful Alfonso in Naples rather than the powerful French. Alfonso was freed just when Martin died. Eugenius, the pope who replaced Martin, had discussions with Alonso Borgia whom he made a cardinal and recognized Alfonso's right to Naples. The pope also legitimized King Alfonso's bastard son Ferrante, a fairy book ending.

Eugenius was replaced by Pope Nicolas, an intelligent, honest, good man who at 49 could have been, in age, Alonso Borgia's son. He confirmed the legitimization of Ferrante. Yet he too died and was replaced--due to infighting between the Orsini and the Colonna--by the last man on earth a bookie would have put his money on, the benign Alonso Borgia himself [called Alonso de Borja at the time], now Pope Calixtus III, age 76.

Calixtus surprised everyone by ordering a crusade against the Turks, but found little following. There had been half a dozen crusades already, all of which, except the first one, had ended in disaster. A cardinal known as Scarampo was named to head the fleet the pope built with the church's money, but ships promised by Alfonso never materialized, turning Calixtus irredeemably against the man who had made him. He refused to allow King Alfonso to divorce his wife of 40 years and he refused, much more importantly for Alfonso, to ratify the bulls legitimatizing Ferrante. As I wrote concerning Lorenzo, when he went to Naples he didn't know if Ferrante would kill him or behead him. This was because Ferrante was a sociopath, the kind only amused by the cruelest butchery. This Calixtus knew because Calixtus had been appointed Ferrante's tutor by the man he now hated, Alfonso of Aragon, Sicily, Sardinia, Corsica and Naples. But Calixtus also refused to legitimize Ferrante because he was a bastard, and a bastard son would not be allowed to reign by the moralistic Spanish, something the Italians accepted without question.

Calixtus also found help against King Alfonso in strange places. He was aided by an indomitable warrior called Skanderbeg of Albania, so invincible against the Turks that he won Venice's favor, until he became so powerful that Venice feared the dominance of Albania over Venice and offered a reward for his head. Incredibly, Skanderbeg had been kidnapped by the Turks as a child and had worked his way up through the janissaries until switching sides. Calixtus was also helped by a character rich in color, known to us today as Dracula.

Vlad the Impaler was known by his father's name, Dracul, meaning son of the dragon. His father ruled Wallachia. He was a warrior who dedicated himself to the protection of Christians against the hordes of Ottomans of whom he is credited with impaling tens of thousands. As a boy he spoke Romanian and learned Greek, German and Latin, combat skills as well as geography, mathematics and science. Vlad and a younger brother, Radu the Handsome, were sent by their father to the Ottomans as hostages and there Radu converted to Islam. The Ottomans taught the boys warfare and horsemanship. Vlad's father was overthrown and Vlad's older brother, who should have succeeded his father, was blinded and buried alive. When Vlad eventually came to power in Wallachia he strove to increase both the defenses of the country and his own political power. He had the nobles he held responsible for his father and brother's murders impaled. When Turks arrived to reclaim tribute from Wallachia he requested that they remove their turbans in respect for his person. When they refused, he had the turbans nailed to their heads, killing them all. The Turks sent an army that Vlad defeated; the soldiers were impaled with the highest stake reserved for their general. The pope and the Venetians--whose trade had been disrupted by the Turks--were wild with joy at the news. But Radu the Handsome, who had converted to Islam, came at the head of janissary battalions to destroy his Christian brother, promising that the nobles in Wallachia who had lost their positions because of Vlad would recuperate their entire wealth. By then Vlad's reputation for evil had spread through Germany and Russia. How much is true will never be known. He was said to have had children roasted and then fed to their mothers, and to have had the breasts of women cut off and forcibly fed to their husbands, before impaling them all. Radu's army refused to cross the Danube when, in horror, they came across thousands of rotting corpses, all impaled.

Dracula

Calixtus, so physically weak he ruled from his bed, followed up his wars with the Turks with his decision to take back the Papal States from the lords, dukes, princes and powerful families, like the Colonna and the Orsini, that ruled the countless entities comprising the Papal States, entities that nonetheless belonged to the church situated in Rome. The States were necessary for the glory of the papacy, but also due to their importance: fertile flatlands crossed by a vital road link between Florence and the Adriatic, the Via Emilia.

For this Calixtus needed men he could count on. As there were none, he turned to boys, namely his sister's sons. One was Pier Luigi Borgia, the other was Rodrigo Borgia, Rodrigo who, when elected pope, the future Alexander VI, would continue the fight to subdue the Papal States with a boy of his own, his son Cesare, Alexander VI who would soon become, along with his successor Julius II, the most powerful popes in the history of Italian Christendom.

For the moment Calixtus made sure the boys were educated, Rodrigo earning even a doctorate in law. Pier Luigi was named head of the troops headquartered in the Castel Sant'Angelo. Rodrigo was made a cardinal and then Calixtus' own personal aid, known as the vice-chancellor--the most important man in Rome, after the pope--at the unheard-of age of 26. He was also made captain-general over all papal troops--in effect Calixtus' minister of war--a position that put his brother Pier Luigi under him. This was accepted by the Colonna and the Orsini because it was through nepotism that they themselves had gained power and prodigious wealth. Pier Luigi was then made prefect of Rome, a post held by the Orsini for generations. Pier Luigi ventured out from Rome to take back the tiny city-states in the environs, ruled by the Orsini, whose hatred for the pope and his nephew were now beyond limits.

The Orsini had ruled over Rome and its surroundings like cave-age thugs for a century. Armed, they took what they wanted when they wanted it, killing whomever they pleased, having their way with any girl that caught their fancy.

The Colonna were thrilled, naturally, and informed Pier Luigi that he could have a Colonna bride whenever he wished. Rodrigo performed his duties brilliantly, the reason he was so easily accepted by the other cardinals. Rodrigo was also awarded the bishopric of Valencia which greatly increased his income.

Then King Alfonso died, a man of great intelligence, a ruler of vision. When Calixtus heard of Alfonso's passing he shouted out, ''At last free!'' As Ferrante hadn't been legitimized, Calixtus simply issued a bull bringing Naples back into the Holy See.

Then two things happened. First, Ferrante moved his army to Naples' borders in preparation for an attack by papal troops, and, second, a murderer entered the scene: the summer months of July and August when the heat provokes fevers that have carried off nearly every pope unable to escape to mountain retreats. With Calixtus too ill to move to the mountains, certain to die, the Orsini took to the streets crying vengeance against all Spaniards, many of whom were killed. Pier Luigi was snuck out of the city under disguise and Rodrigo, bravely, remained next to Calixtus until he rendered his last breath. Rodrigo would be courageous throughout his entire life, no matter the later heinous acts he would be accused off, a fearlessness his son Cesare inherited in its entirety.

The conclave to choose the next pope was set in motion. The Vatican was walled off. The clear winner was thought to be Cardinal d'Estouteville of France, cousin to the King of France and immensely wealthy. On the first vote he received only his own ballot, proof of the maxim: He who enters the conclave pope, leaves a cardinal.

What took place next was pure drama, knowledge of which has come down to us in a document written by the cardinal of Siena, the only time in the history of the church that the contents of a conclave have been divulged. We're told that d'Estouteville offered a part of his fortune to all the cardinals, telling them that the first vote was a fluke, and that he was now but one ballot short of winning. In the secrecy of the latrines, the only private place to talk, he promised something to everyone, promising Rodrigo that he would continue as vice-chancellor. The cardinal of Siena tells us that he [the cardinal of Siena] was so offended by d'Estouteville's latrine shit that he mounted a counter-offensive. He met with Rodrigo, calling him a ''boy'' and a ''fool'' for believing d'Estouteville, assuring him that not only would a Frenchman be the next vice-chancellor, but also that the papacy would be moved back to French Avignon.

In the election the next day the cardinal of Siena was three votes short of winning. The cardinals decided to meet together in silence until one or several broke it by publically changing his secret vote for oral support. The first to do so was Rodrigo himself, who declared for the cardinal of Siena. This was followed by another cardinal. Colonna, seeing that the cardinal of Siena was certain to win and wanting to caste the critical vote that would swing the election and assure Colonna of the new pope's gratitude, rose to do the same. He was halted by d'Estouteville who tried to drag him out of the room. Colonna nonetheless had time to shout out ''I accede to Piccolomini,'' making the cardinal of Siena the new pope, Pius II.

As G.J. Meyer, in his wonderful *The Borgia*, informs us that Rodrigo had admitted to Pius II that he was going to vote for d'Estouteville for reasons entirely of self-interest. Such candor, says Meyer, ''will be characteristic of Rodrigo over the next forty-five years, helping to explain his almost uncanny ability to win the affection of almost anyone who came within his reach.'' Pius reaffirmed Rodrigo in his function as vice-chancellor, took a fatherly interest in the boy, finding in the already fat Rodrigo someone totally open to Pius' teaching.

Pius was one of 18 children, dirt poor, who studied law. His friends reportedly broke up with laughter when he announced that he was to become a monk because his joy in the delights of the flesh had already made him the father of several bastards. He walked with a limp caused by a pilgrimage to a shrine of the Virgin, over ice and through snow.

Pier Luigi was convinced to return to Spain for his own safety and Pius named a Colonna as prefect of Rome, his reward for the Colonna vote. A Pius nephew took over Rodrigo's role as head of the papal army. Readers of Robert Caro's monumental life of *LBJ* will recognize a trait Rodrigo and Johnson had in common: both took every position they fought tooth and nail to acquire not only with fanatical seriousness, but developed it into something colossal, milking it for all it was worth. Johnson worked tirelessly to become president, Rodrigo did the same to become pope. Michelangelo had said of himself, ''I work harder than any man who has ever lived,'' and it was true, a truth that could have been equally applied to Rodrigo Borgia.

Because of continued problems with the Turks, Pius evacuated the problem in Naples by declaring Ferrante its new ruler. He then tried to mount a crusade against the Turks but failed when France, whose claim over Naples had been disregarded by Pius, and Venice who sought peace with the Turks through negotiation, refused to take part. In world history no enterprise suffered more defeats and ended up killing more people--and was a bottomless pit for more money--than the crusades. Christians against Moslems; Christians against Christians, which led even to the sacking of Constantinople by Christians; inhumanity the likes of which have rarely been seen on the face of the earth; acts of horror that have blackened the reputations of kings, like Richard Coeur de Lion, and blackened

Christianity itself. Calixtus had failed; and now Pius II would fail too. He would make it to Ancona where he planned to see the crusade he financed set off, only to die, of fever, perhaps bubonic. Rodrigo would be stricken too but would survive.

But for the moment Pius had left Rome to take the waters in Tuscany, from where he wrote an extraordinary letter to Rodrigo who was back in Siena, stating that Rodrigo had become the laughing stock of Italy owing to his participation in orgies, an example of the pot calling the kettle black, given Pius' own lust and his own sowing of oats when he was Rodrigo's age.

Rodrigo played next to no part of the conclave of 1464 because he was suffering from the aftermath of the Alcona plague. Cardinal Pietro Barbo of Venice was elected, taking the name of Paul II, although originally he had chosen Pope Formosus, meaning beautiful, but had been talked out of it. Son of Eugenius IV through an incestuous coupling with his sister, passed off as Eugenius' nephew, he was made a cardinal at age 23. Meyer says he was ''tall and handsome … lived simply and kept himself free of scandal.'' Most other sources maintain that he spent his life in the company of male prostitutes, that he himself, when pope, organized a carnival that was a nonstop orgy, and that he suffered a heart attack at age 54 while being butt-fucked by his lover, said some, by a favored page claimed others.

Paul II kept Rodrigo as vice-chancellor, as did his successor Sixtus IV. Sixtus was the son of a poor fisherman whose title to glory was built on undreamed of nepotism, bringing to Rome a family of fishmongers and appointing, over the papal troops, a boy who had literally been selling apples on the streets of Liguria when he learned of his uncle's election. Scurrying to Rome the boy quickly rose through the ranks, humping prepubescent girls and marrying into the Sforza of Milan, forcing the hymen of his Sforza bride, Caterina, age 11, with the full consent of Caterina's father whom she adored and who *knew* what was awaiting her. In point of fact, Sixtus' family was an early version of Ettore Scola's *The Down and Dirty [Brutti, sporchi et cattivi]*. Sixtus' only success, as far as his family was concerned, was his raising his nephew, the handsome Giuliano della Rovere, to the dignity of cardinal, at age

18, the future Julius II, arguably the church's most powerful pope ever [Alexander VI weighing in a close second].

Sixtus doted on his family because the family, detecting his intellectual gifts, had pooled their resources to assure the dirt-poor Sixtus' education. Sixtus loved one nephew so much that he was believed to have been both Sixtus' son and his lover, as Sixtus adored boys, one of the reasons for bringing his nephews to Rome. They were louts, yes, but beautiful louts. His son-cum-lover was Pietro Riario. Sixtus turned over bishoprics to the young sire, making him fabulously rich although not enough to cover the boy's debauches, his horse racing, his deprivation. Pietro was a Renaissance man in that he gave himself to both men and women. He was on the most intimate terms with the murderous Galeazzo Maria Sforza of Milan, both eating from the same plate and sleeping in the same bed. The untoward career of the young Pietro ended at age 28--some say due to a fever, others due to indigestion because the boy adored huge banquets, and still others the usual poison--to the incommensurable chagrin of his father/lover Sixtus. Because the pope only trusted his family, the young Pietro was replaced by Girolamo, the lummox who ruptured his wife's hymen at age 11, and named him head of the papal troops. It was the miscreant Girolamo who had had the bright idea of killing Lorenzo de' Medici, the failure of which had seen Sixtus' handsome nephew and new cardinal, Raffaele Riario, at age 26, taken prisoner.

Sixtus did, however, improve Rome by widening the streets and encouraging the construction of new palaces, and by bringing in artists and founding the Sistine Chapel Choir, filling it with beautiful lads.

After this brief excursion into the origins of Rodrigo, the future Alexander VI, we will go back to Lorenzo *Il Magnifico,* who is entering Naples to confront Ferrante, the man who could as easily behead him as kiss him.

In Naples things miraculously worked themselves out in Lorenzo's favor. Ferrante, faced with French desires to take Naples on the one hand and, on the other hand, confronted with Turkish ships that were approaching--as well as being in need of

Medici banking--freed the young man. Also thanks to the Turks, Sixtus decided that he needed Florence at his side in his attempt to mount a crusade against the Muslims. He lifted the excommunication.

Lorenzo allowed the dissident monk, Savonarola, to preach in Florence where he predicted the imminent death of Ferrante of Naples and Lorenzo himself. Lorenzo died in 1492 and Ferrante in 1494. Ferrante had reigned for 36 years and despite being a merciless and treacherous sadist, he died at age 71, perhaps receiving his just deserts in Hell. The cause of death, according to an autopsy in 2006, was colorectal cancer; he had also suffered from a double infestation of two different species of lice, in his head and pubic hair.

PART II

FLORENTINE ARTISTS

[PART ONE]

CHAPTER FIVE

CELLINI AND MICHELANGELO

After the death of Lorenzo *Il Magnifico* de' Medici his son, Piero II, took his place. Weak and incompetent, he and the rest of the Medici were expulsed from Florence. Later, Pope Clement VII, a Medici, was able to impose his bastard son, Alessandro de' Medici over Florence, Alessandro who was followed, after his assassination, by a Medici of distant ancestry, Cosimo I de' Medici.

Cosimo I de' Medici had historian and artist Giorgio Vasari build him a corridor that connected the duke's offices, called the Uffizi, and ran from the Palazzo Vecchio to the Palazzo Pitti, spanning the Ponte Vecchio, the entire length filled with portraits.

The Uffizi eventually became the museum it is today, one on a par with the Louvre and the Vatican Museum.

The Vasari Corridor and the Uffizi Museum, the Palazzo Vecchio in the background.

Vasari was an intimate friend of Cellini and had not only studied under Michelangelo, it was Vasari who designed Michelangelo's tomb. It's because of Cellini's role in the lives of the two men who followed Lorenzo *Il Magnifico*--Alessandro de' Medici and Cosimo I de' Medici--that we will begin with his amazing life and wondrous works.

Alessandro was the first Duke of Florence, Cosimo I the second Duke of Florence, from 1537 to 1569, after which his title was enlarged to Grand Duke of Tuscany. His father was the illustrious condottiere Giovanni dalle Bande Nere, his grandmother the equally illustrious Caterina Sforza de' Medici (16). Cosimo's enemies joined with France to overthrow him, but were defeated and beheaded by the strong-willed duke. Cosimo then joined forces with the Holy Roman Emperor Charles V, whose backing permitted the Medici to remain in power until the death of the last of the Medici, Gian Gastone de' Medici in 1737. Cosimo eventually allowed his son Francesco I to take his place, while Cosimo retired to his villa outside of Florence.

A view of Tuscany, Italy's Paradise.

CELLINI
1500 - 1571

Perseus detail

Giovanni, Cellini's father, was Cellini's first great love, and no son was more adored by his dad than was Benvenuto. He loved the man and the man loved his boy with every fiber of their souls. This was Cellini's first great luck in life. When Cellini went off, they both had tears in their eyes. When he returned, they both wept with joy. In [nearly] the same way, Cellini loved his lovers, boys and men to whom he was fiercely loyal. When Cellini returned to Florence from his first adventures, he came across a former friend who greeted him with kisses and an open bed, and when Cellini went off again, the boy plucked a few nascent whiskers from Cellini's chin to keep in memory.

The second lucky break was being born in Florence. The Florence of that epoch was the most beautiful city in the world, 30,000 Florentines massed between walls that surrounded the town, a space so narrow it could be walked across in an hour. Divided in half by the Arno, where ruddy-cheeked lads swam naked in its refreshing waters, Florence was the birthplace of the Renaissance and home to the hallowed sextet, da Vinci, Michelangelo, Raphael, Botticelli, Donatello and Ghiberti. Nothing surpassed the beauty of the Piazza della Signoria, nor the splendor of the immensely imposing and beautiful Palazzo Vecchio, as well as the Duomo with Brunelleschi's dome, the Baptistery with its Gates of Paradise and the Ponte Vecchio Bridge, spanned by jewelry shops that would one day sell, at prices only the wealthiest could afford, Cellini creations.

At around age two--younger even than a later prodigy, Mozart--Giovanni put his boy to practicing the flute, the rigor of which Cellini hated, but nonetheless became highly proficient at playing, a proficiency that would serve him well when at the end of a long workday of sculpting or jewelry making he would take out his flute, to the wonder of those around him, many who knew nothing of his hidden talents, and enrapture them as the Pied Piper, leading any who might have been hesitant into his welcoming bed.

Cellini's father wanted him to become a musician because all of the great courts of Italy employed them all year round, from festivals to nightly entertainment during dinners. To become a musician was to have assured employment. But when it became clear to Giovanni that his son would never give in, he allowed the boy to join the workshop of Michelangelo Brandini, but took him away after a few months. Cellini may have been removed due to the reputation of artists' workshops, where sex between the master, the apprentices and the models was daily routine. These kinds of relationships were totally par for the course, accepted by parents and society as being the only way boys could learn about life, as girls were shut away. Some workshops, however, gained reputations as nothing more than whorehouses where one could go for sex as one could at any tavern that had rooms.

Florentine sexuality seemed ideal. Men like Cellini passed from boys to girls and back with disconcerting regularity. Today we're used to a world divided sexually, where there are straights, gays and those who are bi. In Greece women served to keep the home and to produce, basically, sons. In Rome women were far better educated but were still homebodies, and homosexual encounters were frequent if somewhat smirked at. A Roman woman, unlike Greek women, could really be a helpmate and sincerely loved. In Florence, as we'll see again and again, men--all men--were intimate with boys and other men, despite laws to the contrary. Cellini usually took his girls from behind, certainly to avoid pregnancies, perhaps for the increased pleasure of a tighter sheath. Cellini ranted about his boys, covering them with every kind of complement and the most sublime of adjectives: beautiful. He never complimented girls, although about a certain Angelica he did say, in his autobiography, ''I enjoyed such pleasure as I never had before or since.''

At age 15 Cellini gained the right to enter the workshop of Antonio di Sandro di Paolo Giamberti, known simply as Marcone. He learned to draw, to work gold, silver and jewelry. As his father paid for his instruction, he was not obliged to perform menial tasks like sweeping the workshop, marketing, preparing food, cleaning the latrines and the hundred other chores involved in the daily care of boys. Cellini tells us he liked the trade so much that soon he had caught up with even the very best of Marcone's craftsmen. But his father was not forgotten. Cellini would return home to play the flute, rejoicing in his father's tears, fulfilling his filial duty ''to give my father contentment.''

By the age of 16 Cellini knew how to protect himself with sword and dagger, as did his younger brother Giovanfrancesco, called Cecchino. ''At that time I had a brother, younger by two years, a youth of extreme boldness and temper.'' In Florence a fight could begin if a boy looked at another a nanosecond too long. For some unknown reason, Cecchino got into a brawl at age 14 and Cellini came to his aid. Several boys were hurt and because boys 13 and over were considered adults, they could have been severely punished. In the Cellini boys' case, they got off easy, with an order to banish them for a period of six months. They went to Siena where the goldsmith Castoro, with Giovanni's permission, took them in. Cellini worked on jewelry while Cecchino wandered around the town whiling away time, hooking up with boys and bothering the girls.

Boys then prided themselves far more on how they dressed than they do today. Some belt buckles were very large, and Cellini made his with sculpted masks and incredibly intricate foliage. Nowhere did boys like to dress up more than in the Florence under the Medici, where costumes for festivals and carnivals were magnificent: Boys' trousers so tight they looked painted on, ample shirts that fell from the collarbones to the upper thighs, taken in by a thin belt at the waist. A headband with perhaps a feather adorned the forehead. Niccolò Machiavelli wrote, "The city's youth, being independent, spent excessive sums on clothing, feasting and debauchery. Living in idleness, it consumed its time and money on gaming and women."

Cellini returned to Florence for a teary reunion with his father. While there he copied a painting by Michelangelo showing soldiers bathing naked in the Arno, a copy that came to the attention of a certain Piero Torrigiano who was in Florence in search of artists needed in London where Piero was living. The story of Torrigiano was singular because Torrigiano had been a sculptor under the patronage of Lorenzo *Il Magnifico*. He was credited with bringing the artistic segment of the Renaissance to England. But through a quirk of human nature, he is known today as the man who broke the nose of Michelangelo. Torrigiano had been one of Michelangelo's lovers and, in a fit of jealousy, smashed the great artist in the face. Knowing how furious Lorenzo would be at his disfiguring Michelangelo, Torrigiano fled. As Cesare Borgia was offering money to new conscripts, and since Torrigiano needed money, he joined his troops. As Michelangelo was Cellini's hero, Torrigiano was sent packing. After working a number of years for Henry VIII Torrigiano went to Spain where he sculpted a Virgin for the Duke of Arcus, but when the duke tried to swindle him, he destroyed it. In revenge, the duke called on the Inquisition that imprisoned Torrigiano for sacrilege. In prison he starved himself to death.

It was now 1517 and seventeen-year-old Cellini had his first real love affair. The boy was Giovanni Francesco Lippi, grandson of the painter Filippo Lippi, and the same age as Cellini. About Giovanni Cellini wrote: ''So much love grew up between us that we were never apart, day or night. For two years or thereabouts we lived in intimacy.''

A new boy and a new workshop. He entered that of Francesco Salimbene. Here he created a silver belt buckle of supreme beauty, about three inches in diameter, showing leaves, vines and masks. Two years passed and he decided to change workshops again ... and boyfriends. The new lover was Giambattista Tasso, a woodcarver, and one day during a stroll ... but let Cellini take over: ''By this time we had reached the San Piero Gattolini gate-- the gate by which one leaves Florence to travel towards the Holy City. We looked at each other, tied our aprons around our waists, and set off along the road. It had been God's will that we came to the gates without noticing that we were that far. On the way I asked him, 'Oh, I wonder what our old folks will say this evening?''' Words that ring as true then as today. ''I had just reached nineteen, and so had the century.''

It could have been the Yellow Brick Road, for it led to a long life of astonishing adventure.

In Rome Cellini and Tasso found work in a shop of Firenzuola. He was well received, especially as he was wearing some of the silver pieces, clasps and a belt buckle that he had made himself. He made a saltcellar that he sold for enough money to wander around the Eternal City and copy the works of art by other artists. He joined a new workshop when his funds were low, that of Paolo Arsago. Firenzuola didn't see things that way and went after Cellini, as he had spent time and money teaching Cellini his trade, but Cellini brushed him off with ''As a free man I'll go when and where I please.'' When Firenzuola lost his temper, Cellini put his hand on the hilt of his sword. ''The dispute waxed warm as Firenzuola was a far better swordsman than he was a goldsmith.'' Luckily a passerby who had been Firenzuola's old master stopped to find out what was going on. He got both talking, and in the end Cellini became godfather to one of Firenzuola's children.

Cellini passed much time wandering around Rome, discovering its hidden corners, adding, always adding new knowledge and new experience to his art, drawing, learning perspective, and the incredible difficulties in making molds and mixing and pouring molten metals. He says he also made a great deal of money that he gave his father.

Cellini landed a commission, the crafting of a silver vase, for the Bishop of Salamanca. He spent months on the *oeuvre* in company of a new lover, this one 14, Paulino, of whom he writes, ''I had a passionate love. He was honest and had the most beautiful face I'd ever seen. The love he had for me and mine for him bordered on the unbearable. His splendor was such that he would have driven the Greek gods themselves mad!'' Paulino's father met Cellini, and although adventures between men and boys were known and practiced by one and all, there's no indication that he suspected Cellini's attachment to his son. On the other hand, Paulino had a sister that his dad hoped would interest Cellini. ''He wanted me as a son-in-law, '' resumes Cellini in his autobiography. While working on the silver vase he continued his studies in sculpture, drawing and architecture.

As Paulino loved music, Cellini spent many a languorous night playing his flute for the fourteen-year-old who was entranced by his lover's talents, artistry and expertise in the art of virile domination--acquired since Cellini himself was but 13--all of which took Paulino's breath away.

Cellini opened his own workshop at age 23. One of his first wealthy clients was Giacomo Bergenario da Carpi, a doctor who made his fortune treating syphilis, called the French disease because it entered Italy at the same time as Charles VIII. The good doctor ordered several silver cups. Thanks to the Bishop of Salamanca's vase and the doctor's cups, commissions flowed in. Cellini nonetheless studied on the side, especially with Cristoforo Foppa, an expert in enameling, thanks to whom Cellini would later make a *chef-d'oeuvre* for François I of France. From here on in Cellini began to make a lot of money, much of which, he says, he sent home to his father.

Cellini attended a party given by Giulio Romano, a painter notorious for his *I Modi* sexual-intercourse drawings. Romano thought it would be amusing to have a dinner in which the men invited their mistresses [whom Cellini reveals later as being, for the most part, whores]. Cellini had none, but he did have a boy of wondrous beauty, 16, whom he dressed as a girl. ''Diego had a handsome figure, and a complexion of marvelous brilliancy. The outlines of his head and face were far more beautiful than those of the antique Antinous. When I begged him to let me array him in women's clothes he readily complied.'' Diego is recorded to have made such a splash that one of the men present fell to his knees before him and said, ''Behold ye of what sort are the angels of paradise!'' One of the mistresses left in a huff, followed by another when one of the men put his hand in the little lady's panties and discovered the truth. The men broke up in laughter and Diego, the ''girl'' of wondrous beauty, was said to have passed an equally wondrous night. [The details of which, alas, are not found in Cellini's book.] The mistress who had left in a huff was a whore named Pantasilea who decided to get revenge against Cellini by seducing one of his boyfriends, the handsome Luigi Pulci. Both Luigi and Cellini were free to go with other boys, but Cellini did not want him to go with Pantasilea. Cellini had met Luigi when the lad was sick with syphilis and provided the best doctors for him, never leaving his bedside until he was well. He, and everyone who met Luigi, fell in love with him. He was said to have had a beautiful voice and sang in public, his beauty and talent attracting even Michelangelo who followed him assiduously from performance to performance, and became his lover. It was because Cellini had nursed the boy back to health that he now got his absolute assurance that he would not sleep with Pantasilea. She nonetheless succeeded in alluring the boy into her bed, an act that infuriated the artist no end, even though, as I said, he partook of any boy who caught his fancy--and they were numerous--no matter if they were connected to one of his friends or not-- meaning that if a friend's back was turned Cellini never hesitated to steal his boy. Cellini therefore decided to waylay the couple and teach them a lesson. Several days later they had all gone to a party but Cellini left while Luigi and the whore were engaged in necking. He went to the whore's house and waited for them outside. His ire mounted when they returned, their bodies as entwined as his and Luigi's had been when they were going steady. Cellini jumped from behind the tree where he was hiding and hit Luigi with his sword, a glancing blow that also struck Pantasilea, ''hitting her full on the nose and mouth,'' wrote Cellini. Cellini was arrested and shouted to Luigi, as he was being marched away, that if he continued seeing Pantasilea he'd break his neck. Shortly afterwards Luigi Pulci was caracoling his horse in an attempt to impress Pantasilea. It had rained and the horse slipped, falling on the boy, breaking his neck.

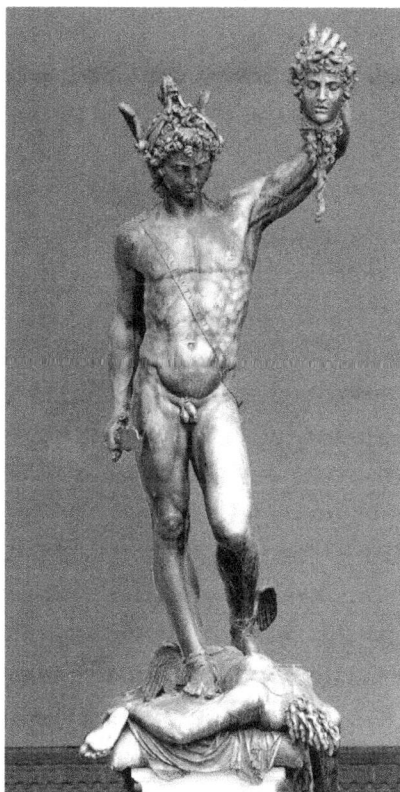

A world wonder: Cellini's *Perseus*

Cellini was released from prison, in time to participate in what is known in history as the Sack of Rome. The sack was carried out by the mutinous troops of the Holy Roman Emperor Charles V. France, Milan, Venice, Florence and Clement VII joined forces to counterman the growing power of Charles. As far as Clement was concerned, he wanted the papacy to be totally free from Charles V's continual intercessions. Charles' troops were persistently victorious but armies cost enormous funds and Charles was late in paying them. The troops were a heteroclite mixture of mercenaries, thieves and deserters, even former soldiers leagued against Charles but who now thought the wages would be better under the emperor. There were also a number of followers of Martin Luther who wished to see the anti-Christ, Clement, at the end of a sword. Before reaching Rome they destroyed other towns, pillaging, raping and massacring. So inured had they become to blood that even the screams of children and babies left them unmoved. In defense of Rome were an estimated 5,000 militiamen and 500 Swiss Guard, mercenaries so valiant and fearless that the popes had taken them as their personal protectors and Michelangelo had dressed them, like a Renaissance Yves St. Laurent. Rome also had artillery, heavy cannon, which was lacking in the rebellious troops. Cellini was present: ''Let it suffice that it was I who saved the castle.'' Somewhere outside the Castel Cellini's brother Cecchino was also wielding arms, but as a professional. In his book Cellini wrote that he too was now trying to decide whether to give up art in favor of arms, as he was thoroughly enjoying himself. It was during this period that a number of jewels went missing, the theft of which would be blamed on Cellini, at a later time, with dire consequences. Cellini claimed that it was he himself who fatally shot the leader of the rebels, Charles the Duke of Bourbon, who prided himself on his all-white cloak, a marksman's perfect target. Another of Cellini's comments, ''I pursued my business of artilleryman, and every day performed some extraordinary feat.'' The attack was terrible and the Swiss lived up to their reputation by fighting until all were dispatched, except the forty-two who accompanied the pope to the redoubtable fortification Castel Sant'Angelo. As for Cellini, ''During just one blast from my cannon I slaughtered more than thirty men.''

The city was looted, every church, palace and wealthy home.

Even peasants from surrounding villages joined in, so great was their hatred of Clement VII whose armies had pillaged their farms and taken their women in order to feed their bellies and satisfy their groins. Clement finally gave in and paid a ransom of 400,000 ducati for his life. The sack continued on for *eight months*, until there was literally no more to steal, no more undiseased women to rape and no more food to eat.

In Florence Alessandro de' Medici, age 19, whose specialty was robbing girls of their virginity, was named ruler of the city by his purported father, none other than Pope Clement VII. To thank the pope and to gain his blessing, Alessandro went to Rome accompanied by a group of boys, louts like him, who came up against even trashier men, the pope's own guard. Among Alessandro's boys was none other than Cecchino, Cellini's brother. The pope's guard arrested one of Alessandro's men--we don't know under what pretense, but Alessandro and his ruffians were known for everything vile, including the mass rape of nuns. The arrested boy, Bertino Aldobrandi, was a friend of Cecchino's--who, like his brother, nurtured extremely intimate friendships with his pals. Cecchino learned, falsely as it turned out, that his friend had been killed by one of the guards. Mad with fury, Cecchino got a description of the man he thought to be the murderer, found him, and "ran him right through the guts," wrote Cellini. Another guard then shot Cecchino in the leg with a harquebus. The wound festered and Cecchino died. Clement wanted Cellini to return to work despite his mourning, saying that Cecchino was now gone and nothing more could be done. But Italians are extremely bound to their families, and Cellini no less so. He found out who had shot the boy and, as he wrote, "followed him as closely as though he were a girl I was in love with." He attacked him with a dagger, a first blow that grazed the neck as the man, aware of an approaching figure, was able to move slightly out of the way. He tried to run but Cellini was on him like a lion on a fleeing antelope, downing him with another blow, to the back, and as he lay on the ground, another and still another to the neck and upper back. He then ran to Alessandro's palace near the Piazza Navona where guards caught up with him. Alessandro explained the motive for the killing and the guards left. Later, the pope simply asked him if he ''had gotten over it now'', and gave him a commission.

Alessandro by Vasari

Cellini opened his own shop on the Via dei Banchi, guarded by a dog given him by Alessandro de' Medici himself. The workshop was burglarized soon afterwards while Cellini was asleep with a girl. He was awoken by the dog's barking and although the animal didn't succeed in stopping the burglar, it did get a whiff of him, and several days later, while strolling through the Piazza Navona, the dog attacked a boy in the custody of two policemen. In order to keep the animal way from him the boy confessed to having robbed Cellini. He returned what he had taken and begged forgiveness, which Cellini granted, but the lad was nonetheless hanged. Alas for Cellini, the girl gave him syphilis: ''It broke out over my whole body at one instant, covering my flesh with blisters of the size of a six-pence and rose-colored.'' The syphilis went away, perhaps permanently, as Cellini lived forty more years.

Alessandro

Cellini got in a row with a jeweler, a certain Capitaneis, with whom he was in competition. Words were exchanged and Cellini scooped up some mud and threw it at him. Cellini *says* that unknown to him there was a stone in the mud and the jeweler was felled. ''Provoked by his ugly words, I stooped and took up a lump of mud--for it had rained--and hurled it with a quick and unpremeditated movement at his face. He ducked his head, so that the mud hit him in the middle of the skull. There was a stone in it with several sharp angles, one of which striking him, he fell stunned like a dead man, whereupon all the bystanders, seeing the great quantity of blood, judged that he was really dead.'' Then a few days later, while sitting with friends outside a shop, Capitaneis happened to pass with some friends. Seeing Cellini, insults and gestures were exchanged. Capitaneis and friends wandered off down the street, giggling. Cellini, despite his own friends who tried to stop him, followed Capitaneis and cold-bloodedly knifed him from behind, Capitaneis' companions too surprised to intervene. Cellini is said to have coolly walked away, but when news got to the pope, Cellini's arrest and execution were ordered. Alessandro de' Medici nevertheless gave him a horse for his escape.

The newly elected pope, Paul III, gave Cellini a pardon and a commission saying, ''Men like Cellini, unique to art, are above the law.'' But a problem arose: the pope's son, Pier Luigi Farnese, a homosexual who had raped even a bishop, was a friend of the man Cellini had murdered, a man who had a daughter that Farnese wanted to marry to his lover, a young peasant boy, in order to confiscate the girl's dowry. Despite what the pope felt for Cellini, Farnese had the power to order Cellini's arrest, which he did. He also hired an assassin to kill Cellini. The assassin met him in a tavern and, seduced by his charm, told Cellini of the plot to kill him. Cellini then immediately fled to Florence and the open arms of Alessandro de' Medici.

Alessandro took advice from no one, living for his own pleasure, his motto being ''They made me duke, so I'll enjoy it!'' By enjoying it he meant wandering the streets at night fully armed, pushing aside anyone in his way, looking for a fight he was destined to win for the simple reason that he had barred the carrying of a sword or a firearm, both of which never left him, nor did his dagger. And he had reason to fear, as the nobility of Florence wanted him replaced by legitimate blood, noble blood. He had gained power at age 19 and had by now fully tasted every perversion, so that what was left was taking the hymen of those who still had one, notably nuns, and that of those who kept guard over theirs, virtuous women. He liked his boys too, for quick, easy couplings, as heated and virile as possible. His favorite companion was his cousin Lorenzino with whom he shared his bed and more when not extinguished from a night of whoring. And when he awoke with a lustful urge, Lorenzino was always conveniently spread out, naked, at his side. This is how Cellini had caught them many times, as the artist was permitted to come and go as he wished, and as Alessandro had no modesty and no need to hide his vices, Cellini was aware of everything that went on. ''Meanwhile I went on making the Duke's portrait and oftentimes I found him napping after dinner with that Lorenzino of his.''

No one knows why Lorenzino turned against Duke Alessandro, aided by a professional assassin, Scoronconcolo. In his play, *Lorenzaccio*, Musset writes that Lorenzo wanted the duke dead so that Florence could become a Republic again. Others suggest that he was just jealous of the duke's powers and privileges. Because Duke Alessandro was so unpopular, he was never without his body armor, weapons and guards. But Lorenzino told him that he had found a Florentine lady of exceptional beauty and, especially, ironclad virtue, who had been abandoned by her husband. Lorenzino would bring her to the duke, and from then on it was up to the duke to prove that he could triumph over virtue. Lorenzino convinced the duke to dismiss the guards for the night, to take off his armor and to slip naked into bed. From then on it was easy for Lorenzino to strike him with a dagger. Afterwards he rode off to Venice, a glove covering a finger Alessandro had nearly bitten off. There, he published his version of what had taken place in his *Apologia*, claiming to be a second Brutus. Lorenzino himself was later stabbed to death by a poisoned dagger on a bridge in Venice.

Due to the events described above and his problems with the pope and the pope's son Pier Luigi, Cellini had had enough of both Rome and Florence. So with two new boys, Ascanio, "the most handsome boy in Rome," and another handsome lad, Girolamo Pascucci, he and they headed for France and the wondrous court of the courtly François I. The trip to Fontainebleau was fraught with dangers. It rained incessantly and at one point one of his horses slipped and fell against another horse where the rider's javelin pierced its neck. At another place a horse and rider fell over a bridge, landing, luckily, in a pool deep enough so that no bones were broken. Naturally, it was Cellini who rode down to the river's edge and pulled the driver free from the torrents by grasping his cloak: "As he had stayed underwater all this time, unable to come to the surface, he lived thanks to my quick actions." Brigands stopped them at one point but were forced to flee thanks to Cellini's drawn sword.

François, who had already lost his virginity to his sister at age 10, was a lad 6 ½ feet tall and so big some girls couldn't accommodate him although most tried, and, it was said, virgins literally lined up around his bed awaiting their chance to be deflowered--his specialty. His bed accompanied him while he was out hunting, using it between kills, to the utter amazement of Henry VIII who had accompanied the king during his visit to France [Henry went far in such things, very far even, but not *that* far]. François took whomever he wanted from the nobility, whether the ladies liked it or not, and apparently not all did as one woman had her husband infect himself with syphilis before infecting her so that she could infect the king. Another woman had her face slashed, which didn't dissuade François as it wasn't her face that interested him.

François I by Jean Clouet. His nose was greatly appreciated by demoiselles tired of their virginity.

François offered Cellini a commission: six colossal gods and six goddesses, all in silver, more than life-size as François wanted them his height, the purpose of which would be to hold candlesticks. That he asked Cellini to create these giant candelabras, holding three or more candles, was a surprise, given the expense of the project, as Cellini was only noted for his belt buckles, silver plates and vases.

Cellini set to work making a clay model of one of the statues, a male figure, that was cast in bronze over which he hammered sheets of silver with a wooden hammer. During this time Cellini had problems with accountants, with jealous artists who badmouthed him and, far more deadly, with Madame d'Étampes, François' mistress, whose ass [to be honestly frank] Cellini just hadn't sufficiently kissed.

The day came for Cellini to present the finished statue to the king and his mistress. ''The Jupiter was raising his thunderbolt with the right hand in the act of hurling it; his left hand held the globe of the world. ''Among the flames of the thunderbolt I had very cleverly introduced a torch of white wax.'' Cellini had the king observe the statue from several angles, informing him that a sculpture should always be viewed from at least eight different standpoints. Cellini had draped some tissue around the statue's private parts, knowing a woman would be present, but when d'Étampes saw the statue she suggested to the king that the tissue was there to hid some imperfection. Cellini had Ascanio take it away. Madame d'Étampes stared at the incredible detail of the pubic bush, balls, penis and ample foreskin, and Cellini asked, ''Do you find it all as it should be?'' Madame d'Étampes left the room in a huff. As soon as she was gone the king ''exploded with laughter,'' says Cellini. The statue had taken four years to make, at the cost of 40,000 francs.

Cellini now had a girl model about whom he wrote, ''I also used to keep her for my bed,'' a far cry from what he said about his boys, ''the most beautiful in Rome,'' ''the sweetest face that ever existed,'' ''the gods themselves would have been mad for him.'' There were plenty of boys for his bed too, as well as at his dinner table. They played tennis on the court attached to his building, a building that François later presented to him as a gift.

The streets of Paris were dangerous and Cellini had to be careful as he wandered through cobbled alleys scarcely large enough for two to walk abreast. He passed under sagging facades suspended overhead like the stomach of Gargantua. Stone walls and latticed windows enclosed an eerie medieval silence. Wind-jostled shop signs depicting wares--a horse head for a *chevaline*, an old frock for a *tailleur*--were unlighted and at night the streets belonged to the thief. At the dawn of each day a dozen night wanderers were found assassinated. Lamp carriers were hired to accompany the rich to the doors of their apartment buildings; the price of the carrier's services sifted through an hourglass fastened at his waist. Returning home on one occasion Cellini was attacked by four armed men, but sent them running when they came up against his sword and drawn dagger.

No matter how beautiful were his boys, a man is programmed by nature to want more and Cellini found it in a girl, Caterina, a girl who served as model, a girl he seems to have been deeply, sexually, attached to. He did what he could to keep her out of the hands of others, fearing she might become pregnant. Alas, coming home early from a dinner he found her *in flagrant delicto* with a boy. He wanted to kill the boy but ''I had so many acts of violence upon my hands that if I killed him I could hardly hope to save my life.'' In her defense, Caterina accused Cellini of sodomy, an offense that was more or less troublesome in Italy, but one that brought death in France. ''I found Caterina and her mother waiting in the courtroom. They were laughing with their advocate. In the presence of the judge I asked Caterina to relate all that happened between us. She answered that 'I had used her after the Italian fashion.' I commanded her to explain precisely how I had consorted with her. The impudent baggage entered into plain details regarding all the filth she lyingly accused me of. I made her repeat her deposition. When finished I cried out with a loud voice: Lord judge I call on you for justice. Well I know that by the laws of his majesty both agent and patient in this kind of crime are punished with the stake. The woman confesses her guilt. I admit nothing whatsoever of the sort with regard to her. Her go-between of a mother is here, who deserves to be burned for either one or the other offence. Therefore I appeal to you for justice. To the stake with her and her mother.'' As Sun Tsu said, the best defense in a good offense. He got off but we know nothing of the hows and whys because the court records have been lost. Caterina was chased from the house, but it suddenly became clear why he didn't want her with another boy. Because Cellini used her as he did his boys, she couldn't become pregnant. And if she ever did, she could sue him for support payments because he obviously couldn't have risked having his head cut off by telling the court that he had abused her anally.

''The following morning Caterina came to our door and knocked so violently that I ran to see if it was a madman. When I opened the creature laughed and fell upon my neck, embracing and kissing me and asked if I was still angry with her. I said No. I supplied her with food and partook of it at the same table in sign of reconciliation. Afterwards she returned as my model, during which occurred some amorous diversions. Then she irritated me and I gave her some beatings. So we went on several days, repeating this around the clock.''

In the meantime, while Cellini was busy on still another project, an enormous statue, Ascanio had fallen in love. The head of the statue was on the ground and was so huge that Ascanio had a bed installed in the head where both he and his beloved hid when her mother, who had learned where she was, came around in search of her daughter. The statue soon gained a reputation for being haunted because, at night, movement could be observed behind its eyes.

There were lodgers in the Parisian palace where Cellini worked, and as he needed more room, he simply threw them, physically, into the street. One of the lodgers went to court. ''The lawsuit tormented me beyond measure and took up so much of my time that I often thought of decamping in despair from France.'' He lost the suit: ''When the decisions of the court were sent to me I perceived that my cause had been unjustly lost. I had recourse for my defense to a great dagger which I carried. The first man I attacked was the plaintiff who had sued me. One evening I wounded him in the legs and arms so severely, taking care, however, not to kill him, that I deprived him of the use of both his legs. Then I sought out the other fellow who had brought the suit and used him also in such wise that he dropped it.'' Because Madame d'Étampes succeeded in poisoning the king's mind against Cellini because of his cold indifference to her and his unwillingness to kowtow, Cellini decided to return to Florence.

There he went to find Cosimo I de' Medici who had replaced Alessandro de' Medici. Cosimo had not been taken seriously as a young man, his priority being himself and the quantities of drink and women his young body could do honor to. So all were surprised when he not only took control of the government, but also had his enemies tortured and beheaded in public. Pleasure and pleasurable surroundings were in the de' Medici blood, and that which was true of all the rich--a need for art in the form of paintings, frescoes, sculptures, drapery, sublime clothing, silverware, magnificent gardens and fountains--was true on an even grander scale for the de' Medici. Cosimo I had nothing of the erudition of the first Cosimo, nor that of Lorenzo *Il Magnifico,* but he appreciated the good things in life enough to offer commissions without end to his suppliants. Alas, he offered much but came through with the minimum, financially, as Cellini would soon discover, and where Lorenzo *Il Magnifico* could charm a serpent, Cosimo I had his foot perpetually in his mouth, a lesser evil to his ceaseless meddling in the execution of the works of art he commissioned. Oh yes, he was also a hunter who slaughtered every living thing he came upon, including hummingbirds!

Cosimo promised that if Cellini produced a great work of art, he would not be disappointed in his reward. Cellini suggested doing the statue of Perseus, Cosimo agreed, and thus began the countdown to Cellini's Immortality. The year was 1545.

Cosimo I.
His greatest gift to humanity was his commissioning the
Perseus of Cellini, found in the Piazza della Signoria along with
Michelangelo's *David*, the works of two sons of Florence.

A place for it was rapidly found, in front of Cosimo's home, the Palazzo della Signoria, facing Michelangelo's *David*. A new boy, handsome, naturally, was found too, a very young lad, Cencio, son of a prostitute who would eventually accuse him of sodomizing her boy in an attempt to extract money. He took on

Bernardino Mannellini, the exquisite head and body of whom would be the model for the future *Perseus*. "He was 18 and I asked him if he would enter my service. He agreed on the spot. He groomed my horse, gardened, and soon essayed to help me in the workshop, with such success that by degrees he learned the art quite nicely. I never had a better assistant than he proved." He decided to enlarge the horizons of Bernardino and his assistants by taking them to the Old Market, the Chiasso de' Buoi, the Tavern Buca and the baths, all pleasure zones where the lads could enjoy both sexes, singly or in bacchanals. In fact, he was, in a sense, making up for lost time. He had kept boy-love to a minimum in France because there the penalty was death, one that seems to have been enforced by François who much preferred female plumbing to that of males. Back home in Florence, he seems to have let out all stops. Be that as it may, Bernardino turned out to be intelligent, loyal and hardworking, and was Cellini's first assistant from then on.

This is the story of Perseus: Acrisius, King of Argos, wanted a son and consulted the Delphic Oracle who told him that his *daughter* would have a boy, but that the boy would grow up and kill Acrisius. So Acrisius locked away his daughter, who was nonetheless impregnated by Zeus who took the form of a golden shower [?]. The son she bore was Perseus. Acrisius refused to kill them both so instead locked them in a chest that he flung into the sea. The chest was netted by fishermen loyal to King Polydectes who reared Perseus. Polydectes wanted to marry Perseus' mother but Perseus refused him her hand, telling the king he would give him whatever else he wanted. The king said he would settle for the Gorgon Medusa, a monster having a terrible face and hair of serpents, a face so horrible that the person looking on it froze with fright. The gods favored Perseus and gave him a sack in which to put the head, winged feet to get to it, a sickle to cut it off, and the helmet of invisibility belonging to Hades. Perseus collected the head and returned [after profuse adventures] to Polydectes who said he had sent the boy away to be killed by the Medusa, and had never planned to give up his mother. Perseus opened the sack, looked the other way, and froze Polydectes to stone. He then returned to Argos where, during Olympic-style games, he threw a discus that rebounded and killed Acrisius.

In 1548 Cellini cast the figure of Medusa and in 1549 work on the rest of the statue began. It was around this time that he hired another handsome youth, Ferrando di Giovanni da Montepulciao, who would cause him much grievance later one. Just before the actual casting he fell sick with fever, brought on, certainly, by the incredible stress related to his work. Luckily Bernardino Mannellini was there to see that things went along correctly.

Perseus comes through as a real living youth, his brow knitted as is Michelangelo's *David*, his look grave. The body of the Medusa is just as living, just as wondrously human.

A marble block had been brought to the workshop in 1549 to serve as a base for *Perseus* and in 1552 Cellini cast two figures which would go into the block, Mercury modeled after Cencio and Danaë modeled by a new girl Dorotea. When Cosimo's wife saw the two figures she wanted them for her own rooms but not only did Cellini refuse, he also sealed the figures into the marble base with such firmness that they could not be removed. Cencio, as *Mercury*, is totally naked and eminently desirable. He had shared Cellini's bed since the age of 12. Dorotea also shared his bed and gave him a son he legitimized. In addition, she accommodated Cencio. All told, Cellini was living and creating, creating and living, in the most beautiful city in the world, under skies warmed by the unstinting generosity of Helios, his *Perseus* complete, his Immortality guaranteed.

Cellini went off on vacation for a few weeks with a new boy, Cesare. On his return he opened the head of a fellow goldsmith, Lorenzo Papi, for reasons unknown, and was sent to the terrible prison of Stinche from whence Cosimo had him released. And then an apprentice, Ferrando di Giovanni da Montepulciao, accused him of ''sexual intercourse on many occasions,'' treating the boy ''as though he were a wife.'' Cellini seemed to have loved the lad, one he had put in his will before some unknown disagreement separated them. ''I take back everything I've done for him,'' Cellini wrote, ''He'll receive nothing. His name will vanish from my will.'' Here Cellini was forced to plead guilty because Ferrando produced witnesses who had actually seen them at it. Cellini tried to flee but the authorities guessed that that was exactly what he'd do and stopped him. He was sentenced to four years in jail but again Cosimo, despite the fact that he was aging and ill and therefore more and more religiously zealous, nevertheless intervened. Cellini received a year of house arrest instead. He entered a religious order, perhaps through his own will, perhaps to please Cosimo, but he left after two years. He then begot another child, a boy, from an unnamed servant, and then still more children by a model, Piera de' Salvatore Parigi, one of which, a boy, he had at age 69. Piera and he married.

The last years of his life seem to have been marked by increasingly ill health and unattainable projects. From Paris the immensely original Catherine de' Medici requested that he return to his Parisian palace to build a tomb for her beloved husband, Henry II and for herself, two kneeling figures. Health and insufficient willpower prevented him, but he was tempted. He was part of a committee that arranged the burial of Michelangelo whose reputation--in death at least--now placed him, in the eyes of mere mortals, among the gods. He made some trinkets, jewelry, seals and buckles as he had as a very young man. He left his fortune to the de' Medici, asking only that they care for the boys in his workshop.

He went to work on his book which, next to *Perseus*, was his greatest triumph. He was aided by a boy, age 14, and seemed to have liked the experience of talking about himself while the lad noted all. Part of his memoirs had been a tell-all outing of the true nature of Cosimo, but he burned the papers, following the French adage: *Toutes les véritées ne sont pas à dire.* In that respect his relationship with the truth was always hesitant, as was his love for women. He never admitted loving boys or anally contenting himself [as well as, certainly, some of his lovers], yet when he loved a boy he was as frank--or even franker--than the times permitted:

"We are never apart, day or night."
"We loved each other more than if we had been brothers."
"My passionate love for the boy."
"'The prettiest face of anyone I have ever met in my whole life."

''He's amazingly beautiful, and the great love he's shown me made me love him in return--almost more than I could bear.''
''His beautiful smile would have driven the gods themselves mad.''
''Extreme personal beauty.''
''The most handsome young fellow in Rome.''

He weakened. He died, accompanied to his resting place by hordes of admirers--I can't say *last* resting place because, for this man who had never stopped moving, it was, in reality, his first. When I entered the Peace Corps, a very young boy, I received a huge box of books, as do all volunteers. One was *The Autobiography of Benvenuto Cellini.* I read it with great pleasure, totally unaware of the volcano who had produced it, only vaguely aware of my own sexuality, never dreaming that I would eventually, like countless other boys, fall in love with this incredible creature, proof that God truly does work in entirely mysterious ways (15).

Perseus

A final word on Vasari: Giorgio Vasari is a hallowed name in art history, as is Plutarch in political science. Born in Tuscany, he started his artistic life as an apprentice in stained glass and then moved to Florence where he was immersed in humanism, an education which is clearly visible in his marvelous work, *Lives of the Most Excellent Painters, Sculptors and Architects.* He was the first to use the word Renaissance in print. He lived in Rome and Naples, learning and painting as he went from confirmed artist to professional in frescoes. Known for his architecture, it was he who built the corridor that connects the Palazzo Pitti to the Uffizi, as earlier stated, built under the order of the Medici who wished to pass from one to the other without being seen, as well as frustrating attempts to assassinate them. He loved to fill his book with anecdotes, like the boy Giotto painting a fly on a painting by Cimabue that the master kept trying to brush away. Julius III built an incredibly luxurious palace, the Villa Giulia, adorned by Michelangelo and Vasari and lesser artists who decorated it with Ganymede and soft-core pornographic satyrs and naked angels.

Vasari's book, paintings and architectural constructions made him wealthy, allowing him to retire to his hometown of Arezzo where he built himself a palazzo that is now a museum. For obscure reasons Vasari turned against Cellini, even though, as Cellini writes in his autobiography, he had provided Vasari with boys on numerous occasions, one of which Vasari badly scratched while in the throes of orgasm. Cellini noted that Vasari didn't even give the lad a single coin in recompense, nor a coin that is normally an old man's gift in exchange for the far-more precious access to a young man's beauty.

Vasari wrote that once one had seen *David*, one need never look at another statue. Yet, at that very moment another statue came to light, one sculpted well before the birth of Christ, unearthed in a field outside Rome in the presence of Michelangelo himself who had been summoned to see it. It is now in the Vatican and is proof that other magnificent creations *are* still worth seeing. It is the *Laocoön*, the story of which can be found in my book *TROY*. Later, in 1527, during a revolt in Florence, *David's* left arm had been broken. It lay on the ground three days until Vasari, then a young boy, ventured out during the fighting and recuperated the pieces that he sent to Cosimo I who, in 1543, had the arm restored.

About Botticelli Vasari tells us, ''Old and useless, ill and decrepit'' he hobbled through the streets of Florence on crutches, an incarnation of the city itself.

And concerning Raphael, "So gentle and charitable was Raphael that even the animals loved him."

Vasari self-portrait.

About Leonardo Vasari wrote, "There is something supernatural in the accumulation in one person of so much beauty, grace, strength and intelligence as in da Vinci." As well as this, "Leonardo had such a great presence that one only had to see him for all sadness to vanish."

MICHELANGELO
1475 - 1564

Few men had lived a longer, fuller life than Michelangelo, perhaps none had bequeathed as much artistic wealth to humanity as this tortured genius, dead at age 89, with a chisel still in his hand, at work right up to the end. The body was destined for burial in the Basilica of St. Peter's still under construction, but was stolen by Florentines in the midst of the night, destination a city Michelangelo had not visited for 30 years, his nonetheless beloved Florence. Paraded through the streets to his last resting place, word of mouth spread as to who it was, and soon the streets were jammed with crowds. At the Basilica of Santa Croce the coffin was opened for the benefit of the crowd. The body within was intact, clean and totally lifelike a month after his passing, proof to the assembled masses of the artist's sanctity. But he had not had the luck of going to his tomb in company of his lover, as da Vinci did with Salaì and Melzi. The love of Michelangelo's dreams, Tommasso, was absent, and the love of his life, Urbino, had preceded him in death.

Michelangelo was born a Florentine and he died a Florentine, even if his birth had taken place outside of Florence in Caprese, and he had been destined for burial in Rome. His full name was Michelangelo di Lodovico Buonarroti Simoni, his father was Lodovico. When his mother died, Michelangelo, age 6, was farmed out to his nanny and her husband, a stonecutter, where Michelangelo was introduced to his art. ''If there is some good in me,'' Vasari quotes Michelangelo as saying, ''it is because I was born in the subtle atmosphere of Arezzo. Along with the milk of my nurse I received the knack of handling chisel and hammer.'' His father was forced to place him in the bustling workshop of the immense painter Ghirlandaio, at age 10. Forced because the lad was headstrong despite, says Ascanio Condivi, a painter and Michelangelo's biographer, Lodovico's ''outrageously beating him''. Lodovico had destined the boy for more literary quests, beginning with the obligatory study of Latin, a language Michelangelo would always regret not having learned as it separated him from the ranks of the nobility he admired, a regret that burned like a coal until the day he died. But he did make it to Ghirlandaio's, as if directed by the hand of God, as Leonardo had been fortunate in finding Verrocchio. Michelangelo's older brother, Leonardo, didn't fare as well. Destined for commerce, his father placed him with an abacus teacher, obligatory for the times, Raffaello Canacci, who sodomized the boy, age 10, ''often and often from behind,'' he admitted to the court. He was fined 20 florins and a year in prison which was dropped because he confessed his sin. Leonardo entered the orders, became a Dominican friar, and disappeared from History. Lodovico had five sons about whom he said, ''None of them would give me the slightest help or even a glass of water.''

In the workshop apprentices learned to look after the tools and keep them clean and in working condition, as well as keeping the shop in order and doing the shopping. They became familiar with the materials used in fresco and tempera, and in the preparation of paints, and how to prepare the surfaces over which the assistants and the master would paint. In exchange for their labor they discovered the secrets of their trade. Michelangelo soon became better than Ghirlandaio, which was bad enough, but he bragged about his superiority in frescoes and tempera to the other boys, earning Ghirlandaio's disdain for the boy's arrogance.

Michelangelo learned about Ghirlandaio's workshop thanks to a boy two years older, Francesco Granacci, who would remain his friend until his death. Together they were sent to work for Lorenzo *Il Magnifico* de' Medici who owed a part of his prestige to his position as patron of the arts. At the moment Lorenzo lacked sculptors and Ghirlandaio sent him the two promising boys. Here Condivi recounts the charming story of Lorenzo coming on Michelangelo as he was sculpting a faun. He pointed out to the boy, then 15, that a faun as old as the one he was creating wouldn't have had a mouth of such perfect teeth. Michelangelo is said to have not been able to hold still until Lorenzo had left so he could knock out a tooth, and then he couldn't wait until Lorenzo returned and admired what he had done. Alas for boy and man, Lorenzo, although still young, had but four years left to live. About Lorenzo the great historian Guicciardini wrote, ''No one, not even his enemies, denies that he was a very great and extraordinary genius.'' Lorenzo provided him and Granacci a room and a place at his excellent and refined table. Yet despite the refinement, Lorenzo's household was run on an extremely informal basis. One was free to come and go as one wished, and to say what one wished, and Lorenzo himself was always available to boys like Michelangelo, whereas visitors of high rank often had to cool their heels for days before being admitted into his presence. A grown man was present, Poliziano, a professor and Latin poet, a founder of humanism. He translated works from the Greek, especially Plutarch and Plato. He was also a rampant lover of boys, and one can only wonder what effect his intelligence and enticing talk had on seducing the young artist, if any. He took an interest in Michelangelo and was said ''to have loved him greatly''. Francesco Granacci, on the other hand, would have made a perfect first friend for Michelangelo [he is painted in the nude in the painting *The Raising of the Son of Theophilus* by Filippino Lippi]. Another boy was also present, Pietro Torrigiano. He too was a sculptor under Lorenzo's patronage, and later he brought the artistic segment of the Renaissance to England where he finished his life. He was also an insufferable bully and when Michelangelo made some disparaging remark concerning his work, he broke the artist's nose, an infliction that greatly diminished Michelangelo's faith in himself, as he felt he was no longer handsome. [Some say he was Michelangelo's boyfriend and the dispute was in reality a quarrel between lovers, as Torrigiano was known for his startling beauty.] Afraid of Lorenzo's reaction, Torrigiano fled to Cesare Borgia who was offering money to enroll new army conscripts, and as Torrigiano needed money and was physically fearless, he joined his troops. Afterwards, as I've said, he went to England where his destiny was fulfilled.

Having his nose broken was the beginning of a series of ordeals for the young Michelangelo. Lorenzo *Il Magnifico* died at age 43, certainly from problems centered around the family plague, gout. How this singular light in the history of humanity, ruler of Florence since the age of 20, so strong, courageous and vibrant could just cease to exist was incomprehensible. An event of far less importance, but one that was nonetheless destabilizing, was a charge by a youth called Mancino who claimed that Poliziano had repeatedly sodomized him. There followed a roundup in the taverns of anyone in the company of boys. Michael Rocke, in his *Forbidden Friendships,* points out that by age 30 one out of every two youths in Florence had been arrested for sodomy; by age 40 two out of every three men had been incriminated. As these acts took place in private, and were therefore rarely discovered, it meant that literally every boy, youth and man was doing it. When the dust following Poliziano's arrest settled, those found guilty were fined and they all went right back to satisfying their loins. Priests ardently preached against sodomy, their eyes bulging with hatred for the vile act, spewing saliva over the faithful in their haste to denounce it, while below the pulpit the choir and altar boys quietly awaited the private behind-doors ceremony to follow, when the priests, aroused by the heat of their sermons, would savagely penetrate one of the less fortunate among them. It took place then as it takes place now, and we continue, like the Florentines, to do nothing.

Lorenzo's son Piero had a footman who ran alongside him as he rode, acting both as groom and bodyguard. Piero described the man as exceptional in his beauty and perfect in body. Michelangelo drew the man, as he did others of great beauty and physical perfection who worked for the Medici. In the closed circle of the Medici, which counted palazzos and villas the size of mansions, immense parks consisting of rivers and lakes, of artists, tutors and in-house philosophers convinced of the singular majesty found in the male body, boys and men were plentiful, available, from laborers to grooms to models and apprentices, most of whom were open to the intimacy that allowed the Medici and their guests, Michelangelo included, a chance to familiarize themselves--during languorous Medici nights--with a male's attributes, his nipples, navel, veins, pubic bush, testicles and foreskin, knowledge of which Michelangelo would need to perfect his future *David*. Michelangelo was said to have been very close to Piero, even though the boy was in no way up to the standards of his father Lorenzo who had founded universities and had had, like his grandfather Cosimo, books translated from the Greek.

Now comes a strange interlude in Michelangelo's life. Charles VIII invaded Italy and appropriated Florence, to the humiliation of Piero de' Medici who tried to deal with Charles but was turned away like a servant. He fled Florence and entered history as Piero the Unfortunate. In fear of Charles' army, Michelangelo escaped to Bologna where he and two friends who accompanied him were jailed because they didn't have the small sum of money needed to buy permission to stay in the city, an important source of taxes for towns like Bologna, one that permitted them to do things like medical dissections which, in Bologna, had been carried out in public for centuries. Somehow an important Bolognese personage recognized him as a Medici sculptor from Florence and paid for his release, taking the boy to his palazzo. Now, Michelangelo would be remembered throughout history as being tight-fisted in the extreme, rarely inviting friends to share a meal, and he never accepted gifts for fear of being placed in a person's debt. But he was also generous to those he loved, literally giving them the shirt off his back. The paradox is that Michelangelo rarely went through life with the same people, no matter how much he had loved them in the past. Only when he was in the throes of love was he fierce and total. Da Vinci, on the other hand, kept loyal to friends and remained close to his lovers until the end, but in a way that may have been too cerebral in comparison to Michelangelo, who loved his boys fully and violently. Be that as it may, Michelangelo was said to have abandoned his two friends in prison and went off to live in such luxury that when Piero de' Medici happened to come to Bologna, Michelangelo didn't even make an effort to see him.

He and his new friend, Gian Francesco Aldrovandi, spent their nights reading Boccaccio, literature as erotic then as it is to us today. A friendship developed … and certainly more. Michelangelo carved three small statues for Aldrovandi's church, St. Dominic, each around 2 feet high, of extreme beauty and intricacy, especially the angel. After a year Michelangelo returned to Florence where the political situation had stabilized, and then went to Rome where he sculpted the *Pietà*, Christ cradled on the legs of his mother, whose portrait is so young she could have been Christ's sister. Michelangelo inscribed his name on a band across her breasts, the first and only time he ever signed a work. The perfection of the faces and the intricacy of Christ's mother's drapery, incredibly complicated, majestic, is beyond human understanding as to how Michelangelo accomplished it. The finish was achieved with pumice stones, a labor of love he would never ever repeat. Michelangelo had sought out the marble himself from Carrara, beginning a lifelong love of the beautiful wooded site that would only grow until his death. He was 25, the new and never to be toppled King of Rome.

The *St. Dominic Angel* and the *Pietà*.

Michelangelo had been called to Rome by Cardinal Raffaele Riario due to a statue Michelangelo had carved and then buried, known as the *Sleeping Cupid*. When experts unearthed it and then maintained that it was an example of ancient Greek mastery in sculpture, Michelangelo revealed that it was he the creator. The statue had been bought by Raffaele who had amassed the greatest collection of Greek and Roman art in Rome. Upon arrival, at age 21, Raffaele took Michelangelo under his wing, proudly showing him through his immense collection, offering the boy the chance to do all the drawings of the statuary he wished. Raffaele had passed through Florence at the time of the attack on the life of Lorenzo and had been arrested because he was a Riario, and some members of his family had plotted in the killing. Very young at the time--his uncle Sixtus IV had made him cardinal at age 16-- and described as being handsome in the extreme, Lorenzo took it upon himself to see that the boy was freed. Now, years later and having lost his beauty, he commissioned a statue, a life-size Bacchus. Since the plot in Florence to kill Lorenzo, Raffaele had become wealthy. Lucky at cards, he had won 15,000 ducats during a night of play, a fortune he used to build an immense palace, the Palazzo della Cancelleria, the columns of which, dating back to the times of Augustus, were taken from the church of San Lorenzo that Raffaele didn't hesitate to have destroyed. He would later lose the palazzo to a Medici pope, Leo X, who remembered Raffaele's supposed role in the assassination attempt against *Il*

Magnifico, and told Raffaele, in other words, your palace or your life. Raffaele offered Michelangelo 150 florins for the *Bacchus*, a small fortune for a boy of 21. After pocketing the money Michelangelo denounced his collaboration with Raffaele, calling him crass and uncultivated, the reason being that Michelangelo needed the backing of the Medici, Raffaele's enemy.

Raffaele Riario by Andrea Bregno and the *Sleeping Cupid* by Michelangelo.

After the *Pietà* Michelangelo was rich but the money was put away in banks or under his mattress. His brother Buonarroto found him living in dingy, humid lodgings, dressed like a beggar. But Michelangelo would always live in avarice, collecting and hiding money, and at his death a whole chest of gold was said to have been found under his bed, a fraction of what he had horded away. He never slept enough, ate enough, or dressed warmly enough. He made it known to those around him that he was penniless, perhaps to keep them from asking for alms.

David was next, carved from a block of Carrara marble that had been awaiting the genius, in Florence, for 40 years. Since his early teens Michelangelo had dissected bodies, learning the secrets of tissue, muscles, veins, skin and bone, a grisly, horrifying experience in times without the least refrigeration, a task he's said to have enjoyed, certainly in the sense of a stepping stone to what would become, at age 26, his and the world's foremost masterpiece, *David,* that will reign until the end of time as the measure of perfect manhood.

A month after he started *David* he requested that a wall be built, allowing him to continue in private. Nearly two years later, it was removed. The problem arose as to where to put it. So great was its immediate impact that a panel of Italy's finest artists and most prominent citizens, 28 in number, including Botticelli, Filippino Lippi and da Vince himself--perhaps realizing that the statue would become the symbol of Florence itself--were united to decide where to put it. Months of discussion ended in accepting Michelangelo's own request to place it in the Piazza della Signoria. It was pulled there over greased wooden beams. It was positioned on a plinth and its genitals covered with a garland, and there it would remain until eventually placed in the Accademia di Belle Arti in 1873.

The first miracle was its creation, the second its perfection thanks to the acceptance of dissection, and the third is that it has gone through riots, revolutions and wars and has come out unscathed, although nearly immediately four louts were imprisoned for throwing stones at it and had to pay heavy fines. Antonio Forcellino, in his wonderful *Michelangelo*, underscores *David's* ''provocative nipples ... a penis full of energy ... testicles full of vigor.'' *David* is the canon of male beauty, now and for always, this gorgeous lad who might have just come out from swimming in the Arno, slightly grimacing at a friend's remark that the water must be cold, judging from his diminished manhood.

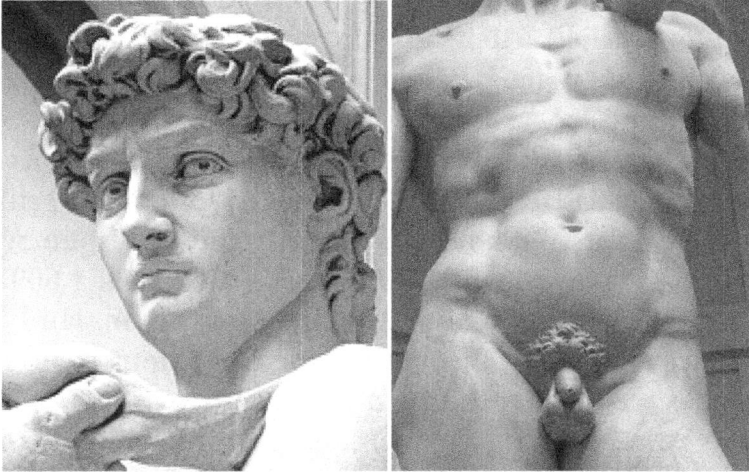

David grimacing and ''a penis full of energy ... testicles full of vigor''.

Vasari wrote that once one had seen *David*, one need never look at another statue. Strangely, at that very time another statue came to light, one sculpted well before the birth of Christ, unearthed in a field outside Rome in the presence of Michelangelo himself who had been summoned to see it. It is now in the Vatican and is proof that other magnificent creations *are* still worth seeing. It is the *Laocoön*, the story of which can be found in my book *TROY*. Later, in 1527, during a revolt in Florence, *David's* left arm had been broken. It lay on the ground three days until Vasari, then a young boy, ventured out during the fighting and recuperated the pieces that he sent to Cosimo I who, in 1543, had the arm restored.

After the *Pietà* Michelangelo did another virgin and child, the *Bruges Madonna*, for a Bruges merchant, and then the *Pitti Tondo,* a virgin and child carved from marble in the form of a sphere, not unlike a bas-relief. Martin Gayford in his wonderful *Michelangelo* claims that the model for this was a man [as was often the case in Michelangelo's works] The chisel strokes are highly visible, supposedly because Michelangelo liked this particular carving in this unpolished fashion.

Julius II became pope, taking Julius Caesar's first name as his own. Julius asked Michelangelo to build his tomb and asked where it should be placed. Michelangelo answered "in St. Peter's that I will build." "At what cost," asked the pope. "100,000 ducats" was the artist's answer. "Make it 200,000" was Julius' rejoinder. Julius had a passion for collecting ancient sculptures, more so even than Cardinal Riario, a friend, the man who had recommended Michelangelo to him. Julius advanced 1,600 ducats, money that Michelangelo immediately invested in land around Rome and property in Florence, especially houses in the Via Ghibellina, as well as depositing a part in the bank. He then went back to the Vatican to beg for more, which infuriated the pope.

He went to Carrara to command the marble. Martin Gayford takes over with this amazing scene: "One day when he was high up in the mountains above the town of Carrara, looking down at the peaks and valleys below and the Mediterranean in the distance beyond, he formed the wish to make a colossus that would be visible to mariners from afar. In other words, Michelangelo wanted to carve a chunk of mountain into a human figure. One guesses, though the subject is not described, that he had in mind a naked male body."

Julius was as impossibly irascible as was Michelangelo. When the artist went to see him and was repeatedly turned away, Michelangelo left for Florence. The pope, furious, sent five horsemen to bring him back, but as Florence was beyond the church's pale, they could do nothing. Political infighting ensued between the pope and Florence, the end result being that Michelangelo was forced to capitulate as no one could conceive of defying the pope. Julius had made the capitulation easier by sending someone to inform the artist that "No one will harm or offend him, and he will be received by us as if nothing amiss had taken place." Then, as would happen again and again, the pope changed his mind, deciding that painting the upper reaches of the Sistine Chapel should come first. He rode off to war with Bologna and, winning, then decided that a statue of himself should mark the event. Michelangelo was called for and actually did cast a huge figure in honor of Julius, a statue that was melted down the moment Bologna was lost. And Gayford writes: ''The tantalizing suspicion is that it must have been a masterpiece.''

Michelangelo returned to Rome and started work on the Sistine Chapel, painted daily on fresh plaster, a technique of such huge difficulty that even da Vinci is suspected of having given up work on his *Battle of Anghiari* because of his failure in mixing the right components, and then, later, making mistakes when doing *The Last Supper* which, consequently, is lost to us forever. That Michelangelo succeeded on just the mechanics, mechanics on such an incredible scale, is in itself a miracle, not counting, afterwards, the choice of the right oils and right pigments. A patch of plaster to be covered during a day's work was called a *giornata*, the seams of which cannot be seen from afar. Errors could be made up for by painting over the dried plaster, *a secco*. Differences in temperature and humidity complicated the making of the plaster, and the mixing of the colors was a daily challenge, especially as the final result could only be verified once the plaster had dried. Mistakes, when not corrected by painting *a secco*, led to the destruction of the day's work, starting again from scratch. Drawings were made on paper and transferred to the fresh plaster in two ways: In the first the paper, called a cartoon, was held against the plaster and holes were pierced along the lines of the drawing with a sharp instrument; the cartoon was taken away and the holes left an outline of the figures to be painted. Or secondly, the cartoon was pierced before being applied against the wet plaster and coal dust applied over the holes with a cloth. The Sistine paintings are a homage to the male body. In the part dedicated to the story of Noah, called *The Drunkenness of Noah*, Gayford points out that not only was Noah painted in the nude, his sons, shown covering the body while averting their eyes, were also painted--for absolutely no biblical reason--stark naked too. Gayford adds an interesting insight into why the church allowed nudity, saying that it was acceptable because God had made Christ as an incarnation of man, and so the body was not a shameful object. ''Here was a theological reason to decorate the chapel with buttocks, penises, biceps and pectorals,'' says Gayford. The surface Michelangelo had covered was 1,200 square meters, his head looking always upward, compensating with each stroke for the distortions caused by the curved surface. The ceiling was covered with nine biblical scenes, from the division of night and day to the creation of Adam and Eve and the Great Flood. The lunettes, half-moon spaces around the chapel, were covered with biblical ancestors, the pendentives, corner triangles, with prophets and prophetesses. Four years later, at the end of his labors, Michelangelo wrote in a letter to his father, ''I work harder than anyone who has ever lived!'' And it was so. At age 37 the King of Rome had become the King of the World.

While Michelangelo and his men were bent over, painting in excruciating conditions, in humidity and the freezing cold--an integral part of churches--Raphael had come onto the scene and had won over Julius who gave him his Vatican apartments to decorate. Raphael was physically beautiful and exquisite in his manners. As opposed to Michelangelo, he treated his assistants as brothers, getting the best out of them at all times. He was eager to learn and immediately absorbed the techniques of other artists. He sought knowledge, his conversation was intelligent, his way with people impeccable. He was sociable--in every aspect the opposite of Michelangelo.

Known for his avariciousness, Michelangelo would also be known for eventually abandoning everyone around him, from assistants to lovers. There were no exceptions. In this case, concerning the Sistine Chapel, he had invited friends from Florence to work with him, childhood friends as it were, paying them 10 ducats a month. But once the Chapel was nearly finished he dismissed them all, perhaps because friends were so much more demanding than strangers, and replaced them with Romans. He then spread the news that it was he, Michelangelo, who, after years of intense labor, had painted the Chapel by himself, a piece of propaganda we see in films even today.

It is said that in the more difficult portions of the ceiling, the lunettes and the pendentives, he would place a handsome boy, naked, before the area to be painted and shine lamplight from behind him, leaving a shadow on the portion of plaster that he would then outline, a technique that immeasurably shortened the usual preparation. The males served for both men and women.

The only hick, near the end, were the guests of rank that Julius would continually send him to be personally shown around the cramped space between the ceiling and the scaffolding, princes, dukes, even kings. Michelangelo was said to have fulfilled his mission with talent.

As mentioned, Lorenzo *Il Magnifico* had his son Giovanni named a cardinal at the ripe old age of 13. He was now 37 and pope, taking the name Leo X, although his coronation had to be put off until he was consecrated a priest, which had not as yet been the case. He is shown, fat, in a painting by Raphael, *Portrait of Leo X*, alongside his handsome brother, Cardinal Giulio di Giuliano de' Medici, son of *Il Magnifico's* assassinated brother, and future Pope Clement VII. Leo X was notorious for both the selling of indulgences and his homosexuality. He summoned Raphael to adorn the Vatican sauna with erotic paintings, in a room called the Stufetta del Cardinal Bibbiena, one of which shows the randy goat-god Pan leaping from the bushes with a monstrous erection.

On the sexual front Michelangelo could solicit whom he wished, although longer, more intense relations were known to have existed with Piero d'Argenta, an assistant, and an assistant known as Silvio, whose bedside he refused to leave when the boy became ill. Antonio Mini, 17, replaced Gherardo Perini, 19, who wrote that he was ready to offer Michelangelo any service. Niccolò da Pescia, "who lives with me," wrote the master, followed. There was Febo di Poggio and then Federico Ginori that Cellini describes as a young man with a fine spirit, noble, with handsome looks, whom a princess later took for lover.

Michelangelo did an enormous number of statues throughout his life. He lived 88 years [nearly 89], and as he said himself, it would have taken four lifetimes to accomplish all he wanted to accomplish. But a lot of time had been wasted, nearly *40 years* on just the tomb of Julius II. Time wasted by popes demanding one thing, only to change their minds in favor of something else. Literally years were spent at Carrara seeking out the best marble. One thing is for certain, after his run-in with Julius no other pope ever treated him like a servant again. He sculpted the Tomb of

Giuliano de' Medici, as well as a male nude [*Day*] and a woman [*Night*] who is nothing more than a male nude with breasts. Then he sculpted the Tomb of Lorenzo di Piero de' Medici showing Lorenzo, along with a male nude [*Dusk*] and another male nude with breasts [*Dawn*]. Michelangelo hadn't tried to make the statue of Giuliano resemble in any way Giuliano, and the same with Lorenzo. When someone criticized this he answered, Who cares? In a thousand years no one will remember what they looked like. He did another statue, *Victory*, a naked boy with a strangely small head.

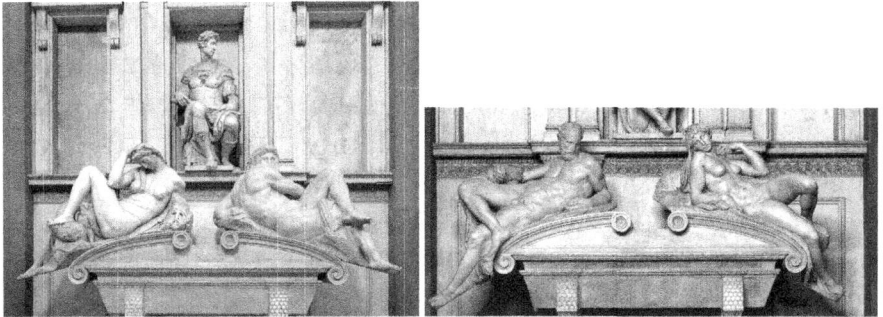

Day and Night and *Giuliano de' Medici / Dusk and Dawn*.

Sexually, he had his models and assistants, all of whom happened to be among the most beautiful and desirable boys found wherever he decided to set down roots. Benvenuto Cellini writes, in his autobiography, about a youth called Luigi Pulci ''whose singing was so lovely that Michelangelo, that superb sculptor and painter, used to rush along for the pleasure of hearing him whenever he knew where he was performing.'' The boy became Michelangelo's lover. Cellini goes on to say that Pulci's father had been beheaded for incest and that the boy had ''just left some bishop or other, and was riddled with the French pox [syphilis].'' Cellini nursed him back to health, Martin Gayford tells us, after which the boy had an affair with the nephew of a cardinal and with Cellini's own mistress, in revenge for which Cellini wounded him with a sword. Pulci was later killed falling from a horse while showing off in front of Cellini's mistress whom the lad was still seducing, as I recounted in the chapter on Cellini. All this is proof again that, in Florence, as in ancient Rome, a boy took advantage of literally any orifice that presented itself. Another source tells us that Michelangelo ''spent time without end helping boys, like Andrea Quaratesi, to learn how to draw.'' As Cicero had said of Plato who insisted he was platonic with boys, ''If his aim was only to teach philosophy, how was it that he chose only handsome boys and never ugly ones?'' The same was true with Michelangelo. Quaratesi was gorgeous, as seen in the master's drawing of him, *Portrait of Andrea Quaratesi*. Cellini tells us that despite the revolts and wars and even the plague, Michelangelo had never seemed more relaxed, and indeed took time to wander around the city, paying special attention to handsome young men.

The *Portrait of Andrea Quaratesi*

He was nonetheless getting old, around 50, and one wonders what his approach to boys was. Did he feel that his talent and willingness to instruct them compensated for his age, and for his need, ever more desperate, it seemed, as he grew older, to inhale their beauty? Could his art have gone on without them? Could he have survived as an artist for the exclusive sake of art? We won't know because to the very end he remained faithful to both, his art and to the blinding beauty of the boys that inspired it.

As Hadrian had found the boy of his life in Antinous, so too Michelangelo found his in Tommaso Cavalieri, who was described as being of incomparable beauty, of having graceful manners, and ''more to be loved the better he is known.'' Vasari wrote that he was "infinitely more than any other friend" to Michelangelo. Michelangelo sent him a letter in which he said, "I promise that the love I bear you is equal or perhaps greater to that I ever bore any man, nor have I ever valued a friendship more than I do yours." Thanks to Tommaso Michelangelo would know his own Renaissance, a new life at age 60, and he still had 30 years left to share it with this young gentleman. Michelangelo immediately set himself to drawing, the most rapid way to offer presents. One was *Tityus*. Tityus was Zeus' son who tried to rape Leto, in punishment for which he was eternally attacked by a vulture. Michelangelo showed him, in Gaylord's words, being assaulted with "the great bird's groin pushed against his buttocks." Next came the drawing of *Ganymede*, being carried off to Olympus where he would serve as Zeus' servant and bedmate. Then came *The Risen Christ*, a full-frontal nude, followed by *Phaeton*, the son of Apollo who nagged his father until allowed to drive the chariot of the sun. He lost control and Zeus had to kill him before he hit the earth, destroying it. Another highly unique drawing was *The Dream*, showing a naked young man surrounded by a ring of vices, a woman [a man with breasts] awaiting copulation, the exquisite buttocks of another young man, and a fully engorged dick. They were gifts to Tommaso, all accompanied by what would turn out to be dozens of sonnets.

Christ Risen and *The Dream*.

His favorite brother Buonarroto, the only one who married, died, and Michelangelo took over the care of his children, two boys of whom only Leonardo survived, age 9, who came to live with him, and a girl that he put in a nunnery until marriageable age. The story of Leonardo is amusing as later, when he was 20, Michelangelo would fall ill and the boy would rush to his side. But the master knew the boy by then, and knew that only his money interested him. He therefore chased him away, telling him, literally, to never darken his doorway again. But as the lad was the very last of the Buonarroti--and Michelangelo wanted the name to go on--he was forgiven. As I've written, at one time or another Michelangelo broke off with nearly everyone he had known. Even when his brother Buonarroto was living Michelangelo said he was disgusted with his family: ''I feel that I no longer have a father or brothers or anyone else in the world.''

Michelangelo served the popes in diplomacy. One of his statues, *Heracles*, was sent to François in France, the same François who held the dying head of da Vinci--and would offer employment to Cellini, as we've seen. The artist was also dispatched to Ferrara where the duke, Alfonso d'Este, was wild with joy to receive him. Alfonso was known to have two interests in life, making cannons in his own personal foundry and parading around town at night, his sword in one hand, his erect cock in the other. His former wife had been so fed up with him that she turned to women for satisfaction. He later married Lucrezia Borgia and at her death he married his mistress, apparently very rare during Renaissance Italy. Due to renewed problems in Florence Michelangelo considered going to the court of François I--he would have been there at the same time as da Vinci--but Florence threatened to jail him if he didn't return home, which he did.

In Florence Michelangelo painted *Leda and the Swan* for his new friend Alfonso d'Este. We see a nude woman in the wings of a swan, its long neck stretched across her belly, prior to inserting it. The result was that Leda gave birth to twins, Clytaemnestra and Helen, from the same egg, half fertilized by Leda's husband and the other half--the half that produced Helen--by Zeus. [You can find the full story in my book *TROY*.] The painting was later destroyed in France because it was found quasi pornographic.

Clement VII died and Paul III took his place. He had been named a cardinal by Alexander VI because he was the brother of Alexander's mistress. The Romans thereby changed his name from Cardinal Farnese to Cardinal Fregnese, ''Cardinal Cunt''. Paul III had been waiting years to get his hands of Michelangelo and did so now by ordering him to paint *The Last Judgment* in the Sistine Chapel, an immense work that would require scaffolding seven stories high and take five years to finish, longer than he had taken on the entire ceiling. In other Last Judgments only the damned were featured naked. Here nearly everyone was, the saved and canonized alike. As Gayford says, ''nude, curly-haired young men with the bodies of Oympic shot-putters passionately kiss and caress. Some of them hug grey-haired elders.'' The genitals and asses were later painted over by Michelangelo's assistant, Danielle da Volterra, after his master's death, his only claim to fame.

To a certain high-ranking critic who was shocked by the

nudity in *The Last Judgment,* and suggested that its place was in a sauna or tavern, Michelangelo painted the critic into a corner, showing a serpent chowing down on the critic's penis.

The serpent biting the critic's member.

Paul III bestowed a yearly salary on Michelangelo that would literally keep him and his family in opulence until the end of their lives. At the same time Michelangelo was offered total control over the restoration of St. Peter's, construction that had gone on for centuries at the cost of untold thousands, most lost through scandalous waste and theft. The new money did not free Michelangelo's mind, for such was his nature that he could never ever distance himself from worry. At the moment it was his nephew Leonardo who was still a problem, as he wouldn't marry. He did prove himself capable, however, of reproduction, as he fathered a son on the wife of a stonemason. Leonardo lived his own carefree existence, fueled by Michelangelo's considerable fortune, but such were the fireworks between the two that Michelangelo could quite literally not stand to be in the presence of the lad. Yet the boy's semen was vital to the survival of the Buonarroti name and Michelangelo seemed crazed by the possibility that the family name would be lost forever. Leonardo, for his part, tried to come to Rome as often as possible to learn-- felt Michelangelo--where every ducat of the artist's money had been invested or squirreled away, every piece of land, every farm, villa and building, every bank as well as what the master hid under his bed, be it drawings, paintings or gold. He wanted to be on hand too, Michelangelo was certain, when the artist's final hour came to make sure that the likes of Urbino, Michelangelo's assistant, much younger than Michelangelo, wouldn't steal everything not nailed down. Nonetheless, here Leonardo drops from our story and from History, but let it be known that he did have a son, Michelangelo, who died, but was followed by another son. Today Italy is full of Buonarroti, but how many hail from the genius is unknown. Another of Michelangelo's problems was the loss of his master builder, Cesare, who had built the *Last Judgment* scaffolding and was a vital aid with St. Peter's. The boy was caught between the legs of a young beauty whose husband dispatched them both with a knife, although the girl survived.

Julius III replaced Paul III. He was a lucky pope in that during his reign Queen Mary was placed on the English throne and Catholicism was restored, all of which led to his glorification and allowed him to live the lazy, dissolute existence he favored. Added to this was the fact that he possessed great administrative talent and as he had been named governor of Rome twice, he had that center too in his corner. He built an incredibly luxurious palace, the Villa Giolia, adorned by Michelangelo and Vasari and lesser artists who decorated it with Ganymede and other soft-core pornographic satyrs and naked angels, as mentioned earlier.

Julius had fulfilled his erotic fantasies thanks to a youngster, Santino, a streetwise urchin of 14 he saw and lusted for. He had his brother adopt the lad who then became his nephew, on whom he showered benefices and named a cardinal, ennobled under the title of Innocenzo Ciocchi Del Monte. He boasted of the boy's prowess in bed, Julius being the bottom to ''his hung boy''.

Of Julius the governor of Milan wrote, ''They say many bad things about this pope, that he is vicious, arrogant and crazy.'' Thomas Beard wrote: ''He makes a cardinal only of those who bugger him.'' The Venetian ambassador to the Vatican, Matteo Dandolo, wrote home to say that ''the pope shared his bed with a boy cardinal.''

After Julius III's death Innocenzo killed two men who had insulted him in some unrecorded way. The newly elected Pope

Pius IV had him arrested and imprisoned for several years, after which he was again arraigned, this time for raping two women. He died in obscurity and was buried, without a funeral, in the Del Monte chapel next to Julius.

Julius III and Michelangelo were about the same age, around 75, and Michelangelo was even closer to him than he had been with Paul III because Julius had more of an aesthetic sense than Paul, and then, both men shared the same erotic interests.

Calamity came when Julius was replaced by Paul IV, father of several children, among whom was a merciless killer and sodomite whose savage rape of a young priest cost the boy his life. The murderous son was Pier Luigi Farnese, who would later nearly totally ruin the life of Cellini. He was primitive, cruel, ruthless, decadent, courageous and daring [the perfect subject for a book that, for the moment, doesn't seem to exist], and at age 17 he was already a mercenary soldier in the pay of Venice, along with his brother Ranuccio. Under his father the pope he was given certain lands that he taxed to death, permitting, among his favorites, theft and murder. The boy was so evil that Pope Clement VI had tried to excommunicate him, only to be dissuaded by the bastard-boy's father. Pier Luigi was named head of the papal army, and another brother, Alessandro, a cardinal. Another of Paul's sons, Ottavio, married the illegitimate daughter of Charles V and his boy Orazio married the illegitimate daughter of Henry II of France. Pier Luigi was finally deprived of his miserable existence by Giovanni Anguissola who stabbed him to death and then threw the body, his neck attached to a rope, from the window of Pier Luigi's palace in Piacenza. After all kinds of ups-and-downs the duchy Pier Luigi ruled over finally went to his son [this one legitimate] Ottavio.

Paul IV called in the Inquisition, saying that he would burn his own father should he be a heretic. He imprisoned many of Michelangelo's free-thinking friends and even, just hours of taking power, cut off the funds that had been awarded to Michelangelo by Paul III, so rapidly that the decision could only have been made before Paul IV became pope, proof of a visceral hatred for the artist. He appointed Pierro Ligorio, a bitter enemy of Michelangelo, to keep an eye on the construction of St. Peter's.

Michelangelo had to put up with all this the best he could, especially as he was no longer armed with the resilience of youth. Cosimo I learned what was going on and immediately sent word to Michelangelo that he would be welcomed back home in Florence. But Michelangelo had become too invested in St. Peter's to withdraw, thinking, perhaps, that his eternal salvation--his place beside God--depended on his continuing God's work. And then, again, he was old, and could allow himself a certain detachment from the earth he would soon be leaving. Since the breaking of his nose and the loss of his adolescence, when all boys, or nearly, are beautiful, he had lost his own beauty, and although boys without number were attracted to the renowned master he was, this was less the case, less because in that domain he now lacked confidence and also, through their beautiful eyes he saw his own decline, unbearable and intolerable and ... ugly.

Then absolute disaster struck. Francesco d'Amadore, whom he called Urbino, died. He had come into Michelangelo's service as a young man when the master was himself but 30. Michelangelo grew to love Urbino, but in a decidedly different way from Tommaso. Urbino was well cared for, fed and clothed, and he did whatever was needed, from the marketing to the grounding and mixing the paints. But he never received a drawing as did Tommaso. Nor did he merit a sonnet. Yet he was always there. Michelangelo would never put on a clean shirt to greet him, nor, when the sap rose while painting his nudes and he wanted relief, would he need more than turn to Urbino. Urbino was always there. Just there. Until he was there no longer. It was then that Michelangelo died, not the biological end that came later. We need God to exist, He must exist in something, and that something, for Michelangelo, was Tommaso de' Cavalieri. He was the love of Michelangelo's life but not *the* love. That was Urbino, the only person permitted to accompany him during the painting of *The Last Judgment.* Just before the end Cellini had pleaded with Michelangelo to return to Florence, leaving Urbino behind to take care of his master's workshop and belongings. As Cellini related in his autobiography, ''Hearing this, Urbino, in an uncouth way, shouted out 'I will never leave Michelangelo, not until either he or I is under the ground'.''

Surrounded by what the world has to offer in supreme beauty, Michelangelo died alone, having pushed away even Tommaso at the end, thusly sparing himself the cruelest of all destinies, seeing his own ugliness reflected in the eyes of those he had cherished most, the eyes of his lovers, models, assistants, apprentices, boys he met and offered to draw or to teach how to draw, boys in taverns and in alleys after dark in a city, Florence, reputed for its warm nights of sublime encounters--with the imperishable boys of imperishable Italy. There would be no Salaì or Melzi at his side, as there had been at da Vinci's passing. Like Hadrian who lost Antinous, he too would meet his maker alone-- the world's supreme artist, not just in his time, but of all time.

HOMOSEXUALITY

CHAPTER SIX

FLORENTINE HOMOSEXUALITY

As we learn in Michael Rocke's marvelous *Forbidden Friendships, Homosexuality and Male Culture in Renaissance Italy*, the Office of the Night was set up to eliminate sodomy in the Florence of 1432 to 1505, the exact period covering the lives of Cellini, Michelangelo and da Vinci. It's true that I will be using "sodomy" in the sense of male-male sexuality, but we must never forget that back then sodomy was anything involving both men and women, beyond straight missionary-style sexual intercourse. Cunnilingus was sodomy, as was mutual masturbation. The ultimate penalties were castration and burning at the stake, but because everyone was doing it, nearly everyone got off with a slap on the wrist. Lorenzo *Il Magnifico* reigned during this time, the dichotomy being that although the Office of the Night opened its doors, never--thanks to Lorenzo--were Florentines more liberal in the acceptance of male-male sexuality. Boys could do whatever they wanted together, under the title of sexual discovery, fully admitted by parents, never considered *homo*sexuality. Boys bathed naked in the Arno river, to the immense pleasure of the participants and the men on the banks observing them.

Lorenzo *Il Magnifico*'s grandfather, Cosimo, had translators translating the Greek humanists, especially Plato, into Italian. He supported the arts, greatly influenced by Greek nudity, and surrounded himself with the great thinkers and writers of the period, one of whom was Antonio Beccadelli who dedicated his *Hermaphroditus* to Cosimo, a work praising love and sex between males.

As Rocke writes, ''sex between males was a common and integral feature of life in'' Florence. Today's divisions of groups into homosexual, heterosexual and bisexual is so accepted that it is difficult to envision a culture, that of Florence, in which a man simply never categorized himself. His quest was pleasure, in whichever direction the quest led him. In this he followed his ancestors the Romans. For them too if a man was randy, he didn't care if the nearest slave at hand was male or female (4).

Florentine sex was an inheritance of Greece and Rome in that it concerned men who copulated with boys. Greeks, Romans and Florentines reserved the passive role to boys, the masculine, virile role to men. Being penetrated has never been considered masculine, and today too he-men are tops, not bottoms. Naturally, in alleys, always dark, men did what came naturally, and although some boys who became men still preferred ''being taken'', this was not considered normal behavior.

Under Lorenzo *Il Magnifico* the penalties for sexual acts between men were relaxed, as said, except for men who sexually abused very young boys, the sentence for which could be castration or burning at the stake. Boys 14 to 18 who allowed themselves to be sodomized were fined 100 lire, while boys under 14 paid 50 lire. Men were fined 500 lire, pimps and even dads who enjoyed their sons paid the same. Foreigners--non-Florentines-- could be beaten to death by whoever found them *in flagrante delicto*, or if brought to justice they could be tortured and burned. Lorenzo was surrounded by homosexuals. Puigi Pulci was a childhood friend and was denounced by three boys he had sodomized. A de' Medici, Franceschino, was repeatedly incriminated for same-sex-erotic-relations. Another close friend, Braccio di Domenico Martelli, was accused by stable boys for having sex with them ''on many and many times,'' often in the outbuildings on Medici land. The teacher of Lorenzo's sons, Poliziano, wrote *Orfeo*, an ode to homosexual love. One of his many lovers was Pico della Mirandola, a writer and philosopher. Both were at first thought to have died of syphilis and were buried together. In 2007 their bodies were exhumed and tests found they had both been poisoned by arsenic. Some believe that Poliziano's student, Lorenzo's son Piero, did the deed, as accusations of their homosexuality were becoming a burden. Others believe Pico's secretary did it because Pico had drawn too close to Savonarola. Still others say that Poliziano died of fever due to the unrequited love of a boy.

Poliziano, born Angelo Ambrogini in Montepulciano, was a Renaissance humanist philosopher who studied under Ficino at his Platonic Academy and later taught at the University of Florence. His father was a jurist murdered by the enemies of the Medici because he championed their cause. Poliziano was a known lover of boys, some very young, and had been charged by Florentine authorities with sodomy, charges dropped thanks to the influence of his patrons the Medici. They too severed their relations with Poliziano [we don't know why] but later reinstated him, leaving one with the impression that he had not been dismissed due to overly affectionate caresses involving Piero and his brothers.

Pico della Mirandola was a humanist philosopher like Poliziano, familiar with Latin, Greek, Hebrew and Arabic. Somewhat like Plato, he claimed that perfection was found in the virtuous love of a boy, with whom the older man shared his knowledge. The problem was that both Mirandola and Plato hid the sexual side of their relationships, pretending it never existed. In the case of Pico, Savonarola found out, and at Pico's death he told his congregation that Pico was now in purgatory, for sins he didn't specify.

Pico died within two months of Poliziano, and although the arsenic found in both is inexplicable, modern historians feel relatively certain they both died of syphilis. The love of Pico's life had been Girolamo Benivieni, who was placed in the same grave as Pico 49 years after Pico's death, Benivieni age 89.

Poliziano with his student Giuliano de' Medici

One Florentine law of incredible precision banned innkeepers [inns being highly favored for trysts] from selling sweets as they attracted men and boys and their "spiciness" encouraged lubricity. Boys under 18 who were bottoms [passive] could not, under the law, be executed. Tops could. A man who obliged another to have sex could be burned at the stake, as well as rapists and men who sexually assaulted minors. The Office of the Night allowed men and boys to give themselves up, thereby winning total immunity [if, at the same time, they fingered those with whom they'd had sex]. The Office of the Night also put up letterboxes, especially in churches in and around Florence, where informers could denounce sodomites. In return the informers received one-fourth of the fines the perpetrators paid. There were normally six Officers of the Night. A majority was needed to convict, but five votes were needed for a conviction that entailed huge fines or imprisonment or banishment or death at the stake. As sex between men was practiced by everyone, it perhaps shouldn't be surprising that the first man convicted, Rocke tells us, was the official who had set up the Office of the Night! As he confessed the crime of butt-fucking fourteen-year-old Francesco di Giovanni, his fine was reduced to 25 florins. Later, under Lorenzo *Il Magnifico*, fines were further reduced to 1 or 2 florins. During the life of Lorenzo *Il Magnifico* the Office of the Night arrested 1,700 men for sodomy. Because lovemaking most often takes place away from enquiring eyes, one can scarcely imagine the thousands and thousands of pleasure-seeking homoerotic affairs that took place in rooms and under the cover of night, but will be forever anonymous. Rocke goes on to precise that ''In the late fifteenth century, by the time they reached the age of thirty, at least one of every two youths in the city of Florence had been formally implicated in sodomy; by age forty, at least two of every three men had been incriminated.'' Again, everyone was doing it.

Only after the death of Lorenzo in 1492, and the expulsion of his nitwit son, Piero, were fines, convictions and other forms of punishment greatly increased.

As in ancient Rome, boys were needed to run the country, to farm it and to provide its cannon fodder. Laws were therefore established to force men to marry around age 30. In 1348, 80,000 Florentines out of a population of 120,000 was killed by the plague. In 1400, 12,000 out of the remaining 60,000 were decimated. Boys were needed to replace them, further reason to combat sex between men. On the religious side, Savonarola was ever present to preach against sodomy. He encouraged burning at the stake or, at the very least, banishment. Florentines considered anal sex the most evil of all sexual sins, even when they themselves were doing it.

A father could advance socially and further his career if his sons attracted the attention of persons in power, persons who would help a father who turned a blind eye to what went on outside the home. After all, a girl's virginity was lost once and forever. And a boy's? How was one to know what a man's son had or had not experienced? Plainly, some men basked in the sun of their sons' beauty, and fully took advantage of it. Like the Greeks, Florentines believed that lust was at its highest between the ages of 14 and 24, when young anuses were believed to be more supple than men's, and, in truth, many boys adored being scratched there where it itched. As a father had often undergone the same thing when he was young, where was the harm?

Boys, then as now, were mantraps: The poet Tibullus tells us that we have no chance against tender youths, who give us ample reason to love them. This boy is pleasing due to the masterly control he has over his horse; this other one causes our hearts to flutter when he breaks the surface of the water, showing his snow-white chest and ass; so and so captures us by his daring; such and such by his peaches-and-cream complexion. At times youths objected for the form when men made advances, even menacing to tell their fathers if the men didn't cease. But once bridled, and the man could find rest after expulsing his lust, it was the boy who sought more, awaking the man from sleep by the gentle entreating of his buttocks. Again satisfied, man and boy plunged back into the arms of Morpheus for an hour before the boy asked if the man would like to do it again. The man would, but when the boy stirred still again, an hour later, it was the man who threatened the boy, "If you don't stop I'll tell your daddy!"

Florence fought against same-sex-erotic-relations by opening whorehouses, literally supplying men with female prostitutes. These areas became major zones where men met, perhaps originally to have sex with women, but wound up doing it together, nearly always anally, and nearly always for free. Other zones for sex were in and outside taverns, dark alleys, the Mercato Vecchio, Borgo Santi Apostoli, Parte Guelfa, the Piazza della Signoria, gardens, covered doorways, stables, under overhanging upper stories, in the baths and the numerous parks. Workshops were ideal places where boys joked about their conquests and exhibited themselves freely, zones of free sex between apprentices, their masters, models, and whoever dropped by to exchange gossip. Some workshops gained reputations as nothing more than whorehouses where one could go for sex as one could at any tavern that had rooms. Everything was at hand at the workshops. They were more or less private and included sleeping quarters. Warm friendships developed between the boys and young men working there, to the extent that literally anything imaginable went on. Michael Rocke mentions a workshop run by Francesco di Giuliano Benintendi, "full of boys," where Benintendi encouraged sodomy on the premises. Florentines considered that in such places boys were simply gaining sexual experience before marriage, around age 30. Boys who slept rough were choice objects, thankful for a meal and warm place to sleep if invited back; if not, the gift of a florin. Churches were often used because they were open, they were shelters and they possessed innumerable recesses. Or a boy simply invited a friend home, often to a room in his parents' house, and as boys shared beds at the time, nothing suspect was necessarily going to take place. Renaissance women cared little or nothing about their husbands straying away, as finding a man to pay for their upkeep was usually sufficient.

I'll end this chapter with a contribution from gay-studies Professor Randolph Trumbach: ''The sodomy which most Florentine males practiced was strictly organized by differences in age. From the time boys entered puberty at 15 [for physiological reason, puberty began later than it does today] until their beards began to grow at 19 or 20, they were anally penetrated by older men. These men were usually unmarried and in their later twenties. Between 19 and 23 there seems to have been a transitional phase when a young man could be both active and passive, but he was always active with someone younger and passive with someone older. Adolescent boys occasionally took turns at being active and passive with each other.'' The assertion that someone older was always active with someone younger is certainly questionable, as many men thrive on being penetrated, and are uncaring about the age of the boy/man who gives him satisfaction.

CHAPTER SEVEN

VENETIAN HOMOSEXUALITY

While homosexuality in Florence under the Medici was treated with wrist-slapping tolerance [and a way for officials to make money], this was not necessarily the case in other regions of Italy. Florence was one extreme, Venice another, and a clearer picture of what was going on in the country as a whole can only be reached by comparing both city-states.

Sodomy will never find acceptance in the public mind for reasons that are summarized in my translation of Antonio Rocco's *Alcibiades the Schoolboy*, in which Alcibiades stigmatized the act as filthy, using the words stink and shit, while Philotime, the

Socratic teacher whose hard-on he does nothing to hide from the boy, refers to ambrosia, in color and odor (22).

For the Serenissima it was the sin of Sodom and Gomorrah, which God utterly destroyed. In committing it the miscreant did not respect God because he didn't have Him always before his eyes, in the same way that we sin against Him by having evil thoughts when mentally undressing a boy/girl.

The sin became so great in the eyes of Venetians that its prosecution was taken from the hands of the Signori di Notte and placed in those of the Ten who severely stiffened the penalties. Guido Ruggioro in his excellent and complete *The Boundaries of Eros, Sex Crime and Sexuality in Renaissance Venice* brings us the case of the lad Giocomello repeatedly abused by a co-worker Pietro. Pietro claimed he had never penetrated the boy [a distinction of life-or-death importance] but Giocomello maintained he did, and often. The problem was that Giocomello kept going to Pietro's bed to sleep, while there were other beds available. Under torture Giocomello stuck to his innocence and Pietro admitted only to ejaculating between the boy's thighs. Giocomello was eventually let off as were many passive participants in sex, and Pietro was burned alive.

The fear of Sodom-and-Gomorrah-like destruction by God was such that sodomy was banned on ships for fear of being sunk by God's wrath, where in times past such acts were part and parcel of naval life. Merchants and bankers also were certain that the reoccurrence of the plague was a direct result of sodomy. Intercrural sex [between the legs] was prevalent, but although there was no penetration two men pleading guilty to it could nonetheless be burned alive, perhaps because it eventually led to anal sex.

The Ten were extremely discreet in repeating details unless they wished to emphasize something especially horrid, like the 8-year-old son of a noble raped by two noble friends of the family. Their act was disclosed in detail, including the screams of the boy and the damage done to his inner passage. It is evident that in this case burning at the stake was a pleasure for the Ten who, it seems, did all they could to strike a balance between a crime and its punishment. Legislation was eventually enacted that *obliged* citizens to report cases of anal injuries. The anal abuse of women was punished [but not by death], something new then, and even today it is considered a natural form of birth control by Italian boys.

Punishment varied greatly. Passive children could get off scot-free, while one boy of 10 received 10 lashes. Nevertheless, as the legal age was 14, most boys caught in passive sex were released with nothing more than a stern warning, while a workman could lose a hand or even an eye as punishment. Banishment was also widely used, three years being the mean, a punishment often reserved for nobles, although nobles were at times burned like others. Or a jail term in addition to banishment was possible. Punitive measures were tailor-made and implacable. There was no space for kidding around in the Serenissima.

When it became evident that boys were practicing their trade freely, without legal constants thanks to their being underage [under age 14], a new law was passed that allowed them to receive a minimum of 3 months in jail and from 12 to 20 lashes in the Venice torture chamber, an experience that certainly put more than one back on the right track. As shown in Florence [and in Rome too] boys made a living from age 9, and de Vinci, Cellini and a huge number of others paid for their services. [In a Fellini film a child scorns a man who lightly fondles his balls through his trousers, until he produces a gold coin that changes the frown to a smile of (im)pure delight.]

Jail today, where one can have his teeth knocked out to facilitate fellatio, is little compared to then. One boy escaped prison and when his father ordered him back he showed him his wounds, an anus and genitals quasi destroyed, and an arm so damaged through torture [by whom and why is not disclosed] that it had to be amputated. Rapes involving men were punished with far greater severity than those involving women, always death by burning. A man was considered lucky if he were beheaded before his body was transformed into ashes, while men who abused women never got more than jail sentences.

A complicated case came up that involved 15 nobles and 3 men who claimed to be clergy, and therefore punishable only by the church. The people, however, wanted them all put to death.

This was the case for the nobles who were duly burned, but not the 3 ecclesiastics. The Ten wrote to the pope who told them to contact the local bishop who would come up with a sufficiently harsh judgment. One of the 3 was judged to have lied about his being a priest and was immediately burned alive, along with the person who had certified that he was one. The bishop, a law-abiding Venetian, decreed that one of the remaining two men be put in a cage and hung from the campanile of San Marco for the rest of his life. Luckily for him, he escaped. The last of the 3 was put in jail on bread and water.

A case that proved the Ten's incredible diligence involved a servant, Lodovico Spetiario and the master he killed, purportedly for his money, the noble Antonio Morosini. Lodovico fled and the Ten offered a large reward for his capture, 500 lire. He was caught in Ferrara and under torture he claimed that he had killed Morosini to preserve his honor when the noble homosexually attacked him. The Ten believed the servant and he was freed.

One man who had a hormonal imbalance felt himself to be more woman than man and dressed himself in a robe, took the name Rolandina, and took on ''an infinite number of men'', which makes some wonder to what extent homosexuality was prevalent in Venice, although men perhaps turned to ''her'' because Rolandina was available for quick sex, nothing more.

The Ten noted that some schools were open after dark, and exactly like the Greeks 2000 years earlier, they ordered their closing during all but daylight hours, ''because it might lead some of these youths to commit prohibited deeds,'' Ruggiero informs us, quoting a text from the period. There would be no private lessons either [the first step the seducer of Alcibiades had taken so that he could convince the lad, once they were alone, to let himself be fondled, which Alcibiades immediately did]. Barbershops were meeting grounds for homosexuals, as they had been in ancient Greece and Rome. Those who assiduously frequented them were tortured, a great number of whom confessed--due to the truth or to escape more pain is unknown, as they were burned alive before they could tell anyone whether they had told the truth or not. In places where men were known to meet, the Ten made lanterns obligatory, decreeing even their number. Not only were places where one drank and played cards suspect, but so were pastry shops [sugar has always been a supposed cause of men's sexual arousal, the reputation that chocolate has today]. Male nudity in paintings and sculptures was forbidden, but the Ten had to back off here, perhaps because men were created in the image of God and therefore not, in themselves, lewd. This tolerance is something I too have always found incredible. I know that *David's* attributes were covered for 200 years in Florence, as pictures of *David* are today in many parts of the United States. But, in truth, it does seem lame to claim that *David* is not sexually arousing, down to his nipples, down to his ample testicles and foreskin, down to the down descending from his navel.

Sex in Florence and the Serenissima most often took place among unwashed bodies, as the bathing purity of the Ancient Romans often gave way to fears that warm water opened the pores to diseases, the worst of which was the plague. And we have this quote from Christopher Hibbert in his *Florence*: ''William Holman Hunt, who had taken a studio in Florence where his wife had died, thought the people 'the filthiest' he had ever known: 'Such stinks meet you on the street and wake you up at night that it seems Pestilence must be on the threshold with destruction for the whole city ... What do you think of a boy of fifteen or sixteen in the blazing sunlight at one o'clock on Sunday, in Kensington Gore say, taking his breeches down for a necessary purpose which he performs while he still goes on with his game of pitch and toss with seven or eight companions some two years old who remain in a circle about two or three yards round him. Then again to an old gentleman of the utmost respectability ... walking across the road at the Duke of York's column and taking down his black cloth breeches for the same purpose.' ''

FLORENTINE ARTISTS

[PART TWO]

CHAPTER EIGHT

LEONARDO DA VINCI, DONATELLO AND RAPHAEL

LEONARDO DA VINCI
1452 - 1519

Leonardo was gorgeous and so were his boys, beginning with Salaì, magnificent in da Vinci's two paintings, *St. John the Baptist* and *Bacchus*, the absolute ultimate in homoerotic art. The beauty of Leonardo can be admired in Francesco Botticini's *Tobias and the Three Archangels*, Leonardo shown as the first angel; and Verrocchio's *Archangel Michael* [although his presence is disputed].

Da Vinci's *Bacchus*.

Salaì was Leonardo's nickname for his boy lover, meaning Little Devil, bestowed when Salaì, unmanageable and stubborn, hotheaded and careless, proved to be a liar and a not-so-accomplished--although highly assiduous--thief. This at the prepubescent age of ten. A very close friend of Leonardo's, Giacomo Andrea, was present during one of the first meals shared with Salaì. It is suspected that Leonardo's idea for the *Vitruvian Man,* the male body made up of two superimposed figures showing four arms and four legs, was originally Andrea's invention, and bares an amazing resemblance to Leonardo himself. Of Salaì Andrea said he was a glutton who ate as much as four monks, spilled the wine and broke whatever his fingers came upon. Another friend, the painter, architect, writer and historian Giorgio Vasari wrote that Salaì was ''a graceful and beautiful boy with curly hair and a delight to Leonardo.'' There is no doubt that he was Leonardo's bedmate, the only question being from what age? Along the line Leonardo drew him with a huge erection, a drawing called *The Incarnate Angel.* But Salaì was such a trickster that he may have drawn in the phallus himself on one of his master's many drawings of him. [Another drawing is entitled *Salaì's Ass,* the boy's buttocks shown surrounded by penises.]

The Vitruvian Man

Numerous times Salaì made off with Leonardo's money, but as the painter had endless commissions, he was rich and, at the end of his life, even wealthy. Salaì is said to have bought clothes with most of the lucre he swiped, at one point possessing thirty pairs of shoes. Throughout his entire life he remained by Leonardo's side, at times replaced, as with the handsome Melzi, Melzi to whom Leonardo left half of his fortune, the other half going to Salaì. But most importantly, both boys remained loyal to the master, both present at his side to witness his last breath.

The Incarnate Angel

Some find it incomprehensible that Leonardo, known for his exactitude [most sources say it took him 4 years to paint the *Mona Lisa*, others as long as 14], painted *John the Baptist* as an erotic young man and not the usual old prophet in most paintings. The surprise is greater still when we learn that in Leonardo's painting the Baptist was at first totally nude, and that only later were animal skins added. At any rate, Leonardo kept the painting with him to the very end, understandable as *John the Baptist* is the most beautiful portrait of a young man that has ever been put on canvas. He kept the *Mona Lisa* until the very end too, at the Chateau of Clos Lucé, a chateau given to him by François I, who is believed to have held his head as he expired, perhaps his last gaze on Salaì at his bedside or Salaì, much younger, the model for *John the Baptist.*

John the Baptist

Maybe his last gaze was on the *Mona Lisa*, one might say. But it didn't matter. Both the *Mona Lisa* and the *John the Baptist* had the same enigmatic smile, because *La Giaconda*, too, may have been of Salaì, a hypothesis forwarded by some. Perhaps stranger still is the painting called the *Monna Vanna*, a lookalike Mona Lisa right down to the smile, but this one thought to have been painted by the boy Leonardo considered his best pupil, the selfsame Salaì, a self-portrait Salaì did of himself, with breasts. At his death the *Mona Lisa* was bequeathed to Salaì and sold to King François I for 4,000 écus. Supposedly a huge number of highly erotic drawings were destroyed at the time by a resident priest, whether under da Vinci's orders or not is unknown, giving credence to those who believe that *The Incarnate Angel* was indeed by da Vinci's hand.

Nude Mona Lisa by **Salaì** [his real name Gian Giacomo Caprotti].

No one will ever know why the child Salaì was chosen by Leonardo. Leonardo himself said he had come upon him while the child was drawing, and seeing potential, he made enquiries into his family. Finding them poor, he made them an offer they couldn't refuse. Leonardo was thirty-eight, an age when a man begins to think of settling down, tired of running after boys his ever-so-slightly decline in beauty was more and more compensated for by a few easy coins, of which, for him, there was no dearth. Already, at age twenty-four, he'd been arrested by the Florentine Office of the Night, he and a gang of his friends, all accused of sodomy. He got off as the charge was difficult to prove, but it shows that, like other Florentines, he was no parvenu to male-male intercourse. His interest for those of his own sex was already well known, as reflected by the male nudes that studded his canvases and notebooks, erotic proof of the mystical attraction men have for each other (11). The boy Leonardo and his friends were accused of sodomizing was an apprentice goldsmith, Jacopo Salterelli, age 17, a notorious rent-boy. Serge Bramly in his *Leonardo* concludes: ''The authorities were prepared to turn a blind eye to various sexual misdemeanors--homosexuality, incest, bigamy: fairly common forms of behavior, after all--on the condition that public order was not disturbed and that a minimum of discretion was observed.'' But Leonardo must have suffered nonetheless now that everyone in Florence knew about his indiscretion, including his father.

Leonardo's exposure to boys was literally limitless. In the workshop artists and their models came and went as they discussed artistic issues and gossiped, most of whom were sexually available. And as Leonardo gained in reputation, he was surrounded by a constantly renewed court of extremely beautiful boys and young men, friends and models, many of which adorned his paintings and notebooks: thighs, buttocks and penises from repose to full erection, or, in his words, ''long, thick and heavy'' to ''short, slim and soft,'' and he continues: The male member ''has a mind of its own. When we desire to stimulate it, it obstinately refuses, or the opposite. When a man is asleep it is awake, and when he's awake it's asleep. It remains inactive when we want action, and wants action when we forbid it.'' He maintains that ''it'' can at times be dangerous, inundating the world with human beings the world in no way needs, as well as being the entry point for diseases [syphilis having reached Italy in 1495]. On one page of his notebook he noted: ''A woman's desire is opposite to that of a man's. She wants the size of his member to be as large as possible, while he wants the opposite [in the woman's sex], so that neither gets what he's after.'' A friend proudly wrote him about the son the man had just given birth to. Leonardo's response was unexpected to say the least, ''I had once thought you to be a prudent man, but now have proof to the contrary, for you congratulate yourself on bringing forth an enemy whose energies will be directed at gaining his freedom, freedom that will only come with your demise.'' Despite his pessimism Leonardo, both gorgeous and good natured, must have made a lot of boys extremely happy.

Vasari wrote that ''there is something supernatural in the accumulation in one person of so much beauty, grace, strength and intelligence as in da Vinci.'' Da Vinci was also said to be preternaturally gentle for the period, kind to rich and poor alike, generous, always in good humor and possessing a sense of humor. Vasari goes on to say, ''Leonardo had such a great presence that one only had to see him for all sadness to vanish.'' As a person he personified what Plato would call the perfect alloy of *virtu*, intelligence and knowledge.

Leonardo was born, out-of-wedlock, in 1473 in the Tuscan hill town of Vinci, near the Arno River that flows through Florence. His father was a wealthy legal notary and his mother a peasant. His full name was Leonardo di ser Piero da Vinci, meaning Leonardo son of Messer Piero from Vinci. He lived his first five years with his mother, then with his father who married four times, but never Leonardo's mother. He was a bastard but that had few ill effects in Renaissance Florence, although bastards couldn't be notaries, the position of his father which would certainly have become his own had he been born in wedlock--to the loss of the entire world had his destiny been such. He couldn't become a doctor, either, a pursuit he might well have chosen, given his love of science.

At age fourteen he was apprenticed to the painter Andrea di Cione, known to the world as Verrocchio, in whose *Archangel Michel* we see the incredibly beautiful Leonardo. The choice of Verrocchio was fortuitous as his paintings are exquisite, the demonstration that Fortune never ever stopped looking over Leonardo's shoulder. Verrocchio's shop was in Florence, another lucky break as it was then, as today, arguably the most beautiful city in the world. Verrocchio never married, but this was true of half of the male population of Florence for whom freedom to live their lives as they wished was of prime importance. Verrocchio's apprentices included Ghirlandaio, Botticelli and Botticini, whose *Tobias and the Three Archangels* features da Vinci. At age twenty Leonardo's father set him up with his own workshop, but his love for Verrocchio was such that they worked together until Verrocchio's death. Verrocchio was a father figure, perhaps the most important man in the artist's life.

Botticini's *Tobias and the Three Archangels,* da Vinci the angel on the left.

Verrocchio was described by Serge Bramly in his marvelous *Leonardo* as "a sort of one-man university of the arts." He knew and taught literally everything with the exception of huge wall murals, the reason for the disastrous destruction of the *Last Supper*, discussed herein later. When Verrocchio was only 17 he had struck a boy, age 14, with a stone, killing him. He was jailed but released when it was proven that the incident had been an accident. Verrocchio was nonetheless haunted by what he had done to the very end, especially as he was a good man, sensitive in the extreme. Verrocchio's father died the year of the accident and Verrocchio found himself at the head of a family consisting of his mother and six brothers and sisters. Years later, now well-off, he was still providing for them as well as his nephews and nieces. Verrocchio was apprenticed to a goldsmith and began learning the skills of drawing, engraving, carving and metallurgy, followed by other jobs in which he would master sculpturing, painting, the basics of architecture and his favorite subject, mathematics. He was commissioned to make the tombstone for the person who started the Italian Renaissance, Cosimo de' Medici. Verrocchio established his own workshop, a large room with all the instruments an artist uses on the surrounding walls, plus sculptors' turntables, workbenches, easels and kiln, as well as shelves bent by the weight of busts and plaster body parts. The production of the workshop was phenomenal as it touched numerous aspects of daily life. Verrocchio and his apprentices turned out banners, coats of arms, caparisons for horses, designs for embroiderers and weavers, pieces of armor, candelabras, bells and furniture, as well as decorating wooden chests and painting canvas for tents. Whatever could be artistically created or ornamented was undertaken by Verrocchio. Around the workshop and upstairs were the living quarters for the boys and the kitchen.

An apprenticeship lasted around thirteen years, which started with sweeping the workshop and cleaning the materials, moved to the rudiments of drawing, making paintbrushes, preparing canvases and pigments freshly ground every day; sculpting, painting, drawing, decorating; even learning how to make salts out of human excrement--from dawn to dusk, seven days a week.

The workshop became the artistic center of Florence where one exchanged ideas, models, recipes for paint and varnishes, where philosophy was disputed and gossip swapped. Of special interest was the new Flemish technique for mixing paint with oil instead of water, making for brighter and more long-lasting colors and smoother gradations of tints. Songs were sung and music was played, as Verrocchio was an accomplished musician. He was truly a kind of Pericles who created the conditions for geniuses to thrive--much of which was perhaps due to his attempt to compensate for having killed a lad of 14.

Like all boys, Leonardo liked to dress up and nowhere in world history was there a better, more exciting city than Florence under the Medici. The costumes for festivals and carnivals [designed by Verrocchio and company] were magnificent. Boys' trousers skin tight, ample shirts that fell from the collar bones to the upper thighs, taken in by a thin belt at the waist, shirts that scarcely covered the piece of cloth over the genitals, held in place by two ribbons.

At age twenty-four, as mentioned, Leonardo was arrested for sodomy. Four years later he moved in with the Medici, with Lorenzo *Il Magnifico*, thanks to whom commissions began to rain down on the lad. From there he went on to the career for which he is known the world over. Salaì followed in his footsteps, helping with his paintings, constructing the machines inspired by the master, keeping shop for the man who would reward him with a golden retirement, providing Salaì with a piece of land and the money on which to build a home. Salaì would later die in a duel, some say by sword, others by firearms, still others by a crossbow.

A saner man than Leonardo would have thrown Salaì out when the boy stole his first lire, or when caught in bed with another of the master's apprentices. But the genius whom we are all acquainted with, the master of every domain that took his interest, revered the boy as his source of inspiration, as the cherished love of his life. Leonardo could see beyond daily tribulations and petty treasons, holding firm to the companion with whom he would walk the rocky path of life, right up to the end. That Salaì was beautiful and beautifully built was important, without doubt, but in a land like Italy, with apprentices he had to turn away in droves, he could have found a dozen replacements. Yet Leonardo knew that in the end one goes ahead alone or one grants the concessions necessary to share the route with another. The alternative is sterile old age, the shipwreck so well described by de Gaulle in his *Memoirs*.

One of the most impressive realities concerning Leonardo's notebooks is that amidst the thousands of pages there is nearly nothing of a personal nature about the master himself. We have only his thoughts, observations, calculations, recipes for mixing oils and ground paint, machines of all nature, fortification, anatomical drawings, male genitalia galore, the texts in reverse left-hand writing, much of which is illegible.

The second love of Leonardo's life was Giovanni Francesco Melzi who became his apprentice around 1508. The boy's father was a senator and a captain in Louis XII's army. Unlike Salaì who only partially succeeded as a painter, Giovanni Francesco Melzi did some remarkable works. As handsome as Leonardo had been in his youth, Giovanni followed his master to the end, inheriting half of his *oeuvre*. The Melzi family property was at Vaprio d'Adda, an enormous mansion, nearly a small Versailles, witness to the Melzi wealth. It was he who informed Leonardo's family of his master's death. Then he returned to Vaprio d'Adda with his master's notebooks and several paintings. He wrote a book drawn from Leonardo's observations about painting, which eventually found its way into the Vatican. The historian Vasari contacted Giovanni for help with the book he himself was writing. About Melzi Vasari wrote, ''Sir Francesco Melzi, a Milanese gentleman, entered da Vinci's service as a young and extremely good-looking adolescent. He was very dear to his master and today is a noble and handsome old man.'' Giovanni left a son, Orazio, who sold off the notebooks bit by bit. His self-portrait, proof of Giovanni Melzi's wondrous beauty, can be found near my own home, at the Musée Bonnat, Bayonne France.

Giovanni Francesco Melzi/self-portrait.

They met when the boy was 15 and Bramly writes that they took to each other immediately. The questions I have on the couple are those expressed by Bramly whom I would much prefer to take over here: ''He addresses his young friend as 'Messer Francesco' on account of his noble rank, but immediately after this polite formula, we read: 'Why in God's name have you not replied to any of the letters I sent you? Just wait till I get back, and by God I will make you write till you are almost sick of it.' By now Salaì must have been twenty-seven or twenty-eight. One wonders how he viewed his master's friendship with this wealthy, presentable, and highborn youth--as different from himself as day from night. It cannot have been easy for him. Harder to understand are the reactions of the Melzi family. Young Francesco soon announced that he wished to follow da Vinci as a pupil, to be initiated into the art of painting. How would his parents take it? It was quite unprecedented for the son of a good Lombard family to soil his hands with paint. Francesco Melzi was never to leave Leonardo's side, nursing him when he was ill, handling studio affairs, taking all sorts of notes from his dictation.''

Leonardo went to Milan where he was happy to put himself under the patronage of Ludovico Sforza who paid him extremely well and allowed him all the time he wanted in order to do exactly what Leonardo himself wished to do, and this for 18 years. Then Louis XII invaded Italy and Ludovico lost it all, eventually imprisoned by the French king until his death. Leonardo returned to Florence, age 48. The Medici had been expulsed and the Republic reestablished. Savonarola had gone up in smoke and a new breed of artist had arisen, led by Michelangelo and later by Raphael. His father was still there, age 74, with his forth wife and eleven children still at home, aged 2 to 24. Leonardo had written him often, always beginning with ''Dearly beloved father...'' a tender loving son, even if the reality of their closeness was perhaps other. At age 50 he hooked up with Cesare Borgia who appointed him military engineer, a position Bramly says he deeply desired. Cesare was a bastard as was Leonardo, and Bramly goes on to say: ''these two bastard children, having created their own lives, respected each other for their intelligence, independence of mind, and scorn for convention. Leonardo must also surely have been susceptible to Cesare's boisterous elegance and superb bearing.'' All certainly true as Cesare was virility personified. But unlike Leonardo, Cesare, age 27, was the adored son of his father, Pope Alexander VI, who would continue to love him even after Cesare murdered his brother, Juan--the son Alexander cherished even above Cesare. To have the backing and limitless wealth of his father, the pope, was a huge morale booster. Cesare went on a conquering spree and Machiavelli accompanied him (17). About Machiavelli's *Prince* Jean Giono wrote: ''It is the most objective study of mankind to date, the study of passions treated dispassionately, as if solving a mathematical problem.'' With the death of Cesare Leonardo returned to Florence where the town leaders, reigning from the Palazzo Vecchio, wanted him to paint a huge wall in the Palazzo itself. He covered the wall with an immense sketch of the *Battle of Anghiari* [won by Florence against Milan]. On another huge wall in the same room Michelangelo, age 29, was commissioned to do the *Battle of Cascina* [won by Florence over Pisa]. Leonardo worked on the sketch and preparations for the painting for three long years. After a first attempt failed due to the preparation of oils [apparently a huge problem before the oils were prepared by stabilized manufacturing], he simply returned to Milan under the auspices of Louis XII who was such an important ally to Florence that the leaders had to bite the bullet over Leonardo's departure. Michelangelo never finished his painting either. Called to the Vatican by the war pope Julius II, he would spend four inhumanly difficult years on the Sistine Chapel. In Florence da Vinci's sketch of the battle was treated as a national monument until the return of the Medici, who had it painted over [by none other than the great art historian--but also painter--Vasari!].

Both Michelangelo and da Vinci had only their love of men in common. The painted nudes of Michelangelo were peaches-and-cream clean, those of da Vinci homoerotic wet dreams [although Michelangelo's statues were, homoerotically speaking, to die for]. The first, da Vinci, had been handsome, the second, Michelangelo, never. The first was now old, the second just starting out on the road to eternal glory. Bramly recounts the story of Leonardo sitting at a café talking about Dante. He was asked a question, but seeing Michelangelo who was walking past said something like, "Ask Michelangelo." The great artist, always on the offensive, perhaps due to his looks and uncouth appearance, answered, "Explain it yourself, you who made a model of a horse you could never cast in bronze and which you gave up, to your shame," a reference to a Milanese commission da Vinci had botched. Bramly's story shows that things were not always peachy between the two men, but Michelangelo's personal relationships rarely were. For that, he had to fall in love. When in love Michelangelo gave himself body and soul; da Vinci was perhaps too cerebral to do so completely.

Vasari tells us that it was around this time that a boy, 20, living in Urbino, decided to forget everything he had ever learned about art and dedicate himself to copying Leonardo's paintings, paintings that had just come to his attention. The boy had a magnificent name, Raphael.

In Milan the French reserved a wonderful reception for Leonardo who, for Louis XII, was the reincarnation of the Renaissance itself. He started the *Mona Lisa* but the history of the painting is far to complicated to be approached here. It's the Churchillian riddle wrapped in a mystery inside an enigma. We're not sure even who ordered it, let alone who sat for it, although many think it was Salaì himself. [Michelangelo always had men pose for his statues of woman, as well as some portraits.]

While battles for and against Louis XII whirled around him, Leonardo was creating another work whose importance would span a period of 500 years: it was a study of the human body, dissected with perfection and drawn with a detail that takes one's breath away. In his own words [and 200 illustrations] he tells of accompanying an old man in his last hours, how the man complained of no physical pain, only weakness, and how he gently slipped from life into death. To find out the cause Leonardo did an autopsy, discovering that the artery supply to the heart and lower members had withered, describing, for the first time in the history of medicine, arteriosclerosis. Bramly takes over: ''One wonders what it felt like to plunge a knife into the thorax of an old man one had been speaking to not long before.'' Later in his notes Leonardo describes examining a hanged man, his penis engorged, of which he made detailed drawings. Leonardo went on to say that even if one had a love for dissecting, one's stomach might find it disgusting, and one might ''be afraid to stay up at night in the company of corpses cut to pieces and lacerated and horrible to behold.''

Politically, there was movement. Ludovico Sforza's son Massimiliano Sforza recovered Milan, expulsing the French back across the Alps. Pope Julius II died and was replaced by Leo X, the youngest son of Lorenzo *Il Magnifico,* enabling the Medici to reconquer Florence after twenty years of disgrace, and bring an end to the Republic. Leo X was destined to die of gout, as did the majority of the Medici, so rich they could afford the richest food [the cause of gout], but Leo X surpassed them all in girth. He had nonetheless brought a cultural revolution to Rome and was flattered by his followers as he who introduced the reign of Apollo, an esthetic age of gold. Leo X's brother, Giuliano de' Medici, one of many patrons of art supposed to have commissioned the *Mona Lisa*, convinced Leonardo to come to the Eternal City where the artist found himself eclipsed by the new stars of the Renaissance, Michelangelo, Titian and Raphael, Raphael who was paid 12,000 ducats for his works, while da Vinci was offered a measly 33 ducats a month, bringing the quip to Leonardo's mouth, ''The Medici created me and destroyed me.'' He was now old, but his greatest triumphs, his *St. John the Baptist* and his *Mona Lisa* were still to come. He spent three unhappy years in the service of Giuliano, part of which was dedicated to building canals that would drain fever-breeding swamps from around Rome--aided by the intelligent Melzi. The works he initiated were completed 300 years later.

Finally came his encounter with the man with whom he would end his life, François I, age 19, a giant at more than 6 feet, who loved war, placing himself in the front lines, and was an insatiable womanizer, whom we met in the chapter on Cellini. He recaptured Milan and Ludovico's son Massimiliano Sforze, but instead of throwing him into a dungeon he welcomed the lad to his court and pensioned him off. Leonardo went to the Loire Valley, but only after the death of Giuliano de' Medici. The year was 1516; da Vinci had 3 years left to him. He became François' tutor, and their days and nights were filled with discussion, often in the presence of Salaì and Melzi, all three immeasurable comforts to the old man, old beyond his years. Personally, I have never, ever come across a life as perfect as de Vinci's; never has there been a man as deserving of the name Man.

The last words will be Melzi's, in a letter he sent to Leonardo's surviving brothers: ''He was the best of fathers to me and the grief I feel at his death is impossible to express. As long as I have breath I shall feel an eternal sadness, for every day he gave me proof of a passionate and ardent affection. Each of us will mourn the loss of a man such that nature is powerless to create another.''

DONATELLO
1408 - 1466

Donatello's art seduced Cosimo--as his body did many a Florentine male--who put up with his every caprice. When a merchant refused a bronze head that Donatello had spent a month producing, arguing that a month's labor wasn't worth so much, Donatello sent it hurling from the heights of a tower where it had been taken to capture the best light, all the while protesting that he was an artist, not some laborer paid monthly wages. Cosimo commissioned a bronze statue of *David* from Donatello, a hero prized by Florentines because he had overcome the tyranny of Goliath, as many Florentines dreamed of the reestablishment of a Republic. The result pleases some; for others it is a girlish body with minimal male equipment. Mary MacCarthy called the androgynous bronze ''a transvestite's and fetishist's dream of alluring ambiguity.'' One can hardly imagine this *David* winning a victory against Mighty Mouse let alone Goliath. Donatello placed his earnings in a basket in his studio and told his assistants to serve themselves with what they needed. Lovers who looked elsewhere for pleasure were threatened with death by the artist who would run after them wherever they fled, a form of exercise that kept him alive until age eighty. He once requested permission from Cosimo to follow one of his runaway boys to Ferrara where he planned to kill him. Cosimo warned the Count of Ferrara who managed to put the boys together, both of whom immediately broke down with laughter and shared a kiss. One of my sources claims that ''laughter'' in this sense was a *mot à clef* meaning to fuck.

Detail of *David* and *David* [please forgive the poor quality of the reproduction].

Donato di Niccolò di Betto Bardi [Donatello] was born in Florence and started his early training in a goldsmith's workshop, followed by a stay in the studio of Lorenzo Ghiberti who spent 21 years completing the bronze doors of the Baptistery of Florence Cathedral that Michelangelo called the ''Gates of Paradise.''

RAPHAEL
1483 – 1520

I will include Raphael in the homosexual history of Florence because he spent a great deal of time there, that historians call his ''Florentine period'', from 1504 to 1508

The first thing to known about Raphael comes from Vasari: ''So gentle and charitable was Raphael that even the animals loved him.''

Self-portrait

The second key is found in those around him, beginning with his student and lover Giulio Romano who became known for 32 drawings called the *I Modi*. Sixteen represented scenes of heterosexual intercourse, 16 others of homosexual couplings. The first 16 were reproduced by the engraver Marcantonio Raimondi and gained such notoriety that they were banned and destroyed under the order of the pope. But they had been more or less well copied by others. The 16 homosexual drawings were considered too outrageous to be copied, and so have been entirely lost [if they had ever existed]. The first 16 came to Shakespeare's notice: In *The Winter's Tale* Queen Hermione mentions, "that rare Italian master, Julio Romano." Besides these, he did some beautiful paintings, for example his *St. John the Baptist in the Wilderness*, a beautiful young boy *à la da Vinci*. His *Jupiter Seducing Olympias* is an oddity, Jupiter's fully engorged penis just inches away from insertion.

Romano's *Jupiter*

The second personage associated with Raphael is Pietro Aretino who wrote dirty sonnets to go alone with the *I Modi*, but is especially known for his satirical writings, so sharp, witty and revealing that Charles V and François I paid him blackmail under the guise of patronage so he wouldn't include them in his satires. He was, if you will, the talented Renaissance Walter Winchell [known by millions but himself so unpopular that only three people attended his funeral]. Aretino too was unpopular with hordes of Italians, barely escaping assassination on several occasions.

The third man is Federico II Gonzaga of Mantua. Mantua, beautiful but dull until the arrival of the duke, became a center of art, as had Milan under Ludovico Sforza, a vulgar condottiere until he visited Lorenzo *Il Magnifico* in Florence. Seeing the splendor of Lorenzo's court and the magnificence of the city-- where, after all, the Renaissance began--Ludovico had an epiphany. Back home, he changed the face of Milan, architecturally first, then artistically, bringing aboard da Vinci himself. Federico II Gonzaga was so afraid of Pietro Aretino that he literally became his pimp in procuring boys, as witnessed in this highly-abbreviated exchange of letters that Federico wrote to Aretino, in answer to a request: ''I would willingly satisfy your wishes regarding this kept boy who you write could remedy your trouble, if I knew who it was, but I do not know this boy Bianchino.'' The duke finds out who the boy is and writes back: ''I truly love you more than any other and the fruits of your splendid intellect have so impressed me that I will never forget them. If I could possibly satisfy your desire for Bianchino I would do so gladly. But having understood his reluctance when I spoke to him on your behalf, I did not think it fitting to plead with him or otherwise to exhort him, and I surely can't order him, it not being either just or honest to command him in this case. So pardon me if I have not pleased you. If I can in any other way, you know very well I am only too glad to do it and you will always find me ready...." It was true that boys who sold their favors could gain not only money but a position in the upper hierarchy of government or church.

Aretino had said of himself: "I was born a sodomist," and it was true. But like all Renaissance men [who normally had a more or less hidden weakness for boys] he too had a weakness, but in his case it was for a woman, a cook. As he wrote Giovanni de' Medici: "My Illustrious Lord, be absolutely assured that I will return to my old ways, and that when I escape from this madness with a woman I will butt-fuck an untold number of men, for me and for my friends." One wonders how he could possibly have had this kind of conversation with Giovanni if Giovanni hadn't shared Aretino's tastes. It's extremely strange to read these letters from civilized highbrows who spent their time screwing boys, boys who were well paid, I hope, for what they had to endure from these often fat, powdered poofs.

Raphael Sanzio [or Sanzi or Santi] was born in Urbino in 1483, the fief of Federico da Montefeltro. Raphael's father was a court artist and it was at court that Raphael, young, learned proper manners and social skills. He was helping his father at age 4, thanks to which he progressed in talent. Of that time Vasari says that the boy "was a great help to his father." His self-portrait at age 16 shows a boy of unsurpassed beauty. He was apprenticed very early, some say around age 8, to Pietro Perugino, "despite the tears of his mother," states Vasari. Around age 11 he went to Florence for 4 years and then around age 15 he went to Rome where he lived until his death, 22 years later. It was there that Pope Julius II put him to work on several Vatican rooms, in one of which he painted his most famous work, the huge mural *The School of Athens*. Here we have the trinity of the times: the Everest of men, da Vinci, followed by the world's Annapurna, Michelangelo, and Raphael. Of da Vinci, Raphael said that the moment he saw his works he gave up all previous knowledge to devote himself to his new master. Raphael was present at the Vatican during the time Michelangelo painted the Sistine Chapel, visiting it during the artist's absences. When Michelangelo found out, he accused Raphael of undisclosed ''plots'' aimed at him, as well as copying his works. No one, and especially not Raphael, denied that he copied the works of others, copying being a way of growth. Michelangelo hated da Vinci too, but the challenge was in finding someone the creator of the God-inspired *David didn't* hate. At any rate, Raphael didn't follow Michelangelo into stilted Mannerism which, happily, had an early death.

The School of Athens

Julius II sent two of Raphael's paintings to François I for reasons of diplomacy and allowed Raphael to do a painting of him, which is sad because the warrior pope comes out looking deathly frail and sick, the antithesis of what he was in earlier life where he lived for war, boys, food and girls, in that order.

Raphael's *Baronci Altarpiece* was seriously damaged by an earthquake but fragments exist, of great beauty, as is the portrait of Giulio de Medici, the future Pope Clement VII, who is seen in the painting of *Leo X*. Along sexual lines, he was summoned to adorn the Vatican sauna with erotic paintings, in a room called the Stufetta, one of which shows the randy goat-god Pan leaping from the bushes with a valiant erection.

Raphael opened his own workshop with, says Vasari, fifty apprentices and assistants, among whom were his lovers, Giulio Romano and Gianfrancesco Penni. Thanks to these boys and men Raphael was able to produce an amazing number of paintings, all of which looked as though they had come from the hand of the master. Raphael was especially noted as someone who would take over the techniques of others, incorporating any and all external influences. He was also a perfect collaborator, establishing peaceful relations between men of extremely varied characters.

After Raphael's death Giulio Romano and Gionfrancesco Penni continued his workshop, their inheritance from Raphael. One of their assistants was Caravaggio. Unfortunately, they separated and died apart. Raphael died of fever, at age 37, supposedly after a night of excessive lovemaking with a mistress, which leaves one dubious.

Pietro Bembo, known, among other things, for his love affairs with Caterina Riario Sforza de' Medici, as well as the notorious Lucrezia Borgia, wrote this on Raphael's tomb: ''Here lies the famous Raphael by whom Nature feared to be conquered while he lived, and when he was dying, feared also to die.'' He was buried in the Roman Pantheon, one of the very rare monuments remaining from ancient Roman times. A hundred painters accompanied the procession, carrying torches. A man deeply loved and revered, his tomb is of incomparable eminence and splendor ... ''for an artist,'' said one contemporary.

Romano was Raphael's star student, whom he taught with ''tender loving care'' Vasari inform us. He soon mastered Raphael's techniques, from the mixing of colors to the secrets of perspective. Romano was not only intelligent and a quick study, he was ''inventive, affable, gracious and had the very finest manners,'' continues Vasari. Raphael would prepare paintings, drawing the basic configuration, and Romano and the other apprentices, but especially Romano, would take over from there, the reason for Raphael's stupendous production. On Raphael's death Romano and Gianfrancesco set their sights on completing Raphael's unfinished works, which were numerous. Then Clement VII decided to build a wonderful palace, eventually known as the Villa Madama, surrounded by parks, gardens and lakes, and named Romano responsible for it all. As an accomplished architect this posed no problem and Romano was excellent at making the drawings for the paintings and frescoes that would decorate the interior, but he lacked the patience to do the work himself as a painting could take months, even years. His paintings are therefore less dynamic, less emotional than his drawings.

Romano's *Two Lovers*

As said, Romano knew the duke of Mantua, Federico II Gonzaga, who, learning that the pope was building a new palace, wanted one too, the future Palazzo Te. How he got Clement to free Romano is not known, but he left Rome for Mantua where the duke provided him with a beautiful home replete with handsome boy servants, as the duke too appreciated healthy lads. With his usual skill, Romano brought the palace to completion and had artists brought in to furnish the interior, all for fantastic sums that the duke had no problem paying. The palace, away from the center of Mantua, was known to be for the sexual pleasure of the duke who nonetheless up and died, giving great pain to Romano as both men had been close, sharing not only girls and boys but also the pornographic sketches for which Romano would become renown. Romano's studio was a popular shelter for apprentices, models, clients and the upper classes who stopped by to slum, to gossip and to pick up boys.

Shortly after the duke's death Romano too died at age 54, leaving but one son who very soon joined his father in the family tomb.

As for Aretino, his power came from introducing himself-- thanks to his talent and wit--into the lives of the great men of the times, where he learned their secrets, procured boys for them, instructed them in the ways of seduction, keeping his eyes open as to what was going on in the palaces he frequented. Soon he could come and go as he wished, someone of so little importance that he was hardly noticed, a little like Cellini who in his autobiography told of entering the bedroom of the ruler of Florence, Alessandro, who was spread out naked "with that Lorenzino of his". Aretino lived on handouts until he turned his observations into satire, bringing disgust and fear into the hearts of those who had fed him. In this he was the original Truman Capote. Capote listened to and made matches for the wealthy wives of powerful husbands who confided in him, until he set his observations into print, observations so brilliant that he is revered throughout America, as Aretino was throughout Europe. Aretino wrote a highly daring play that concerned the marriage of a boy who preferred other boys and was dying of anxiety because he was being forced to perform heterosexually on his wedding night. After a series of silly situations *à la Feydeau*, the boy finds himself in bed with a beauty that turns out to be a hairless lad who makes the night a lustful wonder.

Pope Clement VII was so afraid of Aretino that he made him a Knight of Rhodes. Even the great and extremely wealthy Michelangelo found time for him. Aretino wrote the artist with suggestions on how to paint *The Last Judgment*. Michelangelo responded, saying that his letter gave him great pleasure and his ideas were most worthy, but the letter had come too late, as he had finished the painting.

As attempts to assassinate him accumulated, he was obliged to leave Rome for Venice that he described as "the seat of all vices." He had at last found a place worthy of him and his reputation as the "Scourge of Princes". But as his words could now be produced rapidly on the Gutenberg press, blackmail payments continued, turning his from-hand-to-mouth existence into one of opulence.

Aretino by Titian. He died at age 64, from unknown causes, although his friends maintained that he choked to death from laughing too much.

PART III

CHAPTER NINE

THE LAST MEDICI

MACHIAVELLI

Cosimo I's son Francesco de' Medici [1541-1587] followed him as duke, and although he married, it was for his mistress, Bianca Cappello, that he built the Villa Pratolino, with its Appennine Colossus. She had charms, among them "large breasts, the way they like them here," stated Montaigne. His wife died at age 31, sparking rumors that she'd been poisoned, and Bianca's husband was murdered in the streets of Florence, followed by the marriage of Francesco and Bianca. Although Francesco and Bianca were blamed for the death, she had nonetheless been wildly in love with her husband, whom she married at age 15, but her husband's family, poor, made her do menial work until a prince charming came and swept her off her feet. Francesco was taciturn and graceless, hardly an ideal prince charming, although he did keep Florence out of wars raging elsewhere, and he did found the Accademia della Crusca, dedicated to the study and preservation of the Italian language. He also added a floor to the Uffizi that he turned over to young artists and craftsmen. His own interests centered around alchemy, fireworks, porcelain and glass-blowing. Francesco and Bianca died on the 19th and 20th of October, 1587, Florentines certain they had been poisoned by his brother, although the death certificate stated malaria as the cause. A forensic examination in 2006 found arsenic, small doses administered over a short period of time because there were no traces in Francesco's hair.

Francesco and Bianca.

Francesco was succeeded by his brother Ferdinando I de' Medici who in character was the opposite of Francesco, outgoing, generous and approachable. Ferdinando I encouraged agriculture and commerce, and provided dowries so that poor girls could find husbands. He gained great wealth through Medici banking, a bank in all major European cities, and he fostered agriculture, diverting part of the Arno into a canal between Florence and Pisa, the Naviglio, for irrigation and to encourage trade. He wedded the granddaughter of Catherine de' Medici and married his niece to Henry de Navarre, soon to become Henry IV (2). He added classical statues to the Uffizi collection and bought the gilded sphere now in the Palazzo dei Guidici. He took Galileo into his service, in large part thanks to his inventions and his telescope, but also because his son Cosimo, the future Cosimo II, had been Galileo's student in Padua. In thanks Galileo named the satellites of Jupiter, his discovery, after the Medici: the Sidera Medicea.

The *Appennine Colossus* by Giambologna and an armillary sphere [a spherical astrolabe], of unknown parentage, representing the Earth, Sun and other celestial objects, on display in the Galileo Museum in Florence.

Ferdinando I [1549-1609]

Cosimo II, 1590-1621, the son of Ferdinando I, was a patron of the sciences, having been Galileo's student. He and his wife

Maria Maddalena of Austria had eight children. He died of tuberculosis and was succeeded by his son Ferdinando II.

Ferdinando II was 10 when his father died and was placed under the regency of his mother and paternal grandmother, Christina of Lorraine, who was the power behind the throne until her death, although the titular title went to Ferdinando when he was 18. He was present in Florence during the plague of 1630, which wiped out 10% of the population, remaining in the city, with his brothers, while other nobles fled. He fathered Cosimo III during a period of reconciliation with his wife who had found him in bed with his favorite page.

He had Galileo placed under his care when condemned by the Inquisition and had him buried in Santa Croce alongside Ghiberti, Michelangelo and Machiavelli.

Ferdinando II [1610-1670]
Ferdinando's paternal grandmother was the power behind the throne, leaving him free to follow his two passions, the first an obsession with technology as personified by Galileo whose sentence to life imprisonment by the Inquisition was commuted to house arrest, Ferdinando doing the housing. Ferdinando's brother Leopoldo followed in his brother's footsteps and founded a scientific academy aimed at bringing scientifically-minded Tuscans to Florence where they shared their discoveries. Ferdinando's second passion was boys, which caused his marriage

to sour when his wife found him in bed with a page, Count Bruto della Molera, but by then he'd had a son, Cosimo.

Ferdinando II's son Cosimo III took his place at his death, a boy his mother had educated by priests in an effort to save him from his father's obsession with his mignons. The result was a melancholy boy, fat and mournful, to whom King Louis XIV gave his cousin, a girl in love with another, but Cardinal Mazarin, Louis XIV's minister, wanted to become pope, for which he needed Medici backing. The girl made known her hatred for everything Florentine, beginning with her husband and Florentines, and was finally freed to return home to France after numerous attempts had been made to poison her. She was accompanied by a baggage train filled with everything she had been capable to stealing from Florentine palaces, money, jewels and gold included, which provided the funding of 150 servants and as many lovers as she could open her legs to accommodate.

Cosimo bent to the power of the Inquisition and severely controlled the content of what was taught in universities, forbidding Florentine students from schooling outside of Tuscany. He persecuted Jews, whipped prostitutes who had intercourse with them, while obliging them to buy licenses to walk the streets. It became shameful to not attend religious services and Cosimo himself went to as many as seven churches daily. Taxes were raised to provide money to buy holy relics, although some did go to the acquisition of art for the Uffizi. Alas, he lived on to age 81.

Cosimo III.

Convinced that sexual activity was harmful to his health, he did his duty to produce an heir once a week, under the supervision of a doctor. His wife so hated him that she tried to induce an abortion by starving herself. Cosimo ordered naked statues covered, including that of Michelangelo's *David* that he called "an incitement to fornication."

Cosimo's older son, Ferdinando, had died ten years earlier, a good-looking boy, a musician fond of opera and employed painters like Sebastiano Ricci. He was also deeply attached to his uncle Francesco Maria, who employed young boys dressed as girls, while Ferdinando's true love was a young Venetian castrato.

Cosimo was succeeded by his son Gian Gastone, a man who drank and gambled, although he had a great interest in archeology and botany. Men of science were once again welcome to his court and he ended the influence of religion over daily affairs. He too preferred the company of youths, known as *ruspanti* after the coins he paid for their services. The boys were given free rein of the Pitti Palace, where they romped naked and openly copulated as a way of giving Gastone maximum visual pleasure. Gian Gastone's example freed Florentine men to follow their natural bent, too long held in check by Cosimo I and III, and intercourse between men was so known that it was commented upon from abroad, as it had been in the time of Lorenzo *Il Magnifico*, so that a 1729 earthquake was attributed, by a German, to the Sodom-and-Gomorrah lasciviousness innate in Florentines.

Gian Gastone spoke several languages, among them English. Melancholic in the extreme, abandoned by both parents and often seen weeping by himself in his rooms, he was said to have spent most of his time in bed, waited on and entertained by his ruspanti, his favorite a certain Giuliano Dami who procured him a daily supply of boys and orchestrated the orgies, encouraging the boys "push in! push in!" during intercourse with the duke, each lad inspected for good teeth and a sizable member by Gian himself, each paid 5 ruspi. Dami grew wealthy by deciding who could, or could not, enter Gastone's apartments in quest of the duke's financial favors. Gastone abolished taxes for the poor, repealed laws against Jews and put an end to public executions. Yet Florence descended into poverty during his reign: "There was no town where men live in less luxury than Florence," stated Montesquieu. He turned more and more to alcohol and on the rare occasions he went to church he was seen volmiting into his wig. Like Howard Hughes, he let his hair, fingernails and toenails grow long, but when he died he was mourned because he had favored "new ideas", had allowed the teaching of Galileo at the University of Pisa and had aided the poor.

MACHIAVELLI
1469 – 1527

Born in Florence, Machiavelli was essential during the Renaissance, and no stranger to the love of boys.

Michael Rocke tells us of a letter Machiavelli wrote to a friend, describing, in couched terms, what men did at night in Florence, what Michelangelo certainly did: "A man of my acquaintance went from one site to another that lads are known to frequent, and then wound up finding 'a little thrush' agreeable to being kissed and having 'his tail-feathers ruffled.' After this successful find, the man sealed his conquest," as Machiavelli put it, "by thrusting his *uccello* [dick] into the *carnaiulo* [ass]."

A new Venetian ambassador was sent to the Vatican, Antonio Giustinian, a man of great importance to us because we are informed about much that follows thanks to the thousands of letters he wrote and sent throughout Europe. Around this time too Florence sent a delegation to Cesare Borgia who had just taken Urbino, in order to both calm the young man's ardors for conquest and to get his support in maintaining Florence's authority over Pisa and Arezzo. The delegation consisted of Francesco Soderini, the brother of the courant head of Florence, and a new man destined to leave his mark on the world, Niccolò Machiavelli. Niccolò Machiavelli served Cesare Borgia, which allowed him an eyewitness-view of ruthless government, the basis of his masterpiece *The Prince*, the very foundation of today's political science. We don't know to what extent Machiavelli carried on male-male relations during his adult life, but thanks to Michael Rocke we have this response from Machiavelli to the letter sent to him by a childhood friend who is worried about his son's frequentations, proof of Machiavelli's appreciation of boys during his own adolescence: ''Since we are verging on old age, we might be severe and overly scrupulous, and we do not remember what we did as adolescents. So Ludovico has a boy with him, with whom he amuses himself, jests, takes walks, growls in his ear, goes to bed together. What then? Even in these things perhaps there is nothing bad.'' [*Growls* in his ear: I *adore* that!]

Machiavelli is also said to have exclaimed: ''In your house there are no young boys and women to fuck. What kind of a fucking house is that?''

Machiavelli about Cesare Borgia (17): ''He was the handsomest man of his times.''

Few other times in history were more tumultuous than those known to Machiavelli. Just the mention of names such as the Visconti, the Sforza, the Borgia, Charles VIII, the warrior pope Julius II, the Turks brought instant fear to the hearts of men (20). Battles between the city-states continued without ever a respite. Quarrels between the Medici and their fellow citizens led to the assassination of Lorenzo's brother Giuliano by the Pazzi. Religious unrest caused by the likes of Savonarola, and the miserable decadence of Pope Alexander VI, caused riots and turmoil (17). Privileged youths such as Cesare and his brothers-- and nearly every other boy-delinquent of noble blood--were free to kill, maim and rape. Condottieri were encouraged to recuperate their wages by destroying villages, towns and cities, and to assuage their lust on girls and women. To these inflictions can be added disease and plague--so terrible that noble families farmed out their children until around age seven, the age at which they were allowed to return home had they survived the various ailments of the times. Machiavelli himself was tortured by the usually civilized Medici--with the *strappado*, a torture in five degrees. In the first the prisoner's hands were tied behind his back and he was advised to confess. If he refused, his arms were raised behind his back by a rope attached to a pulley. During this second degree he was lifted off his feet for a short time. If he still refused to confess he faced the third degree, being raised until his arms dislocated. During the fourth degree he was violently jerked. During the last degree, more weights were added until his arms were torn from his body. Machiavelli went as far as the first degree, but as his purported crimes were few, he was let off. [We know nothing of the Medici accusations against Machiavelli.] He then retired from politics and in a letter to a friend he described a typical day of retirement as one in which he entered his study, wearing the formal dress of an ambassador, and there he discoursed with the popes, princes, kings and emperors of old, asking them questions and noting down their answers.

CHAPTER TEN

LEOPOLD II

With so much semen lost between the buttocks of willing lads, the line of the Medici died out [the *direct* Medici line, as there are Medici galore even today], replaced by a foreigner and his army, Francis, Duke of Lorraine. Francis and his wife arrived in Florence in great pomp, giving reception after reception in the Pitti Palace, certainly unaware of the bacchanalias that had so recently taken place there. They stayed three months and then left the city, definitively. Florence was thereafter held by a series of regents.

The Grand Duke Francis' son Peter Leopold replaced his father who died in 1765, and it was from this time that tourism developed in Florence, part of the Grand Tour every boy from a wealthy family felt obliged to conform to, one of whom, later, was Byron, whose Grand Tour took him to Athens where he copulated with so many boys, 200 after his reckoning, that, worn out, he vowed never to bed another (5). Under Peter Leopold new inns, called alberghi, opened to better receive the visitors, mostly Englishmen willing to pay for young Italian boys, plentiful, virile, and far better-looking than the pasty, white-skinned English variety, especially English college boys who were often overweight and effeminate, a far cry from lithe well-endowed Italians to the South of Britain, and strapping, equally well-endowed Germans facing the British Isles, the second most preferred hot-spot [soon to become the first], where English boys found healthy lads and willing soldiers, both in abundance in Berlin (3).

One of the British visitors was Horatio Walpole. Educated in British boarding schools before entering Eton College and King's College Cambridge, his first sexual experiences took place with boys in school dormitories, the perfect environment for a lad to discover his sexuality, homosexual, heterosexual or bisexual, untainted by the presence of adults. The memory of first loves was so strong that even lads who went on to marry--something many did because it was expected of them in British society--thought back with nostalgia to the intimacy between friends, the complete history of which can be found in my book *Boarding School Homosexuality*. The call of manly, non-effeminate boys led Walpole to Italy that he visited with his friend Thomas Gray, although Walpole's preference for Florence, and Gray's for Rome, split them apart. Walpole was an art historian and antiquarian, the son of the first British Prime Minister, Sir Robert Walpole. He was so sexually discrete that one of his biographers thought he may have been asexual (4).

Nights were reserved for restaurants, coffee-houses, the opera [where people of quality met to talk and socialize, turning their backs on the stage] and one of twenty theaters, the evening ending, hopefully, in bed with pleasant company, while days saw the visitors take in the Duomo, the Baptistery, the Uffizi, the Pitti Palace and Ponte Vecchio. The period, the mid-1700s, was so opulent that even liveried servants had servants of their own. The

English found Florentines to be polite but arrogant, an arrogance found even in whores who demanded exorbitant sums, often in exchange for the pox. The use of condoms was on every male's lips, but were so impractical and untrustworthy that they were seldom employed.

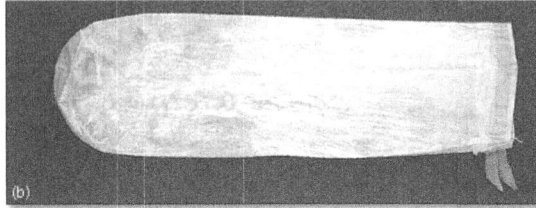

Condoms existed in the 1700s, like this one, but many physicians were opposed to them because they gave little real protection against syphilis, while encouraging men, unaware of their permeability, to engage more often in unsafe sex. On the physical side, there was an evident loss of sensation, and on the moral side condoms were sinful murderers of children [and because of illnesses, plagues and wars--especially the coming Napoleonic wars that would see hundreds of thousands of boys thrown in mass burial pits--children were vital].

While the very first Cosimo de' Medici, along with Petrarch, were the founding fathers of the Renaissance--Cosimo being a man largely unknown outside of historians but a virtual sun in the explosion of life that followed his rediscovery of ancient Greek manuscripts--Peter Leopold also went a long way in giving Florence a hand up. When he arrived he had, in his baggage, many of the art treasures his father had stolen, treasures Leopold restored to the city. He treated Florentines as equals, he spoke Italian, even in private, and he had his son baptized Giovanni, the name of Florence's patron saint. He threw garden parties where all classes were invited, hundreds who could fill themselves with food and wine, while an orchestra played on. He refurbished the hospital, had patients washed and even manicured, and fed them better food than most had in their own homes, care that was free for the poor. He founded new schools, especially in the districts of the poor, as well as new academies of science and the arts. He built libraries and enlarged those already in existence, and even purchased, for public use, the private library of the immensely important Strozzi. He founded a natural-history museum, La Specola, and allotted money to struggling artists, musicians and writers. He drained swamps, improved agriculture and encouraged anything scientific, from ballooning to the crystallization of salt.

But whereas there was no known dark side to the first Cosimo, the same could not be said of Leopold, a religious Tartuffe who demanded morality in daily life, while allowing himself, in private, *le droit de cuissage*, a seigneur's natural right to possess and deflower any girl in his domain. He forbade gambling and swimming in the Arno, where women weren't sufficiently covered and boys skinny dipped. He outlawed prostitution and wore only black. On the other hand, to carry through his hospital-library-academy reforms he taxed the church to the hilt, and suppressed the Inquisition and Jesuit orders.

Then, when his brother the Holy Roman Emperor died in 1790, Leopold packed up to return to Vienna to take his place. He emptied the Pitti Palace, a hundred mules loaded down with Florentine wealth. Once beyond the walls, the city's poor rioted and ransacked the palaces of the wealthy, a revolt ended as rapidly as it had begun, crushed by the nobles and their own armed men. And just in time, as Leopold's son, Ferdinand, came to take charge in 1791, his title Grand Duke Ferdinand III.

In the same way that Elizabeth I had used Francis Drake to divert gold shipped to Spain into Elizabeth's own coffers, so to did the Directory of Paris allow Napoleon to fill French coffers by raping Italy. Napoleon himself had said, ''over there, beyond the mountains, are stores, food, clothes, guns, horses and money to reward us,'' a quote from Hibbert's *Florence*. He entered Florence on the 30th of June, 1796, met with Ferdinand III and promised to respect Florence's declared neutrality, which he did until 1799 when troops entered the city under cheers, and Ferdinand III was expelled. Banquets were given, trees of liberty planted, before the organized sack of the city during which even the gold plate from churches was extracted, along with art treasures, one of which was the *Medici Venus*, another the *Belvedere Apollo*, stolen from Rome, both united in Paris where, in 1799, Napoleon staged a *coup d'état* that would end with his exile to Saint Helena and the death of hundreds of thousands of French boys, most of whom were forced on Napoleon by their mothers, the emperor's most devout followers.

Belvedere Apollo and the *Medici Venus*

The Kingdom of Etruria was founded, with Florence its capital, headed by a king, 28-year-old Louis of Parma. He arrived in 1801 and died in 1803, perhaps of epilepsy. He wife, Maria Luisa, was named regent for their 4-year-old son. Sincere, she did her best to ingratiate herself to Florentines, and on one occasion she invited 200 working-class children to a party, who were allowed to return home with the tableware. Napoleon became emperor in 1804 and King of Italy in 1805. He replaced Maria Luisa with his sister Elisa. Elisa followed in Maria Luisa's footsteps in her attempts to win Florentine support through acts of generosity. But after the defeat of Napoleon at Leipzig, one of his generals, Joachim Murat, formed an alliance with Austria under which Ferdinand III regained his throne in Florence. Elisa left, accompanied by what remained of Napoleon's forces there. Ferdinand died soon afterwards.

Leopold II [1797-1870] was the son of Ferdinand III and was born in Florence. He reigned under the aegis of Austria [the Holy Roman Empire], but tried to minimize Austrian influence. He worked tirelessly for his fellow Florentines and permitted a great amount of freedom of the press, at least in comparison to other autocrats. As demands for political change and a constitution gained support throughout Italy, and revolts broke out, he went as far as the Austrian government would allow him in reforms. Tuscans demanded freedom from Austria, and Leopold II at first backed them to such an extent that there was even a movement to name him king over central Italy. But due to Austria's successes in the field, he was obliged to flee to Gaeta, in the Kingdom of Naples, disguised as a girl, where he was joined by the pope who fled Rome for the same reasons. He finally signed an agreement with Austria that permitted him to return to power in Florence, under which he allowed 10,000 Austrian soldiers onto his lands, putting an end to his popularity. When France attacked Austria many Florentine boys joined them. He was finally forced to abdicate in favor of his son, the last Grand Duke, who ruled from 1859-1860. Historians generally dismiss Leopold II as having been too weak to govern effectively and, philosophically and politically, too close to Austrian Habsburgs to become a veritable liberal. Also, he had demanded Austrian support while at Gaeta, all the while denying having done so.

Leopold II.

Cold and retiring, he was never popular among his subjects, although he gave them more freedoms than other states under Austria, and his administration, deemed excellent, afforded the duchy a high level of prosperity. He was the first ruler to abolish capital punishment and torture. He worked on a constitution said to have influenced that of France after the French Revolution, as well as America's Bill of Rights. He initiated smallpox vaccinations and encouraged the rehabilitation of juvenile delinquents. He fought for the humane treatment of the mentally ill, and was the first ruler to allow hospitals to care for the mentally insane. He built a hospital and placed at its head a physician and humanitarian, Vincenzo Chiarugi. His attempt at political freedoms ended when he replaced his beloved brother as Holy Roman Emperor in 1790. He died two years later [amidst the usual rumors of his having been poisoned or otherwise murdered].

Leopold II introduced gas street lighting, a huge boon in progress, cutting nightly murders while leaving enough unlit sections for prostitutes to earn a living. He drained swamps and imported merino sheep to boost the Tuscan wool industry. He widened streets and enlarged piazzas. He built housing for 300 poor and provided statues for the arcades outside the Uffizi. He was kindness personified, whose subjects, according to visitors, took advantage of him, as in this extract offered by Hibbert in his *Florence*, recounted by a man invited to one of the duke's dinners: ''The English would seize the plates of *bonbons* and empty the contents into their coat pockets. The ladies would do the same with their pocket handkerchiefs. But the Duke's liege subjects carried on their depredations on a far bolder scale. I have seen large portions of fish, sauce, and all, packed up in a newspaper and deposited in a pocket. I have seen fowls and ham share the same fate, without any newspaper at all. I have seen jelly carefully wrapped in an Italian countess's laced *mouchoir*!''
He died a natural death at age 73.

It was under Leopold II that visitors flooded back to Florence, among them Chateaubriand, Shelley, Champollion, thanks to whom Leopold ordered the building of the Egyptian Museum in the Museo Archeologico. But the most notorious was Lord Byron, whose life will be briefly recounted here, as he is an ideal example of the age's bisexuality.

BYRON

Byron lived in an age when men were hanged for their love of males and/or pilloried, caged in public and punched by sticks, eyes stove in and throats pierced, at times causing death. The high and mighty in England didn't necessarily escape [although most did], as shown by Oscar Wilde's trial for homosexuality, a man whose plays were immensely popular then as they are today. There was also the threat of blackmail that led to many suicides. To be hanged, both penetration and ejaculation had to be proved in a court of law, no easy affair. In France laws against sodomy were dropped after the Revolution, in 1791, and many other countries like Italy and Spain followed. But not England. Yet school was a protected sanctum, where boys could enjoy their puberty more or less unhampered. Boys were locked in their dormitories at night, left to themselves, at times exhausting their young bodies in orgies that would have impressed the Romans. *All* boarding schools were rife with sex. H. Montgomery Hyde, who later lost his seat in the House of Commons because of his plea for understanding concerning homosexuals, quoted a student, Addington Symonds: ''The talk in the dormitories and studies was of the grossest character, with repulsive scenes of onanism, mutual masturbation and obscene orgies of naked boys in bed together. There was no refinement, just animal lust.'' The first order that Makepeace Thackeray received on his first day at school from a schoolmate was ''Come & frig me,'' he wrote later. Byron had innumerable lovers, and it is believed that his sex life began as early as age 9 when a servant aroused him sexually by taking him in her mouth. It had long been a custom in Sardinia for mothers to soothe their baby boys by taking the entirety of their sexual apparatus in their mouths, a measure said to have instantly calmed their sons. Later Byron claimed to have read Arabian erotica at age 10. His earliest pre-school crushes seemed to have been with girls, and girls would bring him pleasure throughout his life [pleasure for Byron's friends too, as Byron would often turn his mistresses over to them]. Had not the dangers of the pillory, hanging, blackmail and public scandal been real, he might have had far more homosexual experiences than heterosexual (4).

In 1808 he decided to go to the Orient. Boys he met along the way stirred him sexually and even in Falmouth he wrote to friends at Cambridge about the remarkably handsome lads, one of which he compared to Apollo's lover Hyacinth (1). He employed the word coitus throughout his letters, perhaps taking it from the *Satyricon* where Eumolpus tells how, after much trickery, he had full and complete intercourse with the boy he had been after [*plenum et optabilem coitum*]. He went to Albania where he found the most splendid boys he had ever seen, and then went on to Athens where he heard the story of Hadrian and Antinous (9), and where he went from boy to boy, writing home that he had had 200 couplings ["two hundred *pl and opt Cs*"], so many that he was becoming tired of them, he wrote. In Athens he visited the site of the two lovers Aristogeiton and Harmodius. He went on to Leuctra where the Sacred Band of lovers defeated the Spartans and then to the Thermopylae where Leonidas saved us all from Persian barbarism at the head of 150 Spartan couples formed of lovers and their beloveds (21). He swam in the Hellespont and went on to Troy, battlegrounds of Achilles and Patroclus (10). In a letter, he regretted that the shepherds in his day did not resemble, in beauty, Paris, the abductor of Helen.

He had to be careful in what he wrote home: In one letter he admitted to receiving "as many kisses as would have sufficed for a boarding school." In another "one boy had ambrosial curls hanging down his amiable back" and in another place he and a boy "traveled very much enamoured." In still another letter he asks the reader to tell a friend that he had finally "had" a Greek boy they had known at Cambridge, whom Byron looked up in his native Athens, one of the few he didn't pay for.

He returned to England where men were being hung for "unnatural crimes," two per year. Prison and blackmail, as well as being ostracized by one's peers, were current. The accusation of having committed a homosexual crime would bring out a mob of hundreds into the streets, and the accused had to be protected by large numbers of police. A lieutenant was caught amusing himself with a drummer boy of 16, two years after Byron's return; both were hanged. In the crowd observing the hanging was the Duke of Cumberland, who just missed inheriting the English throne. Nine months before the hanging his valet had been found dead, killed by the duke, thought some, because the valet was blackmailing him for having sex with another of the duke's male servants--every reason for Byron to make good use of whatever heterosexual blood he had within him when seeking pleasure. That he did not exclusively do so is proof of his deep attraction to boys.

With the publication of *Childe Harold* Byron became a world-renowned poet, and attracted a succession of women mistresses, from Caroline Lamb, who tortured him with her public scandals, tantrums and spying, to the Countess of Oxford, and then his own half-sister Augusta Leigh, the most perverse and perhaps the deepest of his female attachments. He then took up with Annabella Milbanke who knew about his homosexuality and perhaps thought she could save him. He apparently did too because they married.

As feared, Caroline Lamb decided to avenge herself, at first accusing Byron of being a homosexual, then of committing incest. Annabella, it seems, spent her time trying to keep him from killing himself. Incest was illegal, but the penalty was far less severe than for homosexuality; that Byron had entered into an incestuous relationship, so venerated by the pharaohs, so heinous for us, was proof that for this boy there were really no earthly limits, and worse would come when he tried to penetrate the 11-year-old daughter of one of his mistresses.

He went to Geneva where it is said he was shunned, while in London a newspaper, the *Champion,* related that Byron was involved in a scandal but placed itself above printing the exact nature. There followed around seven years of largely heterosexual activity, including four years in Italy with a certain countess. He had met her at age 31, she 20, and her husband 54, who appealed to the pope when she left him, but because of Byron's celebrity the pope refused to intervene. Byron was happy with what the publicity was doing for his reputation as a heterosexual in Britain, but as Molière had so rightly written, *Tout le plaisir de l'amour est dans le changement*. Byron therefore decided to return to Greece, and to boys.

There he met the Chalandrutsanos family, consisting of a mother who had fallen on bad times, her three daughters and Lukas, her 15-year-old son who was busy fighting the Turks for Greek independence. Youths from all over Europe, Germany, France, Spain and Italy were flocking to Greece to help the Greeks win their freedom, but due to Greek incompetence, whose who survived returned in rags. Byron took Lukas in hand and wherever they went Byron was well received, thanks to his reputation and wealth. He provided the boy with a uniform and pistols, and welcomed him into his entourage as a page, the usual cover for rent-boys. He had Lukas read ancient Greek texts, certainly those tainted with Greek love, and like any boy Lukas's age, and having lived under the Turks, the boy certainly recognized the intentions behind Byron's largesse.

Even at age 23 Byron had envisioned suicide, but at that age he was sexually fulfilled, and so such thoughts meant little in comparison to now, nearly 36, his hair thinning, his teeth bad and his body fat. He was far from sexually satiated now, so thoughts of suicide, on the battlefield, alongside his Lukas, were attractive. The revenge of age is total. Byron's reputation and money could buy him consolation, but the mirror was there to remind him of the inevitable ravages of time. Lucky were those like Achilles, like Patroclus, Alexander and Hephaestion (19), who left early, in possession of their physical force and beauty.

Lukas was perhaps there to console him because he shared Byron's bed, as related by numerous sources. But Lukas appeared unhappy, and Byron's gifts to him, pistols, gold-laced jackets and a beautiful saddle, seemed to have done little to lessen what appeared to have been the boy's disdain for Byron. Perhaps the boy didn't share Byron's bent, perhaps he would have preferred someone younger with a beautiful body. A man throwing himself at a disdainful boy is sad, especially for a boy who had known the luxury of love and fulfilled desire since his early puberty, as had Byron.

Byron wrote poems to the boy, so sexually discreet that it's difficult to know what he's talking about, yet in the reality of his daily life he was telling friends that his "cock still has spring in it".

This may have been so, but there was daily less spring in his health. He suffered from fevers, perhaps the malaria he had contracted in the South of France as a boy, and syphilis. He had dizzy spells and weakness. Bloodletting, still popular, didn't help, and some say it even eventually killed him. In 1824 he was carried away by fever, certainly not to a better place since it's difficult to imagine a destiny as fulfilling in love, in art, in sexual bliss as that having been lived by Byron. He died at 36, the exact age of his father. A few months later, victim of the Greek War for Independence, Lukas followed.

Byron is remembered as being physically beautiful, a man who has won the admiration of generations through his poetry. In reality he had himself painted when he was in flower, rare moments between bouts of obesity. His rage knew no limits when he suffered the pain of his clubfoot and found out that the reason was his mother's corsets, trying to limit her own spread, uncaring of the physical damage to her son, as he too would be uncaring of how he damaged others. The world owed him a never-ending debt for his handicap, placing him above laws and rules, allowing him to force himself on children and to bed his sister; his money permitted every excess, his position every depravity. And in the end he found himself slavering at the feet of a boy, one that not even the gifts of silver pistols, gold-threaded jackets and fine leather saddles could entice to favor the foul-breathed, fat baron at his feet.

[His full life can be found in my book *Christ has his John, I have my George, The History of British Homosexuality*.]

CHAPTER ELEVEN

ITALIAN UNITY:
VICTOR EMMANUEL, GARIBALDI, CAVOUR,

VICTOR EMMANUEL

Florence had known an advance in tourism under Leopold II and in 1865 came a horde of new inhabitants, thanks to the arrival of Victor Emmanuel, former King of Piedmont, named king of the new capital of Italy, Florence, a decision made in 1860 and now acted upon with Victor Emmanuel's entry into the city. Accompanied by thousands of new bureaucrats, Florentines saw their wealth make huge gains as they increased rents and the price of staples, horses and carriages, especially as the new arrivals loved to show off in daily displacements, the ostentation of their costumes and jewelry infuriating Florentines, a bit like the pan calling the kettle black, as until then it had been Florentines who had set the stage for Italian fashion, and that since Lorenzo *Il Magnifico*. New boulevards had to be cut through older quarters, new piazzas created, parks, gardens and new markets, a revolution that saw much of old Florence disappear. Victor Emmanuel took possession of the Pitti Palace, his mistress, the newly ennobled Contessa di Mirafiori, nearby. In addition, his reputation for relieving virgins of their noisome virginity rivaled that of François I, who even took his bed with him when out hunting [briefly alluded to in the chapter on Cellini], apparently having no difficulty in filling it as the size of his nose, huge, was known to one and all [his full life and prowess found in my book *Cellini*].

Victor Emmanuel threw gala dinners, but nothing was comparable to the balls organized by Laetitia Marie Wyse Bonaparte, wife of Urbano Rattazzi, one of Italy's founding fathers. Other lavish parties were given by other wealthy newcomers. Clubs, casinos and cafés like the Caffè Michelangiolo burgeoned.

The reunification of Italy took place between 1815 and 1871, when Rome became the capital of the Kingdom of Italy [with a few holdouts until the end of W.W. I when, with the Armistice of the Villa Giusti, there was complete unification]. In essence, Italy reverted back to the unity known under Romans from the third century B.C. There were three fathers of unification, Victor Emmanuel, Garibaldi and Cavour.

Victor Emmanuel in caricature and in life.

Victor Emmanuel, 1820-1878, was the first King of Italy since the founding of the country itself by Romulus in 753 B.C. [the full history of which can be found in my book *Catiline*]. As such, Victor Emmanuel was called the father of the fatherland, *padre della patria*. He started out as King of Sardinia-Piedmont when his father abdicated the throne. He nominated Camillo di Cavour as his prime minister who, with Garibaldi, would be known as Italy's liberators. To bolster ties with Britain and France, Victor Emmanuel joined them in the Crimean War against Russia. He joined forces with Garibaldi whose conquests enabled him to assume the title of King of Italy, Turin his capital. Rome and Venice had remained outside of his rule but with Prussian help he won over Venice, after which Florence took Turin's place as capital in 1864, as reported above. When Rome fell in 1870 it became the capital it had been in Roman times and is today. Victor Emmanuel, now residing in the Pantheon, was succeeded by his son Umberto I.

GARIBALDI

While Laurence of Arabia had his Lowell Thomas to inform the world of his exploits, Garibaldi had a slew of admirers, from Victor Hugo to Alexandre Dumas to George Sands, none of whom had the means of popularizing him, no big screen, no Peter O'Toole to immortalize him with O'Toole's immortal beauty. Born in Nice, fate led Garibaldi to encounter revolutionary figures, and at age 26 he received his first death sentence *in absentia* for an insurrection in Piedmont, alongside Giuseppe Mazzini. He sailed to Brazil where he fought for the independence of certain Brazilian regions, then moved to Montevideo Uruguay where he adopted his trademark gaucho clothing, and where he struggled for Uruguayan independence. He became a Freemason, whom he considered a band of progressive brothers and who offered him hideouts. He adopted guerilla tactics that he put in use when he returned to Italy during the turmoil of 1848. He fought against Austrians and the French, and after losing his first battles, one of which obliged him to leave Rome that he was trying to hold, he turned to other pursuits in order to make a living. He went to America where he worked in a candle factory, to Peru, to the Pacific hauling guano, to China, Manila, Australia and England where he traded in coal, and back to the States with copper from Chile. Sickened when Cavour gave his native Nice to the French, he encouraged riots there during the rest of his life. He raised troops to free Sicily when revolution broke out, and then embarked for Naples that he captured. He handed over his conquests to Victor Emmanuel whom he believed Providence had designated to unite Italy, proclaiming him king. [The need for kings has continued into our own days, and even France, after its Revolution, not only reverted to kings, but also emperors, a quirk democratic England lives under in our own time, and even Spain allowed a dictator, Franco, to impose a monarchy over it, one that exists to this day.] As for Garibaldi, he offered his services to America during its Civil War, something the Americans agreed to until he demanded that he be placed over Lincoln's armies. He organized the International Legion, bent on freeing any people anywhere in Europe, and in 1867 declared that he wished to eliminate the papacy, ''the most harmful of all secret societies.'' In 1870 he was given command over a French army in its fight against Prussia, a fight the French lost. He was in favor of the emancipation of women and universal suffrage. Sexually, he was fully Italian in his promiscuity, fathering a number of children and marrying several times, one 18-year-old he abandoned just after the ceremony, when she announced she was pregnant by another man. He died at age 74, having been wounded several times in battle.

Giuseppe Garibaldi, 1807-1882

CAVOUR

Cavour [Camillo Paolo Filippo Giulio Benso, Count de Cavour, 1810-1861] was one of the fathers of Italian unification and its first prime minister, dead three months into office. From a wealthy aristocratic family, he was so headstrong that at age 10, when placed in a military academy, he was put on bread and water for three days when found reading banned books. He was neither reactionary nor liberal, was religious but believed in the separation of church and state. He favored free trade and freedom of thought, yet employed friends, bribed newsmen, rigged elections, his biographers excusing the wrongdoings as par for the course for the times. He was convinced that economic progress was the key to political change, and so thusly encouraged the growth of railroads, canals and stream engines.

Cavour never believed in the unification of Italy, at least not in his lifetime, but he did believe in its expansion, and to help it forward he went to extremes, like entering the Crimean War on the sides of Britain and France in the hope they would back Italian unification. He gave up Nice to Napoleon III, to the fury of Garibaldi who had been born there, and even enticed his cousin, a known beauty and artist, to become Napoleon III's mistress [among other women, some spies, he placed in the emperor's bed!].

During this time Garibaldi was busy taking Sicily and capturing Naples, the most populous city in Italy, proclaiming Victor Emmanuel King of Italy. In 1861 Cavour was named prime minister of the Kingdom of Italy, despite Garibaldi who had never liked Cavour, especially after he'd engineered the loss of Nice, calling him ''a low intriguer'', while Cavour called Garibaldi ''a savage''. That same year Cavour contracted what may have been malaria and insisted on being bled, a later report stating that he'd insisted until ''it was nearly impossible to draw any blood from him.''

Cavour ordered his own bleeding to death.

MAZZINI

Giuseppe Mazzini, 1815-1872, was the philosopher behind Italian unification, his dream ''One, Independent, Free Republic,'' based on a popular uprising, his motto God and the People. His striving towards popular democracy and Europeanism [the first man to see beyond individual nations to a loosely federal Europe] influenced men like Woodrow Wilson, Ben-Gurion, Nehru and Gandhi. Born in Genoa, he entered university at age 14 and graduated a lawyer at age 21. He formed

Young Italy, a secret society (21) aimed at Italian unification, with 60,000 members in 1833, among whom was Garibaldi. He was part of an uprising that year which failed, 12 participants executed and Mazzini sentenced *in absentia* to death.

He was obliged to be continually on the move, Switzerland, Paris and London. He renamed his society Young Europe, aimed now at freeing and unifying Germany, Poland, Switzerland and even Turkey. He promoted and took part in revolts throughout the continent, all ending in failure, often with the death of Mazzini's closest friends, while he himself always managed to escape. With the rise of Victor Emmanuel and Cavour, he became more of a spectator than an actor, and because he was in disagreement with how Italy was being governed, he refused entry into Victor Emmanuel's government. Sentenced to death countless times, it was pleurisy [inflammation of the lungs and chest cavity] that finally took him, at age 67.

Giuseppe Mazzini.
He supported class collaboration, not class struggle, which made him an enemy of Karl Marx who called him ''that everlasting old ass''. Religious, he defined the Fatherland as ''the home where God has placed us, among brothers and sisters linked to us by the family ties of a common religion, history and language.''

MUSSOLINI

Mussolini, the 36-year-old son of a blacksmith, entered Florence in 1919 to boos. But fascists gained power due to post-W.W. I chaos and the rise of atheistic Bolshevism. In 1920 passers-by who refused to give the fascist salute were beaten and in 1922 Mussolini marched on Rome while in Florence the fascists set up barricades and took over public buildings. Once Mussolini in power in Rome, the murders of a series of opposition leaders in Florence ended in a crowd of 100,000 who showed up in the Piazza della Signoria when he returned in 1930, this time to cheers. D.H. Lawrence was living in Florence, where he wrote *Lady Chatterley's Lover*, first published in Florence. He recorded the disorder under socialism, its strikes and the rudeness of even servants and cabdrivers, the absence of law and order, all of which the fascists had promised to put an end to--and eventually did.

Other homosexual writers were present, Somerset Maugham and his lover Gerald Huxley, Reginald Turner, Norman Douglas, E.M. Forster, Osbert Sitwell, all of whom will complete this book as they were hugely influenced by Florence, its history, and the boys skinny dipping in the Arno. Despite their presence, anti-British sentiment ran high, and the names of hotels, many in English, were expunged, down to English Tea Rooms, a must until then for establishments wishing to attract British tourists as well as Florentines.

Mussolini came back again, this time in 1938 with Hitler, a visit planned six months in advance by Mussolini's minister Count Ciano. German and Italian flags were distributed by the thousands. Hitler avidly visited the museums, in the forced company of Mussolini caught mostly yawning, while it was reported that at various places along the route naked women were waiting in nearby rooms, awaiting Mussolini's sexual satyriasis, a form of nymphomania for men. Like a later Kaddafi, Mussolini's end would be nearly on a par with Italian Renaissance hanging, disemboweling, quartering and beheading.

PART IV

When Florence became Victor Emmanuel's capital in 1865 efforts were made to modernize it. Medieval houses were torn down and new streets, piazzas and parks were built, as reported, the whole culminating in a triumphal arch under which the new king made his entry. British inhabitants were joined by Americans, Russians and Germans who, like most Florentines, mourned the loss of what had made Florence so beautiful and unique, the old habitations and alleys. Florentines had always considered themselves more lovers of art than interested in politicians and political intrigue, but when the bureaucrats left for Rome, their money was sorely regretted. A recession followed and the population actually declined from 200,000 to 167,000. Then an epidemic of cholera struck in 1884, reducing the citizenship by a further 8,000. Florence nonetheless rebounded, and just before the turn of the century the population was again 200,000 and tourism exploded: Dickens, Robert Browning, Francis Trollope, Mark Twain, James Fennimore Couper, Harriet Beecher Stowe, Henry James and the Goncourt brothers. There was a woman among the new arrivals, Maria Louise Ramé, who called herself Ouida, the author of over a score of books, who rented expensive villas and threw parties where ''morals and umbrellas were left in the hall,'' states Hibbert. She competed with other women for the affections of the homosexual Marchese della Stufa [aging matrons, always wealthy, have often placed themselves under the influence of homosexuals, men who dress impeccably, can dance the night away, have perfect manners, are witty and masters of the perfect complement, men like bisexual Byron who used one in order to have access to her 11-year-old daughter (5); or use them as sources, as did Capote his swans (7); down to the recent Bettencourt scandal, involving the richest woman in the world, a French president and the jailing of a renowned homosexual photographer (8)].

Johann Winckelmann and Giacomo Casanova--an adept of Florentine carnivals--were present, and as Casanova's promiscuity was the incarnation of Florentine lovemaking, we will pause in order to reveal some of the lesser known aspects of his life.

CHAPTER TWELVE

GIACOMO CASANOVA

Casanova was not a beauty, but possessed endless charm.

The best résumé of the sexuality of Casanova is found in Wikipedia, that ranges his biographers into three categories: ''Casanova's first editor, Jean Laforgue, ruthlessly censored every reference to the autobiographer's homosexual activity. Since then critical reaction has varied widely, from John Masters who cites Casanova's limited admissions of same-sex eroticism as proof of his essential bisexuality, to J. Rives Childs who strains to divorce Casanova's sexual practice from his sexual orientation by ascribing his 'rare act of pederasty' less to inclination than curiosity, to Michel Delon who sidesteps the question of Casanova's possible homosexuality altogether, associating his behavior with traditional early modern libertinism in which a mature man's erotic attentions might be directed indiscriminately toward women or boys without compromising his sexual identity.'' Meaning that Casanova was a man clearly of his times (4), in no way immune to a pair of charming--most probably hairless--buttocks.

Homosexuality wasn't aided by religion which cast a leaden curtain over sex between males, even when such sex was *the* major outlet for priests and cardinals. Added to this is the age-old prohibition against incest, which has for its basis the evolutionary need for the survival of the species, a survival that is endangered by consanguinity and, especially, the waste of a man's seed in male-male sex and in onanism, all of which Casanova was guilty.

Ian Kelly, in his *Casanova: Actor Lover Priest Spy*, 2008, writes: ''The modern concept of bisexuality, no less than of homosexuality, didn't really exist in the 18th century, and the conception of sexual preference was on the whole a much more fluid affair. It seems that Casanova was a man who in sex, as in life, wanted to taste all the flavors on offer.'' Kelly goes on to suggest that if Casanova didn't go into more detail concerning his encounters with men and boys, it was ''to quash rumors afoot in Venice that his rise to prominence was courtesy of his having been the rent boy of his first patron, Meteo Giovanni Bragadin.''

Casanova slept with few men and women, perhaps 130 in all [compared to Don Giovanni's 1,003], but his lasting influence is thanks to the erotic way in which he wrote about his conquests in his memoirs, an example being two sisters he would possess: ''two buds who only wait for a breath of love to come into bloom.'' [A boy, in any of today's dormitories, can outdo Casanova in a year, although even dormitory athletes have difficulty keeping up with the brilliant novelist George Simenon who had had 10,000 (11).]

Billions of years of evolution has placed the survival of the species as the number one exigency, as said, something easily, too easily, relegated, today, to an act of secondary interest. Here Casanova hit the nail on the head when evoking the very ''soul'' that was the foundation of his existence, ''soul'', in Casanova's case, referring to his dick. His dick was his *raison d'être*, as it is ours--*évolution oblige*. [''I live for, with and by my balls'' Errol Flynn would later proclaim (12).]

One overlooks, too, Casanova's immense literary output: He wrote 42 books and plays, he translated the *Iliad*, penned a 5-volume science-fiction novel, wrote treatises on mathematics and even opera libretti, all in addition to his 12-volumn *The Story of My Life*, a bestseller then as today, written in French, the language most used at the time.

Born in 1725 in Venice, he was stimulated sexually very early on by the daughter of the family who adopted him, although his first penetration would wait until age 17, when it took place with two sisters. He came 4 times with one, her trusting husband asleep in a room nearby, and then took her virgin 17-year-old sister, just weeks before her wedding. He had wanted to enter the clergy, but was expulsed when found in bed with a fellow seminary student. He went on to have a child, a girl he would later impregnate. At age 19 he traveled to Constantinople where he and a friend spied on a group of naked harem girls, the friend, a Turk, manipulating Casanova's aroused member through his clothing. ''It would have been impolite to refuse,'' wrote Casanova, ''I would have shown myself ungrateful.''

One of his most extraordinary conquests was of Bellino, a girl who passed as a boy, doting herself with an artificial penis. Casanova was attracted by both her feminine and masculine attributes, discovering that it was a girl only at the time of penetration, an act that would leave her with a child she later--still posing as a boy--said was her brother. Even the supposed love of his life, a certain Henrietta, had at first attracted him when he saw her disguised as a man, during her flight from a brutal husband.

At age 28 the Venetian Inquisition received word from various sources of Casanova's preference for younger and younger prey, boys often from the nobility he was tutoring. He was arrested and sent to the Leads, an escape-proof prison he miraculously escaped from. He went to the Paris of Louis XV, himself a debauched lover of orgies. It was there Casanova thought up the idea of a national lottery, which would make him rich enough to carry on his career of international seducer. His charm, his daring escape from prison, as well as the relating of other adventures, made him an indispensable guest at dinners, as would later be the case for the likes of Oscar Wilde and Truman Capote. His deep involvement in the mystical and mysterious Cabbala provided him with powers of healing and the ability to bestow eternal life, an enormous aphrodisiac to the countless--and extremely wealthy--women he possessed, one of whom he even promised to transmigrate into the body of a male infant. One woman, a Marquess, took her pleasure in watching Casanova take the virginity of the young girls she offered him [deflowering virgins would soon become his greatest pleasure]. He gambled, he screwed, and he had the inevitable duels that went along with his seducing the wives of others.

Due to depression and his syphilitic body, he decided to do away with himself, intending to jump from the Westminster Bridge, his pockets weighed down with lead shot. The year was 1763 and he was 38. A passer-by, a friend, unaware of what Casanova was planning, invited him for a meal. Restored, Casanova went on to additional exploits, one being the impregnation of his own daughter, a service he rendered her because her husband was unable to father children. She thusly had Casanova's.

He lost his looks, and his fortune through gambling, and took on work as a librarian, dying, alone, at age 73.

He never stopped imagining ''that something better was coming along'' wrote his biographer Ian Kelly, which is, I might add, the motor of us all.

JOHANN JOACHIM WINCKELMANN

Winckelmann, a frequent visitor to Florence, was of extreme importance in raising archeology to a science, that he applied to art history, paving the way for the neoclassical movements of the 1700s, the whole built around his founding work, *The History of Ancient Art* (1764). Born in extreme poverty, his father a cobbler, he worked his way through several universities, his interests Greek and Roman art--based on the study of the male nude in Greek and Roman sculpture--and Greek literature. He served as a private tutor to rich families whose sons, his pupils, were the objects of his love.

Winckelmann, 1717-1768

Openly homosexual in his tastes and moderately homoerotic in his writings, we have no proof of whether or not he entered into some form of physical contact with his students: the act of seduction is an art, some had it like Casanova and the more recent Gore Vidal who, as I've written elsewhere (7), would not hesitate to tell a boy, any boy, that he was the most beautiful lad he'd ever seen, and then see what went down from there. Others, like Nietzsche, were all thumbs where enticing boys was concerned. And then, Nietzsche was in no way handsome, while young Vidal was gorgeous, which helps.

Thanks to his studies and publications, Augustus III of Poland gave Winckelmann a pension of 200 thalers so he could study in Rome, which he did in 1755. It was there he discovered the *Belvedere Torso*, ''the utmost perfection of ancient sculpture,'' said he, which I chose for the cover of my book *Greek Homosexuality*. He stayed on in Rome to work in the libraries of several cardinals, since by then Winckelmann was fluent in Latin and, as one cardinal, Passionei, stated, ''his Greek writing was superb.''

We know he lived with the painter Anton Raphael Mengs, and that he had a liaison with one of Meng's acolytes, about whom Winckelmann wrote: "I can be satisfied with my life. I have no worries other than my work, and have even found someone with whom I can speak of love: a good-looking, blond young Roman of sixteen, half a head taller than I am; but I only see him once a week, when he dines with me on Sunday evening." At age 45 Winckelmann fell in love with Friedrich Rheinhold von Berg, 26, about whom Winckelmann wrote to a friend, a certain Goethe: "I have fallen in love, and how!" About Winckelmann Goethe wrote, "Winckelmann felt himself born for a friendship of this kind--not only capable of it, but in the highest degree in need of it." Berg, seeking the excitement of Paris, left Winckelmann who wrote him, "As a solicitous mother inconsolably mourns her beloved child, so, my sweet friend, I deplore our separation with all my heart. My beloved and very beautiful friend, no name by which I might call you would be sweet enough or sufficient for my love; all that I could say would be far too feeble to give utterance to my heart and soul. Truly friendship came from heaven and was not created by mere human impulses. My one friend, I love you more than any living thing, and time nor chance nor age can ever lessen this love."

Another, later friend, Bartolomeo Cavaceppi, persuaded Winckelmann to leave his beloved Italy, the time to benefit from his growing renown. Winckelmann went to Vienna where he received honorary medals from Empress Mary Theresa. On his way back to Italy, in Trieste, he met a café waiter, Francesco Arcangeli, to whom he showed his medals from the empress, between bouts of love making, and this over a period of a few days. Arcangeli was a thief and realized that the only way to steal from someone well known like Winckelmann, and get away with it, was to kill him. He bought a length of rope and a knife, and when both were in bed, Arcangeli held Winckelmann in his arms, Winckelmann's back to Arcangeli's chest. Arcangeli encircled Winckelmann's throat with the rope and pulled. When Winckelmann put up more resistance than Arcangeli had planned, he reached for the knife and plunged it repeatedly into Winckelmann, the coroner later maintaining that Arcangeli had especially aimed at Winckelmann's groin. Arcangeli fled and Winckelmann was able to gather enough strength to leave the room, shouting "Look what he did to me!" before collapsing dead. Arcangeli, 31 and pockmarked [the antithesis of the ideal ephebe], was arrested and, the following month, broken on the wheel.

CHAPTER THIRTEEN

JOHN SARGENT, GEORGE DOUGLAS, SOMERSET MAUGHAM, E.M.FORSTER, REGINALD TURNER, FRANCIS SITWELL AND HAROLD ACTON

JOHN [SINGER] SARGENT

A renowned visitor to Florence was the artist John Sargent, 1856-1925. Sargent was blessed with American parents who, thanks to a heritage, decided to spend their lives in travel, Sargent himself born in Florence Italy. His father was a noted eye surgeon who was also a medical illustrator and his mother was an amateur artist, both passing their skills on to their son. Fruitless attempts were made to see to his formal education, but his parents decided that visiting museums and seeing paintings found in churches would be an acceptable substitute. He observed and copied the works of Tintoretto, da Vinci, Titian, Michelangelo, Velázquez in Spain, and scores of others from the originals. He studied landscape painting under Carl Welsch in Germany and received instruction from Bonnat in Paris where Sargent *himself* was admired by Degas, Rodin and Monet. By age 17 he was fluent in French, Italian and German [and English, of course] and already had a lover, James Beckwith.

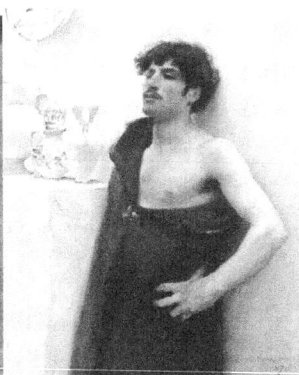

James Carol Beckwith and Sargent's *Young Man in Reverie*, a Caprese boy.

After becoming world famous through expositions, he established himself in London where clients came from the world over to pay around $130,000 in today's dollars for a painting that took from 5 to 7 sittings, while Sargent exchanged amicable conversation interspersed with tea and Sargent at the piano, as he was an accomplished musician. Robert Louis Stevenson sat for him, as did Woodrow Wilson, Teddy Roosevelt and John D. Rockefeller. He did everything himself, from stretching the canvas to packaging and mailing off the finished painting. As he became well-to-do he collected impressionists, especially Monets. Museums began snapping up his works, beginning with the Tate, the National Gallery, the Uffizi in Florence and the Harvard Fogg Museum.

Sargent by Léon Delafosse.

In 1907 at age 51 he closed up shop, free to travel, free from the obligation to entertain and to always be in companionable humor when painting his subjects. But the demand was so great for his work, and clients so wealthy, that he did dash off charcoal sketches, in the hundreds, to those who could pay. He called them "mugs", treasured today in museums and collections around the world.

He died in England in 1925 from heart disease, and is buried in Surrey (5).

Sargent's sketch of Yeats.
The painter Jacques-Emile Blanche knew Sargent during his young years and described his sex life as ''notorious in Paris, and in Venice, positively scandalous. He was a frenzied bugger,'' while a client, Betty Wertheimer, said that in Venice he ''was only interested in Venetian gondoliers.''

GEORGE NORMAN DOUGLAS

George Douglas, 1868-1952, took his life on Capri (13), the inscription he wanted on his tombstone, an ode by Horace: *omnes eodem cogimur, We are all driven to the same end.* And his final *living* words, before taking an overdose: ''Get those fucking nuns away from me!''

Born in Thüringen Austria, Douglas was raised mostly in Scotland. He did diplomatic service in St. Petersburg from whence he was expulsed for supposedly heterosexual activity involving well-connected Russian wives. The year before he wrote his best-known book, *South Wind* (1917), he jumped bail in London and fled to Italy, having been accused of an indecent assault on a 16-year-old boy, what Douglas said was an excessive punishment for ''giving him some cakes and a shilling.'' Perhaps true, but as we know, had the boy not gone to the police, an attempt at sodomy would have most probably followed the giving of the coin. This charge was reinforced by another that came at the same time, an accusation of sexual offences [we don't know the details] against two brothers, aged 10 and 12. [At age 31 he had had a sexual affair with the 15-year-old son of his mistress, and admitted to a friend, concerning his preference for young boys, ''I've always liked a small possession (small lads), attached to a very large possession (dicks).''] Douglas's friends Joseph Conrad and Compton Mackenzie had counseled him to jump bail. [A word on Compton Mackenzie in passing. He lived on Capri and wrote books with lesbian themes. One can only dream of a life like Compton Mackenzie's. Compton derives from the stage name his family adopted, Henry Compton, for example, a known Shakespearean actor. Among his hundred books is one on the Battle of Marathon, another on the Battle of Salamis. His comic novel *Whisky Galore* spawned a film and t.v. series, and his *Sinister Street* influenced writers from George Orwell to Henry James. *Thin Ice* evokes the life of a homosexual politician and four of his books were on his years in British Intelligence. His autobiography consists of ten volumes and in 1952 he was knighted.]

Douglas had married and his wife, in requesting custody of their children, accused him of pedophilia, consisting of the ''rather faunesque pursuit of young boys,'' she testified.

Homosexual scandals in Italy obliged him to leave for the French Riviera before becoming a Caprese. Author John Sutherland wrote that his prose, before becoming outdated, made him ''one of the smartest things going'', a fashion that lasted ''the whole of his long depraved life, one jump ahead of the law.''

His book *Together* is a travel account of his summer in Austria just after W.W. I, with observations on rural life, descriptions of mountains and forests, pretty boring and uneventful, except for the fact that he made the trip with René, a 15-year-old Italian lad.

Douglas lived a good number of years in Florence where he worked with Florentine bookseller and publisher Pino Orioli, who published his works as well as the first edition of D.H Lawrence's *Lady Chatterley's Lover*. He also helped Orioli write his autobiography.

SOMERSET MAUGHAM

Somerset Maugham was a habitué of Florence, visiting Reginald Turner there just seven months before Turner's death [his life follows], as well as using the city and its surroundings in his play ''The Circle'' and book *Up at the Villa*, among others.

The defining feature of Maugham's life [1874-1965] was certainly the loss of his mother, at age 8, whom he adored and whose picture never left him throughout all his years on earth. His father died two years later and Maugham was farmed out to a cold uncle who put him in a boarding school where he was ridiculed for his small size and his inadequacy in English, as he had been born in Paris where his father was a legal expert at the British Embassy.

At 16 he went to Heidelberg University where he had his first sexual relations--most likely outside of those mandatory in boarding schools--with John Ellingham Brooks, 26, a Cambridge graduate in law and a pianist who would later spend time with Maugham on Capri, starting 1895: ''I came for lunch and stayed for life.'' About Brooks Maugham wrote: ''He can discover nothing for himself. He intends to write but has neither the energy, imagination or will. He is weak, vain and profoundly selfish.'' [So much for love.] In Capri Brooks shared his digs with Edward Frederick Benson, 1867-1940, known as Fred, a novelist, archeologist and short story writer. Benson was an exceptional athlete, representing Britain in figure skating. Given the times, there were only the slightest allusions to homosexuality in Benson's writing. Of Benson's five brothers and sisters, all were ''queer'', as he himself put it, which was indeed the case.

Benson, the photo on the left taken at Eton by Baron Corvo.

Maugham went on to study medicine and became a doctor, but the success of his first novel allowed him to devote all his time to writing, eventually making him the highest paid writer of the 1930s. But his time as a doctor had been vital: ''I saw how men died. I saw how they bore pain. I saw what hope looked like, fear and relief.'' By age 40 he had written 10 plays and 10 novels. His lifelong lover was Gerald Haxton who remained with Maugham until his death, 30 years after their meeting.

Maugham traveled widely, writing the *Moon and Sixpence*, the life of Gauguin, and was a part of MI6 from which experience he wrote a series of short stories having for hero a sophisticated gentleman spy whom Fleming used for his James Bond. He lived the rest of his life at Cap Ferrat, the most exclusive and beautiful part of the French Riviera.

During his time with Haxton he had another lover, Alan Searle. He adopted the boy as his son, making the lad literally filthy rich at Maugham's death at age 91, [even if the adoption was later overturned to protect the interests of Maugham's daughter whose mother had married Maugham because she said he had made her pregnant, after which they divorced]. Maugham had also been deeply in love with Harry Philips, and so afraid were they of being exposed in an Oscar-Wilde-type scandal [Maugham had been 21 during Oscar's trial] that they only met in Paris for their sexual trysts. In 1919 Haxton was deported from Britain for being caught in a homosexual act. What happened was this: In November 1915 the military police, looking for deserters, burst into Haxton's hotel room and found him *in fragrante delicto* with a young man, John Lindsell. Haxton, an American born in San Francesco, was deported as an undesirable alien. The reason for the deportation has always been attributed to the hotel incident, but many historians are unsure. What is certain is that the Haxton dossier has been placed in a special ''100-year category'' and will therefore not be disclosed in my lifetime, at least.

Thereafter Haxton and Maugham met only during Maugham's travels, which were extremely frequent.

Haxton, and Haxton with Maugham [pictures of Philips and Searle are, alas, unavailable, and even these are atrocious].

Losing his mother, and school trauma, left Maugham extremely shy and caused a stutter. He said Haxton was indispensable to him in his writing because he was an extravert who interviewed the people Maugham shied away from. Haxton was said to have been obnoxious to Maugham, ordering him about, telling him to fetch his drinks [Haxton was an alcoholic] and ran up gambling debts that Maugham, wealthy, had no difficulty, nor hesitancy, covering. It was evident that Haxton was the *raison d'être* of Maugham's life, and friends claimed that Maugham's eyes would light up the moment Haxton entered the room. On the other hand, Maugham was reported to have treated Searle as badly as Haxton treated him, but Searle, described as rough trade, appreciated Maugham's collection of pornography and the pool parties Maugham threw. For although Maugham was repeatedly said to have been timid, his villa in France was *the* center for boys, obligatorily bathing naked in his pool, and the orgies that took place there rivaled those of Gloeden's at Taormina, with local French lads filling the place of Gloeden's Italians.

A photo taken at Maugham's Riviera pool, amidst 9 acres of gardens, the boys catered to by 13 servants. Maugham was at times absent, in Switzerland, having injections of sheep fetus cells, supposedly to help him keep up with the lads.

In the heyday of story writing Maugham was paid $2,500 for each by Hearst magazines, and one story, ''Rain'', brought in $1 million in royalties, a fabulous sum for 1923 [worth, in fact 14 million of today's dollars], when it was made into the film that launched the career of Joan Crawford. In all, 98 films were made from his material, just in his lifetime! Yet, about himself, Maugham was perhaps right: ''I know just where I stand: in the very front row of the second-rate.''

E.M. FORSTER

E.M. Forster, 1879-1970, spent a great deal of time in Florence, his sojourn in the pension Bertolini the inspiration for his *A Room with a View.*

Forster was above all a humanist, acknowledged as such when named President of Cambridge Humanists in 1959 and a member of the British Humanist Association from 1963 until his death in 1970 at age 81. A great aunt left him £800,000 in today's money, which freed him from any form of servitude. He was an on-the-fringe member of the Bloomsbury Set, and a King's College, Cambridge, student. His name is associated with several men, among them Christopher Isherwood (7) and Benjamin Britten.

His travels took him throughout Europe, especially Italy, which inspired two books, *Where Angels Fear to Tread* and *A Room with a View*. He was secretary to a maharaja and several visits to India inspired his most read book, *A Passage to India*.

Among what is called his "loving relationships" was a very long one with a married policeman.

He was nominated for the Nobel Prize 13 times and he wrote his last book at age 35.

Forster

The problem with E.M. Forster's book *Maurice* was that it had a happy ending. Maurice meets a gamekeeper, they fall in love, decide to remain with each other throughout life, *and do so*. Had the book ended in the usual homosexual tragedy Forster might have decided to have it published, as then everyone could plainly see the consequences of immoral love.

The book begins with prep-school boarding-school love and goes on to university love [Greek texts encouraged by horny tutors], the whole apparently based on the true lives of Edward Carpenter, 1844-1929, and his lover George Merrill. It was finally published in 1971, a year after his death, 60 years after its creation.

Interestingly, Maurice tries to cure himself of his love of boys through hypnotism before deciding to be of service to the working class by running a boxing gym, the compensation being the naked lads under the showers.

A humanist like Forster, Edward Carpenter chose to aid the

lower classes, as well as finding his sexual companions among them: ''the grimy and oil-besmeared figure of a stoker'' or ''the thick-thighed hot course-fleshed young bricklayer with a strap around his waist.'' He also doted on Parisian rent-boys.

He decried the industrial smog of Sheffield that was killing thousands and realized that only a strong socialist movement had the potential of putting things right.

Educated at Brighton College and Trinity Hall, Cambridge, at his father's death he inherited enough to become financially independent. He bought a farm that he worked, while writing his book of poems, *Towards Democracy.*

He met George Merrill, a working-class man without a formal education, in 1891 at age 47, and they lived together 27 years despite the hysteria due to the Oscar Wilde trial and the Criminal Law Bill that outlawed all forms of homosexual contact. Concerning Merrill he wrote, in his *Intermediate Sex*: "Eros is a great leveller. Perhaps the true Democracy rests, more firmly than anywhere else, on a sentiment which easily passes the bounds of class and caste, and unites in the closest affection the most estranged ranks of society. It is noticeable how often [homosexuals] of good position and breeding are drawn to rougher types, as of manual workers, and frequently very permanent alliances grow up in this way, which although not publicly acknowledged have a decided influence on social institutions, customs and political tendencies." The book was the foundation of the LGBT movement [lesbian, gay, bisexual and transgender].

Merrill and Carpenter.

Carpenter's last years were devoted to homosexual rights, as well as the protection of the environment and animals, the benefits of a vegetarian diet and the necessity of pacifism. George Orwell attacked him as representing ''every fruit-juice drinker, nudist, sandal wearer and sex maniac'' in the Socialist movement.

Merrill died in 1928, bringing on a stroke that kept Carpenter paralyzed until his own death in 1929.

Merrill and Carpenter's tombs.

Forster became a close friend of both men, as did John Addington Symonds.

Forster's tombstone.

REGINALD TURNER

The most salient characteristic of Reginald ''Reggie'' Turner's life, 1869-1938, was his gift for table conversation, Max Beerbohm writing, ''one forgot to eat while he spun his fantasies,'' seconded by S.N. Behrman who said, ''He was one of those men who talk like angels.'' To which Somerset Maugham added, "Reggie Turner was, on the whole, the most amusing man I have ever known."

Reggie penned 12 books, few of which were reprinted, which prompted Turner to observe that it was not his first editions that were scarce, but his second ones. Behrman agreed, stating that although he talked like angels, he "wrote like pedestrians."

He never knew the identity of his parents and was raised by the owner of *The Daily Telegraph*, the Levy-Lawsons, one of whom had most probably fathered the boy. Turner is portrayed by Colin Firth in the 2018 film *The Happy Prince*, the life of Oscar Wilde.

Homosexual, Turner was a close friend of Somerset Maugham and one of the few who supported Wilde, as a friend and financially, until his death. Wilde's trial encouraged Turner to leave England for France and Italy, his last home Florence where he died at age 69 and was buried in the Cimitero Evangelico degli Allori.

FRANCIS OSBERT SITWELL

Francis Sitwell, 1892-1969, united with his brother and sister in producing anthologies. He survived W.W. I, where he wrote poetry in the trenches in France, followed in England by short stories, novels and collections of his poems. One of his poems was entitled *Rat Week*, an attack on the Duke and Duchess of York, [King Edward VIII and Wallis Simpson], as well as an attack on those who deserted both when Edward abdicated in order to marry Simpson. Deemed too libelous to be published, he spent a number of years fighting publications that printed sections [although always highly censored sections]. The poem was finally released after the death of all concerned, by which time few cared enough to read it.

According to Sitwells' biographer, John Pearson, "David dressed superbly, had an amusing line of gossip about all the best people, which he recounted in an engagingly basso profundo voice, and after leaving Cambridge was soon floating, as unattached, good-looking, upper-class young Englishmen could float in those more gentle, far-off days, through a rarely failing world of dinner-parties, long weekends and holidays abroad. He was the perfect guest, the ideal ornament for any party, charming to women and agreeable to men, better connected and far better read than the usual run of gilded social butterflies, and equally at home in the best society in Paris or in London." Sitwell also served as a Squadron-Leader in the Royal Air Force during W.W. II, no mean accomplishment.

He spent most of his life with his lover David Stuart Horner, and died outside of Florence, at his castle at Montegufoni. He too was buried in the Cimitero Evangelico degli Allori.

Horner died in 1983, 14 years after Sitwell who didn't leave him the castle as promised. In spite, Horner sold 951 letters written to him by Sitwell.

HAROLD ACTON
1904 - 1994

Acton was born and died in Florence, and spent his time between the citadel of the Medici [his most famous historical work being *The Last Medici*], Paris and London, although it was to N.Y. University that he bequeathed his Florentine Villa La Pietra. He claimed that an Acton descendent had been the prime minister of Naples under Ferdinand IV and his *magnum opus* was on the Kingdom of Naples in the 18th and 19th centuries. Educated at Eton and Oxford, he knew George Orwell, Oliver Messel, Ian Fleming and Brian Howard, an Eton cross-dresser whom Evelyn Waugh amalgamed with Acton in his character Anthony Blanche in *Brideshead Revisited*--"2/3rds Brian, 1/3rd Acton" wrote Waugh. Anthony Blanche is a flamboyant and stereotypical queer who dresses as a girl and dines with Proust. An "aesthete par excellence" who dons "colorful robes" and affects a stutter--it was definitely not a compliment to be compared to Antony Blanche. In addition to sex, Howard and Acton were drawn together by a limitless love of Diaghilev's ballets. They also shared the beds of Anthony Powell and Cyril Connolly. Waugh dedicated his *Decline and Fall* to Acton, "in Homage and Affection." Acton had a younger brother, an artist, who committed suicide in 1944.

Acton was part of the Eton screamers, an effeminate dandy, that today one would call a raging queen, who dressed outrageously *à la* Oscar Wilde. He was open about his homosexuality, if for no other reason that it was so evident, but how active he was sexually is disputed, some claiming he was asexual, others that he had been a scandalous debauchee during a trip to China. But Acton does seem to have had as many Chinese boys as his virility could sustain, followed afterwards by Indian lads when the war kept him away from Peking. In the picture to follow he is seen in Peking on a visit to Desmond Parsons and Robert Byron.

He spent the end of his life in maintaining his Florentine villa and in receiving the likes of Churchill, Greene, Huxley, Henry Moore, Beaton, D.H. Lawrence and others. He died at age 90.

CHAPTER FOURTEEN

RECENT TIMES

Sex in Italy, following W.W. II, is best illustrated by this extract from my book *American Homosexual Giants*:

Rome was one of Vidal's favorite haunts, and what went on there had been going on since Aeneas, fleeing from Troy, founded the city (10). Vidal wrote that the boys of Rome would gather at certain places in the hundreds, "a sexual paradise", especially as girls at that time were locked away until marriage. He had a Jaguar convertible and boys everywhere would surround it in admiration. Then, author Tim Teeman tells us, he would make his choice and say "You're the most beautiful boy I've ever seen," and see how that worked. His boys were always straight and muscular, thankful for the money and clothes he gave them, as American clothing was impossible to come by. Gore wrote that Italian boys went for $20 [$265 today for 1945 dollars]. Later in life Gore said that Italian boys had changed. Gone were the innocent kids who were deeply contented when told "You're the most beautiful boy I've ever seen."

Christopher Hitchens, an extremely prolific British journalist [later an American citizen], knew Gore and Tennessee Williams in Rome and wrote that they picked up rough trade along the Via Veneto that "Gore would take from the rear and then thrust into the room next door where Tennessee would suck them dry." It bears remembering that Gore was of such great beauty that had these boys been gay and not in need of money, he could have had them for nothing [but then he would have had to reciprocate sexual act for sexual act, something money freed him from doing].

Rome was the ideal site for Gore. The architecture, the pale colors of the buildings, the narrow, winding alleys where one could come upon a beautiful fountain or a beautiful face. He loved the language and was surrounded by Italian friends, writers, journalists, the brightest of the lads he had picked up, and from America came a steady stream of visitors who had marked Gore on their map as they had designated the Coliseum and Trevi Fountain as a must-see. A friend, Harry Mathews, wrote, "You could pick up young men on the streets, and for very little money. Gore liked anonymous sex, and that was plentiful. Many were repeat customers, and friends in a way." A Yale friend of Gore, Thomas Powers, said that "sex in Rome was hugely important for Gore, a daily addiction." His residence in Rome was the Palazzo Origo with what Jay Parini, in his excellent, perfectly-titled book *Empire of Self*, 2015, called "a staggering view" of the city. No one cared what went on in Gore's apartment because the Italians have always been a people who live and let live, ever on the edge of anarchy. End of extract.

Today Italian boys fully understand their worth, and their Hersey-bar readiness has given way to intense arrogance [except for those in the hundreds, boys and girls, who display their attributes on roads leading into and out of the major cities]. Here is an extract from my autobiography, *Michael Hone: His World, His Loves*: One day his neighbor Aldo invited him to Ventimiglia to look for whores. Aldo was so excited he dribbled spittle from the corners of his mouth. Boyd [my middle name is Boyd] knew he "worked" the cafés and markets, chatting up salesgirls, while his wife Roseland and their daughter were off at the Narval to be made a fuss over by the servers, cheap Italian labor from across the border. Boyd had accompanied them once. Perhaps considered a potential rival, he got an unselfconscious toe-to-head look-over from the waiters, who appeared dead serious about their "courting" of the two women. Were it not for a cold, he felt sure he would have caught the whiff of their semen-stained jeans. He had seen the Italians often enough in the showers to imagine their cocks, too big and thick when hard to be pulled through their flies, gently swaying while their owners lowered their trousers, preparatory to propping the girl up against the door of the café john, ready to discharge in a minimum of strokes. Too bad if the girl didn't get much out of the quick plugging, they'd have the compensating surprise of watching what dribbled out later in uncanny abundance. Because the salty air filled Boyd's mind with such salacious thoughts, he had agreed to ride off with Aldo. In Ventimiglia the man did the negotiating from his car window, but the prostitutes were too sordid for even Aldo's wants, and the price, it seemed to the boy, sky high for the rundown border town. Back at the quay, Aldo went in search of his wife. Twenty minutes later their boat left the port, something it did only when he needed a quiet place to hump undisturbed. The daughter was left alone on the quay, but never for long.

Italian girls felt they had diamonds in the place of their cherries. Assured of the attention they aroused, the girls paraded as if on continual presentation, *à l'italienne*, chest and buttocks thrust out, in provocative oscillation. Once he had heard an Italian mother scold her six-year-old son: "Why don't you look at the *donnas*? You must look at them when they pass!" She stopped just short of calling him a queer. Young girls, those without approved beaux, were forced to toe the line if they didn't want their adored brothers to give them a fat lip when they disobeyed. Once married, they were relegated to the kitchen where an excess of food and repeated childbearing left them spread out over two chairs, while their aging husbands escaped the conjugal hearth on the arm of "fresh flesh," young girls paid to find them ever manly. Who cared now if their wives' hair reeked of olive oil, or if the odor of sour milk seeped through their pores, or the fustiness of garlic soaked through the matted tufts under their armpits? Even then the women strutted forth, in their mind's eye as desirable as the divine Garbo. End of extract.

If the reader is looking for a magnificent tourist stop, Florence is definitely it. If he's looking for sex, go to Myconos

173

and/or Amsterdam. I could go into great detail as to why Florence fails in this area, but as I have nothing good to say, I prefer to remain benignly silent. The museums, the piazzas and the cafés are your best bets, parks and the Arno River at night are beautiful but risky.

SOURCES

(1) See my book *Greek Homosexuality*.
(2) See my book *Henry III*.
(3) See my book *German Homosexuality*.
(4) See my book *Omnisexuality*.
(5) See my book *The History of British Homosexuality*.
(6) See my book *Caravaggio*.
(7) See my book *American Homosexual Giants*.
(8) See my book *French Homosexuality*.
(9) See my book *Hadrian and Antinous*.
(10) See my book *TROY*.
(11) See my book *Phallus*.
(12) See my book *The Garden of Allah*.
(13) See my book *CAPRI*.
(14) See my book *Boarding School Homosexuality*.
(15) See my autobiography *Michael Hone His World, His Loves*.
(16) See my book *Five Renaissance Wonders*.
(17) See my book *Cesare Borgia*.
(18) See my book *The Sacred Band*.
(19) See my book *Alexander and Hephaestion*.
(20) See my book *Renaissance Homosexuality*.
(21) See my book *Homosexual Secret Societies*.
(22) See my book *Alcibiades the Schoolboy*.

Abbott Jacob, *History of Pyrrhus*, 2009.
Ady, Cecilia, *A History of Milan under the Sforza*, 1907.
Aggleton, Peter, *Men Who Sell Sex*, 1999.
Aldrich and Wotherspoon, *Who's Who in Gay and Lesbian History*, 2001.
Aldrich, Robert, *The Seduction of the Mediterranean*, 1993.
Andress, David, *The Terror*, 2005.
Aristophanes, Bantam Drama, 1962.
Aronson, Marc, *Sir Walter Ralegh*, 2000.
Baglione, *Caravaggio*, circa 1600.
Baker Simon, *Ancient Rome*, 2006.
Barber, Richard, *The Devil's Crown--Henry II and Sons*, 1978.

Barber, Stanley, *Alexandros*, 2010.

Barré, Jean-Luc, *François Mauriac, Biographie intime*, 2009.

Bawlf, Samuel, *The Secret Voyage of Sir Francis Drake*, 2003.

Beachy, Robert, *Gay Berlin*, 2014. Marvelous.

Bellori, *Caravaggio*, circa 1600.

Bergreen, Laurence, *Over the Edge of the World. Magellan.* 2003.

Bicheno, Hugh, *Vendetta*, 2007.

Bierman, John, *Dark Safari, Henry Morton Stanley*, 1990.

Blanchard, Jean-Vincent, *Éminence, Cardinal Richelieu and the Rise of*

Boswell, John, *Christianity, Social Tolerance, and Homosexuality*, 1980.

Boswell, John, *Same-Sex Unions*, 1994.

Boyd, Douglas, *April Queen*, 2004.

Boyles, David, *Blondel's Song*, 2005.

Bramly, Serge, *Leonardo*, 1988. A wonderful book.

Bret, David, *Errol Flynn, Gentleman Hellraiser*, 2004

Bret, Davis, *Trailblazers*, 2009.

Bull, Lew, *Memoirs of a Hustler*, 2010.

Burg, B.R., *Gay Warriors*, 2002.

Burg, B.R., *Sodomy and the Pirate Tradition*, 1989.

Bury and Meiggs, *A History of Greece*, 1975.

Calimach, Andrew, *Lover's Legends*, 2002.

Callow, Simon, *Charles Laughton*, 1995.

Capote, A Reader, Abacus, 1989.

Caro, Robert, *The Years of Lyndon Johnson*, Vol. 4, 2012.

Carpenter, Edward, *The Intermediate Sex*, 1912.

Carroll, Stuart, *Martyrs & Murderers, The Guise Family*, 2009.

Carter, William, *Proust in Love*, 2006.

Cartledge, Paul, *Alexander the Great*, 2004.

Cate, Curtis, *Friedrich Nietzsche*, 2003.

Cavel Benjamin, *Rumble, Young Man, Rumble*, 2003.

Cawthorne, Nigel, *Sex Lives of the Popes*, 1996

Cellini, Benvenuto, *The Autobiography of Benvenuto Cellini*.

Ceram, C.W., *Gods, Graves and Scholars*, 1951.

Chamberlin, E.R. *The Fall of the House of Borgia*, 1974

Clark, Adrian and Jeremy Dronfield, *Queer Saint, Peter Watson*, 2015.

Clark, Christopher, *Iron Kingdom*, 2006.

Clark, Gerald, *Capote*, 1988.

Clerc, Thomas, *Maurice Sachs, Le Désoeuvré*, 2005.

Cloulas Ivan, *The Borgia*, 1989.

Cooper, John, *The Queen's Agent*, 2011.

Cowan, Thomas, *Gay Men and Women Who Enriched the World*, 1988/

Crompton, Louis, *Byron and Greek Love*, 1985.

Crompton, Louis, *Homosexuality and Civilization*, 2003.

Crowley, Roger, *Empires of the Sea*, 2008. Marvelous.

Cruickshank, John, *Montherland*, 1964.

Curtis Cate, *Friedrich Nietzsche*, 2002.

Dale, Richard, *Who Killed Sir Walter Ralegh?*, 2011.

Davidson, James, *Courtesans and Fishcakes*, 1998.

Davidson, James, *The Greeks and Greek Love*, 2007.

Davidson, Michael, *The World, The Flesh and Myself*, 1977.

Davis, John Paul, *The Gothic King, Henry III*, 2013.

Dover K.J. *Greek Homosexuality*, 1978.

Duby, George, *William Marshal*, 1985.

Edmonson, Roger, *Boy in the Sand, Casey Donovan*, 1998.

Eisler, Benita, *BYRON Child of Passion, Fool of Fame*, 2000. Wonderful.

Ellmann, Richard, *Oscar Wilde*, 1987.

Erlanger, Philippe, *Buckingham*, 1951.

Erlanger, Philippe, *The King's Minion*, 1901.

Evans, Robert, *The Kid Stays in the Picture*, 1994.

Everitt Anthony, *Augustus*, 2006.

Everitt Anthony, *Cicero*, 2001.

Fagles, Robert, *The Iliad*, 1990.

Fiore, Carlo, *The Brando I Knew*, 1974.

Forellino, Antonio, *Michelangelo*, 2005. Beautiful reproductions.

Fothergill, Brian, *Beckford of Fonthill*, 1979.

Fraser, Antonia, *The Gunpowder Plot*, 1996.

Frieda, Leonie, *Catherine de Medici*, 2003.

Gayford, Martin, *Michelangelo*, 2013. A beautiful book.

Gidel, Henry, *Cocteau*, 2009.

Gillingham, John, *Richard the Lionheart*, 1978.

Gilmore, John, *Laid Bare*, 1997.

Gilmore, John, *Live Fast—Die Young*, 1997.

Goldsworthy Adrian, *Caesar*, 2006.

Goldsworthy Adrian, *The Fall of Carthage*, 2000

Goodman Rob and Soni Jimmy, *Rome's Last Citizen*, 2012.

Gore-Browne, Robert, *Lord Bothwell*, 1937.

Graham-Dixon Andrew, *Caravaggio*, 2010. The book is fabulous. A genuine

Graham, Robb, *Strangers*, 2003.

Grant Michael, *History of Rome*, 1978.

Grazia, Sebastian de, *Machiavelli in Hell*, 1989.

Grèce, Michel de, *Le Vol du Régent*, 2008.

Guicciardini, *Storie fiorentine (History of Florence)*, 1509.

Halperin David M. *One Hundred Years of Homosexuality*, 1990.

Harris Robert, *Imperium*, 2006

Herodotus, *The Histories*, Penguin Classics.

Hesiod and Theognis, Penguin Classics, 1973.

Hibbard, Allen, *Paul Bowles*, 1993.
Hibbert Christopher, *Florence, the Biography of a City*, 1993.
Hibbert Christopher, *The Borgias and Their Enemies,* 2009. I love
Hibbert Christopher, *The Rise and Fall of the House of Medici*, 1974.
Hibbert, Christopher, *Florence, the Biography of a City*, 1993.
Hibbert, Christopher, *The Days of the French Revolution*, 1981.
Hibbert, Christopher, *The Great Mutiny India 1857*, 1978. Fabulous.
Hicks, Michael, *Richard III*, 2000.
Hine, Daryl, *Puerilities*, 2001.
Hirst, Michael, *The Tudors*, 2007.
Hochschild, Adam, *King Leopold's Ghost*, 1999.
Hofler, Robert, *Party Animals*, 2010.
Hofler, Robert, *The Man Who Invented Rock Hudson*, 2005.
Hogan, Steve, *Completely Queer, Gay and Lesbian Encyclopedi*a, 1998.
Holland Tom, *Rubicon*, 2003
Holland, Tom, *Persian Fire*, 2005.
Hughes Robert, *Rome*, 2011.
Hughes-Hallett, *Heroes*, 2004.
Hutchinson, Robert, *Elizabeth's Spy Master*, 2006.
Hutchinson, Robert, *House of Treason*, 2009.
Hutchinson, Robert, *Thomas Cromwell*, 2007.
Isherwood, Charles, *The Life and Death of Joey Stefano*, 1996.
Isherwood, Christopher, *Christopher and His Kind*, 1976.
Isherwood, Christopher, *Diaries*, vol. one, 2011.
Jack, Belinda, *Beatrice's Spell*, 2004.
James, Callum, *My Dear KJ...* edited by James, 2015.
Johnson, Marion, *The Borgias*, 1981.
Jouhandeau, Marcel, *Ecrits secrets*, 1988.
Kanfer, Stefan, *Marlon Brando*, 2008.
Katz, Jonathan Ned, *Love Stories*, 2001.
Kearns, Michael, *The Truth is Bad Enough*, 2012,
Kelly, Ian, *Casanova: Actor Lover Priest Spy*, 2008.
Knecht, Robert, *The French Religious Wars 1562-98*, 2002.
Köhler, Joachim, *Zarathustra's Secret*, 1989.
Korda, Michael, *HERO The Life and Legend of Lawrence of Arabia*, 2010.
Lacey, Robert, *Henry VIII*, 1972.
Lacy, Robert, *Sir Walter Ralegh*, 1973.
Lahr, John, *Prick Up Your Ears, The Biography of Joe Orton*, 1978
Lahr, John, *Tennessee Williams, Mad Pilgrimage of the Flesh*, 2014.
Lambert, Gilles *Caravaggio*, 2007.
Landucci, Luca, *A Florentine Diary*, around 1500, a vital source.
Lawday, David, *Danton*, 2009.
Lawday, David, *Napoleon's Master,* 2007.

Lev Elizabeth, *The Tigress of Forli*, 2011. Wonderfully written. I love
Lewis, Bernard, *The Assassins*, 1967.
Livy, *Rome and the Mediterranean*
Lubkin, Gregory, *A Renaissance Court*, 1994.
Lyons, Mathew, *The Favourite*, 2011.
Macintyre, Ben, *The Man Who Would Be King*, 2004.
Mackay, James, *In My End is My Beginning, Mary Queen of Scots*, 1999.
Mackay, John Henry, *The Hustler*, 2002.
Mallett Michael and Christine Shaw, *The Italian Wars 1494-1559*.
Malye, Jean, *La Véritable Histore d'Alcibiade*, 2009.
Manchester William, *A World Lit Only By Fire*, 1993
Mancini, *Caravaggio*, circa 1600.
Mann, William, *Men Who Love Men*, 2007.
Mann, William, *The Men from the Boys*, 1998.
Manso, Peter, *Brando*, 1994.
Marchand, Leslie, *Byron*, 1971.
Martin,Brian Joseph, *Napoleonic Friendship*, 2011.
Martines Lauro, *April Blood-Florence and the Plot against the Medici*,
McBrien, William, *Cole Porter*, 2000.
McCann, Graham, *Rebel Males,* 1991.
McGilligan, Patrick, *A Double Life--George Cukor*, 1991.
McLynn, Frank, *Richard and John, Kings of War*, 2007. Fabulous.
McLynn, *Marcus Aurelius*, 2009.
Merrick/Sibalis, *Homosexuality in French History and Culture*, 2012.
Merritt, Rich, *Secrets of a Gay Marine Porn Star*, 2005.
Meyer G.J. *The Borgias, The Hidden History*, 2013.
Meyer, G.J. *The Tudors*, 2010.
Meyer, Jack, *Alcibiades*, 2009.
Miles Richard, *Ancient Worlds*, 2010
Miles Richard, *Carthage Must be Destroyed*, 2010.
Miller, David, *Richard the Lionheart*, 2003.
Minichiello, Victor and John Scott, *Male Sex Work and Society*, 2014.
Mitford, Nancy, *Frederick the Great*, 1970.
Money, James, *Capri, Island of Pleasure*, 1986.
Moore Lucy, *Amphibious Thing*, 2000.
Moote, Lloyd, *Louis XIII, The Just*, 1989.
Mortimer, Ian, 1415, *Henry V's Year of Glory*, 2009.
Nelson, Craig, *Thomas Paine*, 2006.
Nicholl, Charles, *The Reckoning*, 2002.
Niven, David, *Bring on the Empty Horses*, 1975.
Niven, David, *The Moon's a Balloon*, 1971.
Noel Gerard, *The Renaissance Popes*, 2006.
Norton, Rictor, *My Dear Boy*, Love Letters edited by Norton, 1998.

Oosterhuis, Harry, *Homosexuality and Male Bonding*, 1991.
Opper Thorsten, *Hadrian*, 2008.
Ostrow, Steve, *Live at the Continental*, 2007.
Paladilhe, Dominique, *Le Prince de Condé*, 2005.
Paring, Justin, *The life and times of Samuel Steward*, 2010.
Parini, Jay, *Empire of Self, A Life of Gore Vidal*, 2015.
Parish, James Robert, *The Hollywood Book of Death*, 2002.
Parker, Derek, *Cellini*, 2003, the book is beautifully written.
Parker, Peter, *Isherwood A Life*, 2004,
Pascal, Jean Claude, *L'Amant du Roi*, 1991.
Payne, Robert and Nihita Romanoff, *Ivan the Terrible*, 2002.
Pearce, Joseph, *The Unmasking of Oscar Wilde*, 2000.
Pernot, Michel, *Henri III*, Le Roi Décrié, 2013, Excellent book.
Petitfils, Jean-Christian, *Louis XIII*, 2008, wonderful.
Peyrefitte, Roger, *Alexandre*, 1979.
Peyrefitte, Roger, *Propos secrets,* Volumes 1 and 2, 1977, 1980.
Plimpton, George, *Truman Capote*, 1998.
Plutarch's Lives, Modern Library.
Pollard, .J., *Warwick the Kingmaker*, 2007.
Polybius, *The Histories.*
Porter, Darwin & Roy Moseley, *Damn You, Scarlett O'Hara*, 2011.
Porter, Darwin, *Brando Unzipped*, 2004.
Porter, Darwin, *Paul Newman*, 2009. (All Porter books are fabulous.)
Rader, Dotson, *Blood Dues*, 1974.
Read, Piers Paul, *The Templars*, 1999.
Reed, Jeremy, *The Dilly*, 2014.
Reid, B.L., *The Lives of Roger Casement*, 1976.
Renucci Pierre, *Caligula*, 2000
Reston, James, *Warriors of God, Richard and the Crusades*, 2001.
Revenin, Régis, *Homosexualité et Prostitution Maculines à Paris*, 2005.
Rice, Edward, *Captain Sir Richard Francis Burton*, 1990.
Ridley, Jasper, *The Tudor Age*, 1998.
Robb, Graham, *Rimbaud*, 2000. Superb.
Robb, Peter, M – *The Man Who Became Caravaggio*, 1998.
Robb, Peter, *Street Fight in Naples*, 2010.
Rocco, Antonio, *Alcibiade Enfant à l'Ecole*, 1630.
Rocke Michael, *Forbidden Friendships*, 1996, both indispensible and
Roen, Paul, *High Camp*, 1994.
Rolfe, Frederick, Letters to Charles Kains Jackson, *My Dear KJ...*, 2015.
Romans Grecs et Latin, Gallimard, 1958.
Ross, Charles, *Richard III*, 1981.
Rouse, W.H.D., Homer's *The Iliad*, 1938.
Royle, Trevor, *Fighting Mac, The Downfall of Sir Hector Macdonald*.

Ruggiero, Guido, *The Boundaries of Eros*, 1985.
Sabatini, Rafael, *The Life of Cesare Borgia*, 1920.
Saint Bris, Gonzague, *Henri IV*, 2009.
Saslow, James, *Ganymede in the Renaissance*, 1986.
Sawyer-Lauçanno, *An Invisible Specter, Paul Bowles*, 1989.
Schama, Simon, *Citizens* 1989.
Schiff, Stacy, *Cleopatra*, 2010.
Schom, Alam, *Napoleon Bonaparte*, 1997.
Scurr, Ruth, *Fatal Purity*, 2007.
Setz, Wolfram, *The Sins of the Cities of the Plain*, 1881.
Seward, Desmond, *Caravaggio – A Passionate Life*, 1998.
Seymour, Craig, *All I could Bare*, 2008.
Shakespeare, Nicholas, *Bruce Chatwin*, 1999.
Shapiro, James, *1599*, 2005.
Sharaf, Myron, *Fury on Earth: A Biography of Wilhelm Reich*, 1983.
Shaw, Aiden, *Sordid Truths*, 2009.
Shelden, Michael, *Graham Greene, The Man Within*, 1994.
Sheridan, Alan, *André Gide*, 1999.
Shilts, Randy, *And the Band Played on*, 1987.
Simonetta Marcello, *The Montefeltro Conspiracy*, 2008. Wonderful,
Sipriot, Pierre, *Montherlant sans masque*, 1982.
Skidmore, Chris, *Bosworth*, 1988.
Skidmore, Chris, *Death and the Virgin*, 2010.
Soares, André, *The Life of Ramon Novarro*, 2010.
Solnon, Jean-Fançois, *Henry III*, 1996.
Spoto, Donald, *The Kindness of Strangers*, 1997.
Stewart, Alan, *The Cradle King, A Life of James VI & I*, 2003.
Stirling, Stuart, *Pizarro Conqueror of the Inca*, 2005.
Strathern, Paul, *The Medici, Godfathers of the Renaissance*, 2003. Superb.
Suetonius, *The Twelve Caesars*
Tacitus, *The Annals of Imperial Rome*.
Tacitus, *The Histories*.
Teeman, Tim, *In Bed with Gore Vidal*, 2013.
Thucydides, *The Peloponnesian War*, Penguin Classics.
Tibullus, *The Elegies of Tibullus*, translated by Theodore C. Williams
Tuchman, Barbara, *A Distant Mirror*, 1978.
Turner, Ralph, *Eleanor of Aquitaine*, 2009.
Unger Miles, *Magnifico, The Brilliant Life and Violent Time.s*
Unger, Miles, *Machiavelli*, 2008.
Vanderbilt, Arthur, *Best-Kept Boy in the World*, 2014.
Vasari, We would know next to nothing if it were not for him.
Vaughan, Richard, *John the Fearless*, 1973.
Vernant, Jean-Pierre, *Mortals and Immortals*, 1991.

Vidal, Gore, *Palimpsest: A Memoir*, 1995.
Violet, Bernard, *Les Mystères Delon*, 2000.
Virgil, *The Aeneid*, Everyman's Library, Knopf, 1907.
Viroli, Maurizio, *Niccolo's Smile, A Biography of Machiavelli*, 1998.
Walsh, Kenneth M., *wasn't tomorrow wonderful?* 2014.
Ward-Perkins Bryan, *The Fall of Rome*, 2005
Warren, W.L., *Henry II*, 1973.
Weinberg, Williams and Pryor, *Dual Attraction*, 1994.
Weir, Alison, *Eleanor of Aquitaine*, 1999.
Weir, Alison, *Mary, Queen of Scots,* 2003.
Weir, Alison, *The Princes in the Tower*, 1992. Marvelous.
Weir, Alison, *The Wars of the Roses*, 1995.
Wheaton James, *Spartacus*, 2011.
Whyte, Kenneth, *The Uncrowned King*, 2008.
Wikipedia: Research today is impossible without the aid of this monument.
Williams Craig A. *Roman Homosexuality*, 2010.
Williams John, *Augustus*, 1972.
Wilson, Derek, *The Uncrowned Kings of England*, 2005.
Winecoff, Charles, *Anthony Perkins, split image*, 1996.
Wolff, Geoffrey, *Black Sun: The Violent Eclipse of Harry Crosby*, 1976.
Woods, Gregory, *Homintern*, 2016.
Worthington, Ian, *Philip II of Macedonia*, 2008.
Wright, Ed, *History's Greatest Scandals*, 2006.
Wroe, Ann, *Perkin, A Story of Deception*, 2003. Fabulous
Xenophon, *A History of My Time*s, Penguin Classics.
Xenophon, *The Persian Expedition*, 1949.
Zachks, Richard, *History Laid Bare*, 1994.

INDEX

Please note that the page numbers are *passim*. An example, the Ponte Vecchio, 76 – 102, means that the Ponte Vecchio is found within these pages, but not necessarily on *every* page.

A Manual Of Military Surgery

A

MANUAL

OF

MILITARY SURGERY,

OR

HINTS ON THE EMERGENCIES OF FIELD, CAMP AND HOSPITAL PRACTICE.

By S. D. GROSS, M. D.

Professor of Surgery in the Jefferson Medical College, of Philadelphia.

J. W. RANDOLPH,
121 MAIN STREET, RICHMOND, VA.
1862.

In view of the great want of some convenient work on Military Surgery, we present a valuable little Treatise recently published by Dr. S. D. Gross, of Philadelphia. The book trade between the two sections of the continent having been interrupted, it has rendered it impossible for Dr. G's. publishers to furnish the work to the Southern Public. We avail ourselves of the copy recently published in the *Southern Medical and Surgical Journal*, Augusta, Geo.

C. H. WYNNE, PRINTER, RICHMOND.

MILITARY SURGERY.

CHAPTER I.

HISTORICAL SKETCH OF MILITARY SURGERY.

The duties and requirements of military are essentially similar to those of civil surgery. It is founded upon the same knowledge of anatomy, medicine and the associate sciences; it demands the same qualifications, physical, moral and intellectual. The difference consists in the application of our knowledge rather than in its range or depth. The civil surgeon remains at home; the military follows the army, examines recruits for the public service, and superintends the health of the troops. If the former is well educated, he will be quite as competent, at any time, as the latter to perform these duties; for the emergencies of civil are often not less trying than those of military practice, although they may not be on so large a scale.

The best civil have often also been the best military surgeons. In proof of this assertion it is necessary only to refer to the names of Pare, Wiseman, Schmucker, Kern, Larrey, Guthrie, Charles Bell, Alcock, Thomson, Ballingall and Macleod, of Europe; or to those of Rush, Jones, Thacher, Mann and Horner, of our own country.

Military surgery occupies, at the present day, a deservedly high rank in the estimation both of the profession and of the public. The war in the Crimea, the mutiny in India and the recent convulsions in Italy, all attended with so much

waste of blood and life, have attracted to it the universal
attention of the profession; and the revolutionary movements
now in progress in our own country invest it with a new and
fearful interest to every American physician. Its praises have
been sung by Homer, and, in all ages of the world, govern-
ments have extended to it a fostering hand. As a distinct
branch, however, of the healing art, it dates back no further
than the early part of the sixteenth century, when it was
inaugurated by Ambrose Pare, by the publication of his
treatise on "Gunshot Wounds," the fruits of his observations
in the French army in Italy. This man, who was surgeon to
four successive kings, was an eye-witness of the numerous
French campaigns, from 1536, down to the battle of Moncon-
tour, in 1569, a period of thirty-three years. His popularity,
both as a civil and military surgeon, was, up to that time,
without a parallel. The soldiers worshipped him; and the
success of more than one siege, as well as of one battle, was
due almost exclusively to the wonderful influence of his presence. His treatise on "Gunshot Wounds" appeared towards
the middle of the sixteenth century, and, after having passed
through various editions, was ultimately incorporated in his
surgical writings, published nearly a quarter of a century
later.

In England, the earliest work on military surgery was that
of Thomas Gale, entitled a "Treatise on Gunshot Wounds,"
designed chiefly to confute the errors of some of his contem-
poraries, respecting the supposed poisonous nature of these
lesions. Gale was born in 1507, and after having served in
the army of King Henry VIII., at Montrieul, and also in
that of King Philip, at St. Quintin, finally settled at London,
where he acquired great distinction in his profession. In
1639 appeared the work of J. Woodall, "The Surgeon's
Mate; or, Military and Domestic Surgery." He was surgeon
under Queen Elizabeth, by whom he was sent to France,
along with the troops that were dispatched to the assistance of
Henry IV. and Lord Willoughby. In 1676, Richard Wise-

man, sergeant-surgeon to King Charles II., published his famous "Chirurgical Treatises," one of which was expressly devoted to the consideration of gunshot wounds. Two years after this a treatise on gunshot wounds was published at London, by John Brown, also surgeon to Charles. He was a man of eminence, and served with much credit in the Dutch war of 1665. The next English work on military surgery appeared in 1744, from the pen of John Ranby, sergeant-surgeon to George II., under the title of "The Method of Treating Gunshot Wounds." After Ranby came the imperishable work of John Hunter, familiar to every reader of English surgical literature. The part relating to gunshot wounds was founded upon his observations made while serving as staff-surgeon at Belleisle and in Portugal, and is one of the most precious legacies of the last century, near the close of which it appeared.

The present century has supplied quite a number of works on military surgery, as is shown by the publications of Larrey, Hennen, Hecker, Augustin, Guthrie, Thomson, Hutchison, Ballingall, Baudens and others, which have contributed so much to the elevation of this department of the healing art. Some of these works have been re-issued in this country, and have acquired a wide celebrity.

We must not forget, in this rapid enumeration of works on military surgery, the "Manuel de Chirurgien d'Armee" of Baron Percy, published at the commencement of the revolutionary war in France. It is a model of what such a treatise ought to be.

The only work on this department of science yet furnished in this country, is that of the late Dr. James Mann, published at Dedham, Massachusetts, in 1816. It is entitled "Medical Sketches of the Campaigns of 1812, '13 and '14," and forms a closely-printed volume of upwards of three hundred octavo pages.

The latest treatise on this subject in the English language is that of Dr. George H. B. Macleod, now Professor of Surgery at Glasgow, entitled "Notes on the Surgery of the War in the Crimea; with remarks on the Treatment of Gunshot Wounds." It is a work of intense interest, written with great ability by an accurate and diligent observer, and is worthy of a place in every medical library. To this work frequent reference will be made in the following pages.

To Dr. Lewis Stromeyer, Physician of the Royal Hanoverian Army, we are indebted for the most recent German work on military surgery. It was issued in 1858, under the title of "Maximen der Kriegsheilkunst," in two duodecimo volumes, to which a Supplement was added in the early part of the present year. A more valuable contribution to this department of surgery could hardly be imagined.

Besides the above more recent works, the reader should carefully study the "Principles of Military Surgery," by the late Dr. John Hennen, one of the most zealous and, distinguished military surgeons that Great Britain has yet produced; a man of vast experience and of the most enlightened views upon everything he has touched with his pen.

Perhaps the most systematic work on the subject in the English language is that of Sir George Ballingall, entitled "Outlines of Military Surgery," the last edition of which, the fourth, appeared only recently at Edinburgh, where the author held for many years the chair of military surgery; for a long time, we believe, the only one in Great Britain. It is a production of much merit, and is destined to maintain a very high rank in this species of literature.

The works of the late Mr. George Guthrie also deserve attentive study; they are written with great clearness and ability, and embody the results of an immense experience, acquired during many years of arduous and faithful labor and observation in the British army. I have always regarded the works of this great man as among the most valuable contributions, not only to military surgery, but to surgery in general, in the English language.

With these works before him, the student of military surgery cannot fail to make himself in a short time perfectly familiar with everything pertaining to the subjects of which they treat. He should also provide himself with a copy of the excellent little volume entitled "Hints on the Medical Examination of Recruits for the Army," by the late Dr. Thomas Henderson, formerly Professor of Medicine in Columbia College, Washington City. A new edition of it was published a few years ago by Dr. Richard H. Coolidge, of the United States army.

Although we have long had one of the most respectable and thoroughly organized army and navy medical staffs in the world, our country has, nevertheless, not produced one great military surgeon; simply, it may be presumed, because no opportunity has occurred since the establishment of our government in which the men in the public service could distinguish themselves. Their aid has been required in the duello and in skirmishes rather than in great battles, such as have so often characterized the movements of the armies of the Old World. We make no exception in this remark in favor even of the battles that were fought during the Revolution, and during the Late War, as it has usually been designated, with Great Britain. Those engagements were, for the most part, comparatively bloodless. Happily living under a flag which, until recently, commanded alike the respect and the admiration of all nations, belonging to a government which was at peace with all foreign powers, the medical and surgical staffs of the public service had little else to do than to prescribe for such diseases as are incident to civil practice. America has never witnessed, and we trust in God she never may witness, such carnage as that which attended the footsteps of Napoleon at the bridge of Lodi, at Leipzig, at Dresden and at Waterloo; or which, more recently, characterized the exploits of the English, French and Russian forces in the Crimea; or of the French, Italian and Austrian armies in Italy; or of the English soldiers during the late rebellion in India. Nor has she ever been engaged in one great naval battle similar to that of La Hogue, Toulon, Trafalgar or Aboukir. A number of

highly respectable physicians accompanied our army to Mexico, but they returned without any special laurels, and without any substantial contributions to military medicine and
surgery.

CHAPTER II.

IMPORTANCE OF MILITARY SURGERY.

It is impossible for any civilized nation to place too high
an estimate upon this branch of the public service. Without
the aid of a properly organized medical staff, no army, however well disciplined, could successfully carry on any war,
even when it is one, as that which is now impending over us,
of a civil character. No men of any sober reflection would
enlist in the service of their country, if they were not positively certain that competent physicians and surgeons would
accompany them in their marches and on the field of battle,
ready to attend to their diseases and accidents. Hence military surgery, or, more correctly speaking, military medicine
and surgery, has always occupied a deservedly high rank in
public estimation.

Dionis, a surgeon far in advance of his age, in referring to
the value of medical services to soldiers, exclaims, with a
burst of eloquence : " We must then allow the necessity of
chirurgery, which daily raises many persons from the brink of
the grave. How many men has it cured in the army! How
many great commanders would have died of their ghastly
wounds without its assistance! Chirurgery triumphs in armies and in sieges! 'Tis true that its empire is owned; 'tis
there that its effects, and not words, express its eulogium."

The confidence reposed by soldiers in the skill and humanity of their surgeon has often been of signal service in supporting them, when exhausted by hunger and fatigue, in their

struggles to repel the advancing foe, or in successfully maintaining a siege when the prospects of speedy surrender was at hand. Who that is versed in the history of our art does not remember with what enthusiasm and resolve Ambrose Pare, the father of French surgery, inspired the souls of the half-starved and desponding garrison at Metz, in 1552, when besieged by 100,000 men under the personal command of Charles V.? Sent thither by his sovereign, he was introduced into the city during the night by an Italian captain; and the next morning, when he showed himself upon the breach, he was received with shouts of welcome. "We shall not die," the soldiers exclaimed, "even though wounded; Pare is among us." The defense from this time was conducted with renewed vigor, and the French army ultimately completely triumphed, through the sole influence of this illustrious surgeon.

No man in the French army under Napoleon rendered so many and such important services to the French nation as Larrey, the illustrious surgeon who accompanied that mighty warrior in his various campaigns, everywhere animating the troops and doing all in his power to save them from the destructive effects of disease and injury. His humanity and tenderness was sublime; and so highly was his conduct, as an honest, brave, and skillful surgeon, appreciated by Napoleon, that he bequeathed him a large sum, with the remark that "Larrey was the most virtuous man he had ever known."

CHAPTER. III.

QUALIFICATIONS AND DUTIES OF MILITARY SURGEONS.

It is of paramount importance that none but men of the best talent and of the highest education should be received into the public service. Rigid as the examination of the

army and navy medical boards already is, there is need of increased rigor, in order that none may be admitted who are not
thoroughly prepared for the discharge of their responsible duties. Equal vigilance should be exercised in regard to the
introduction of physicians and surgeons into the volunteer service. Every regiment should be provided with an able medical head, a man ready for every emergency, however trying or
unexpected; a man skilled in the diagnosis and treatment of
diseases, and competent to perform any operation, whether
small or large, on the spur of the moment. To do this, he
must be more than a mere physician; he must be both a physician and surgeon, in the true sense of the terms, otherwise
he will be unfit, totally unfit, for his position. He must have
been educated in the modern schools; be of undoubted courage, prompt to act, willing to assume responsibility, humane
and sympathizing, urbane and courteous in his manners; in
short, a medical gentleman, as well as a medical philosopher,
not hesitating, if need be, to perform the most menial services,
and to do all he can to preserve the health and the lives of
the soldiers committed to his care. The white-gloved gentry,
such as figured in some of the regiments that went to Mexico,
have no business in the service; their time can be much better spent in the discharge of their domestic duties, in the
practice of their neighborhood, and in the contemplation, at a
distance, of the miseries of war.

It is much to be feared that, from the rapid manner in
which our volunteers have been hurried together, many medical men, old as well as young, have already been admitted into
the service utterly unfit for the office. If this be the case, let
our authorities, warned by the past, be more circumspect in regard to the future. Above all, let them see that the medical
staffs of the brave volunteers of the country be not defiled by
charlatans and unworthy men, between whom and the regular
practitioners there cannot possibly be any professional, much
less social intercourse, either in civil or military practice.
The medical men should be on the best possible terms with

each other; all causes of discord and bickering among themselves should be studiously obviated, and speedily suppressed, if, unfortunately, they should arise. Concert of action on the part of the medical corps is indispensable to the success of the medical operations of an army.

Every regimental surgeon should have at least two assistants in time of peace, or during the inactivity of the troops under his charge; when on active duty, on the contrary, the number should at least be double, especially in the face of an anticipated bloody engagement. These assistants should be selected solely with reference to their competency; they should, like the principal, be eminently intelligent, and ready, in case of emergency, to perform any operation that occasion may demand. Every brigade should have its brigade surgeon, who should exercise a supervisory control over the regimental surgeons, principals as well as assistants; as every State should have its surgeon-general or medical-director, whose duty it should be to superintend the whole medical arrangements, seeing that the candidates for the medical department of the service be subjected to a rigid examination, attending to the purchase of medicines and instruments, providing suitable nurses, inspecting the quarters, stores and provisions, that nothing of an unwholesome character may find its way into the ranks, pointing out the proper location of camps, and the construction of hospitals, and giving general instructions in regard to military hygiene, or the best means of avoiding disease and accident.

Prior to every engagement at all likely to be severe or serious, a proper number of men should be detailed for the purpose of rendering prompt assistance to the wounded, and carrying them off the field of battle to the hospitals, or tents, erected for their accommodation and treatment. Unless this be done as a preliminary step, much suffering will inevitably be the consequence, if not great confusion, highly prejudicial to the issue of the combat. So fully aware are the leaders and sub-commanders of our armies of this fact, that they never permit any man to fall out of the ranks, during an engagement, to perform this service.

While the battle is progressing, it is the duty of the surgeon and of his assistants to remain in the rear of the combatants, as much as possible out of harm's way, but at the same time ready and on the watch to render the promptest possible aid. They must be Argus-eyed, and in the full possession of their wits. One of the leading differences between military and civil practice is the instantaneous action so often demanded by the one and the delay so frequently admitted by the other.

The first duty of every surgeon is to the officers and men of his own corps; but on the field of battle, or soon after the battle is over, he is often brought in contact with the members of other regiments, or even with the wounded of the enemy; and under such circumstances the dictates of humanity, not less than the usages of war, demand that he should render his services wherever they may be likely to be useful. The medical officers of the contending parties sometimes meet upon such occasions, and, when this is the case, their conduct should invariably be characterized by the courtesy of the gentleman, not the asperity of the enemy. They should not forget that they are brethren of the same noble profession, acting in the capacity of ministering angels to the sick and dying. Country and cause alike should be forgotten in generous deeds.

By the usages of war in all civilized countries, the surgeons are always respected by the enemy if, during an engagement, they happen to fall accidentally into their hands. Their lives are regarded as sacred, the more so, as they are comparatively defenseless. They are not, however, during the rage and smoke of the battle-field, always easily distinguishable from the other officers, or even the common soldiers. The green sash, their distinctive badges of office, does not always afford them immunity, because it is not always recognized; and it is worthy of consideration whether, as an additional safeguard, the word "surgeon" should not be embroidered in legible characters upon a piece of cloth, to be thrown across the chest in time of battle. The significance of such a badge could not be mistaken by friend or foe, and would be the means of saving many valuable lives.

CHAPTER IV.

MEDICAL EQUIPMENTS, STORES AND HOSPITALS.

Every regiment, or body of military men, should be amply provided, in time of war, with the means of conveying the wounded and disabled from the field of battle. For this purpose suitable carriages and litters should constantly be in readiness. The carriages should be built in the form of light wagons, drawn each by two horses; with low wheels, easy springs, and a large, wide body, furnished with a soft mattress and pillows, and capable of accommodating not less than eight or ten persons, while arrangements might be made at the side for seating a number more, as in the French *voiture*. As a means of protection against the sun and the rain, it should have a light cover of oil cloth or canvas.

A great number of *litters*, or bearers, will be found described in treatises on military surgery; but I am not acquainted with any which combine so much simplicity and cheapness, with lightness and convenience, as one which, after a good deal of reflection, I have just devised. It consists of two equal parts, conducted at the ends by stout hinges, the arrangement being such as to permit of their being folded for the more easy transportation on the field of battle. Each part has a side piece of wood, three feet four inches long, by two inches in depth, and an inch and a half in thickness, the free extremity terminating in a slightly curved handle. The side pieces are united by four traverses, and the entire frame is covered with ducking, twenty-four inches in width. Thus constructed, the apparatus is not only very light, so that any one may easily carry it, or, indeed, even three or four at a time, but remarkably convenient both for the transportation of patients, and for lifting them in and out of the wagons, which should always be at hand during an engagement. Moreover, by means of side straps, provided with buckles, it will answer extremely well for a bed-chair, so necessary in sickness and during convalescence, the angle of flexion of the two pieces thus admitting of ready regulation. In carrying the wounded off the field, the labor may easily be performed by two men, especially if they use shoulder-straps to diffuse the weight of the burden. The body, in hot weather, might be protected with an oil cloth, while the face might be shielded from the sun with a veil or handkerchief. A pillow for the head can be made with the coat of one of the carriers.

Besides these means, every regiment should be furnished with an *ambulance*, or, as the term literally implies, a moveable hospital, that is, a place for the temporary accommodation and treatment of the wounded on the field of battle. It should be arranged in the form of a tent, and be provided with all the means and appliances necessary for the prompt succor of the sufferers. The materials of which it consists should be as light as possible, possess every facility for rapid packing and erection, and be conveyed from point to point by a wagon set apart for this object. The ambulance, for the invention and improvement of which we are indebted to two eminent French military surgeons, Percy and Larrey, is indispensable in every well-regulated army.

This temporary hospital should be placed in an open space, convenient to water, and upon dry ground, with arrangements for the free admission of air and light, which, next to pure air, is one of the most powerful stimulants in all cases of accident attended with excessive prostration. The direct rays of the sun, in hot weather, must of course be excluded, and it may even be necessary, as in injuries of the head and eye, to wrap the patient in complete darkness. A properly regulated temperature is also to be maintained, a good average being about 68° of Fahrenheit's thermometer.

As engagements are sometimes begun after dark, or are continued into the night, an adequate supply of wax candles should be provided, as they will be found indispensable both in field and hospital practice, in performing operations and dressing wounds and fractures. Torches, too, will frequently be needed, especially in collecting and transporting the wounded. Bed-pans, feeding-cups, spoons, syringes, and other appliances usually found in the sick chamber, will form a necessary part of the furniture of such an establishment.

The object of the ambulance is, as already stated, to afford prompt succor to the wounded. Here their lighter injuries are speedily dressed, and the more grave subjected to the operations necessary for their cure. In due time, the former are sent back to the ranks, while the rest are conveyed to suitable lodgings or to permanent hospitals.

As soon as practicable, after the hurry and confusion attendant upon a combat are over, the surgeon should classify the wounded and disabled, taking care that those laboring under similar lesions are not brought in close contact; lest, witnessing each other's sufferings, they should be seized with fatal despondency.

Larrey, in order to meet the exigencies of the grand army in Italy, constructed a *flying ambulance;* an immense, and, at first sight, a very cumbersome establishment. It consisted of twelve light wagons, on easy springs, for the transportation of the wounded; some with two, others with four wheels. The frame of the former, which were designed for flat, level countries, resembled an elongated cube, curved on the top; it had two small windows on each side, with a folding door in front and behind. The floor of the body, separable and moveable on rollers, was covered with a mattress and bolster. Handles were secured to it laterally, through which the sashes of the soldiers were passed in lifting the sick in and out

of the carriage, when, on account of the weather, their wants
could not be relieved on the ground. Each vehicle was
thirty-two inches wide, and was drawn by two horses; it
could conveniently accommodate two patients at full length,
and was furnished with several side-pockets for such articles
as might be needed for the sufferers.

The large carriage, drawn by four horses, and designed for
rough and hilly roads, was constructed upon the same principle
as the small; it had four wheels, and could accommodate four
persons.   The left side of the body had two long sliding-doors,
extending almost its whole length, so as to permit the
wounded to be laid in a horizontal position.

These carriages were used for conveying the wounded from
the field of battle to the hospitals of the lines, and combined,
it is said, solidity with lightness and elegance.

The number of men attached to the flying ambulance was
113, embracing a soldier's guard with twelve men on horseback, a quartermaster-general, a surgeon-major, with his two
assistants and twelve mates, a police officer, and a number of
servants.   The flying ambulance was, in fact, a costly and
imposing establishment, devised by the humanity and ingenuity of the great and good Larrey, who could never do too
much for the wounded soldier, and whose presence, like that
of his illustrious countryman, Pare, always served to animate
the French troops.   At one time three divisions of the flying
ambulance, equipped upon this grand scale, were upon the
field in different parts of Italy.

It is not deemed necessary in a work like this, to give an
account of the construction of hospitals, properly so termed;
for, with the railroad and steamboat facilities which we now
possess, there can be little difficulty in obtaining comfortable
accommodations for the sick and wounded soldiers.   Lodgings
can almost always be procured, in nearly every portion of the
country where a battle is likely to be fought, in houses,
churches, and barns. Temporary sheds might easily be
erected in a few hours, with such arrangements as would

serve for the more pressing wants of the wounded. The chief points to be attended to, in their construction, are sufficient elevation of the ground floor for the free circulation of air, windows for light and ventilation, and such a position of the fire-place as not to annoy the inmates.

The *medical stores* of the military hospital, whether temporary or permanent, include medicines, instruments, and various kinds of apparatus, as bandages, oiled silk, and splints.

It would far transcend my limits were I to enter fully into all the details connected with these different topics. A few brief remarks under each head must suffice for my purpose.

1st. In regard to *medicines*, a few articles only, well selected and arranged for ready use, will be necessary. It is bad enough, in all conscience, for a man to be severely shot or stabbed, without physicing him to death. Let him by all means have a chance for his life, especially when he has already been prostrated by shock and hemorrhage. Food and drink, with opium and fresh air, will then do him more good than anything else. I shall enumerate the medicines upon which, in my judgment, most reliance is to be placed in this kind of practice, according to their known effects upon the system.

1. Anodynes :—opium, morphia, and black drop, or acetated tincture of opium.

2. Purgatives :—blue mass, calomel, rhubarb, jalap, compound extract of colocynth, and sulphate of magnesia. Some of these articles should be variously combined, and put up in pill form for ready use.

3. Depressants:—tartrate of antimony and potassa, ipecacuanha, and tincture of veratrum viride.

4. Diaphoretics :—antimony, ipecacuanha, nitrate of potassa, morphia, and Dover's powder.

5. Diuretics :—nitrate and carbonate of potassa, and colchicum.

6. Antiperiodics :—quinine and arsenic.

7. Anæsthetics :—chloroform and ether.

8. Stimulants :—brandy, gin, wine, and aromatic spirits of ammonia.

9. Astringents :—acetate of lead, perchloride of iron and alum, tannin, gallic acid, and nitrate of silver.

10. Escharotics :—nitric acid, acid nitrate of mercury, (Bennett's formula,) and Vienna paste.

2d. The surgical *armamentarium* should also be as simple as possible. It should embrace a small pocket case, with a screw catheter; a full amputating case, with at least three tourniquets, two saws of different sizes, and several large bone-nippers; and, lastly, a trephining case. Several silver catheters of different sizes, a stomach pump, small and large syringes, feeding-cups and bed-pans should also be put up.

3d. Under the head of *apparatus* may be included bandages, lint, linen, adhesive plaster, splints, cushions, wadding, and oiled silk.

The *bandages*, composed of tolerably stout muslin, should be free from starch and selvage, well rolled, on an average, from two inches and a quarter to two inches and a half in width by eight yards in length. The bandage of Scultetus, very serviceable in compound factures, can easily be made, as occasion may require, out of pieces of the common roller.

Of *lint*, the patent, or apothecary's, as it is termed, is the best, as it is soft and easily adapted to the parts to which it is intended to be applied. Old linen or muslin also answers sufficiently well. Charpie is now seldom used.

An abundance of *adhesive plaster*, put up in small cases, should be provided. Collodion will not be necessary.

Splints, of binders or trunk-maker's board, and of light wood, should find a place in every medical store, as frequent occasions occur for their use. In fractures of the lower extremity special apparatus may be required, which, however, as it is cumbrous and inconvenient to carry, may generally be prepared as it is needed.

Cushions are made of muslin, sewed in the form of bags, of variable size and shape, and filled with cotton, tow, sawdust or sand. They are designed to equalize and ward off pressure in the treatment of fractures of the lower extremities.

Wadding is a most valuable article in surgical practice, both for lining splints and making pads, as well as in the treatment of burns and scalds, and cannot be dispensed with.

Oiled Silk is a prominent article in the dressings of the present day; it preserves the heat and moisture of poultices and of warm water-dressings, at the same time that it protects the bed and body-clothes of the patient.

Oil-cloth, soft and smooth, is required in all cases of severe wounds and fractures, attended with much discharge.

Air-cushions should be put up in considerable numbers, as their use will be indispensable in all cases of disease and injury involving protracted confinement.

Bran and saw-dust will be found of great value in the treatment of compound fractures, ulcers, gangrene, and suppurating wounds, as an easy support for the injured limb and a means of excluding flies.

Medical *case-books* should be put up along with the other articles, for the accurate registration of the names of the sick and wounded, the nature of their lesions, and the results of treatment. The medical officers should also keep a faithful record of the state of the weather, the temperature of the air, the nature of the climate, the products of the soil, and the botany of the country through which they or in which they sojourn, together with such matters as may be of professional or scientific interest. The knowledge thus acquired should be disseminated after their return for the benefit of their professional brethren.

Finally, in order to complete hospital equipments, well-trained *nurses* should be provided; for good nursing is indispensable in every case of serious disease, whatever may be its character. The importance of this subject, however, is now so well appreciated as not to require any special comments here.

The question as to whether this duty should be performed by men or women is of no material consequence, provided it be well done. The eligibility of women for this task was thoroughly tested in the Crimea, through the agency of that noble-hearted female, Florence Nightingale ; and hundreds of the daughters of our land have already tendered their services to the government for this object. No large and well regulated hospital can get on without some male nurses, and they are indispensable in camp and field practice.

It is not my purpose here to point out the qualities which constitute a good female nurse. It will suffice to say that she should be keenly alive to her duties, and perform them, however menial or distasteful, with promptness and alacrity. She must be tidy in her appearance, with a cheerful countenance, light in her step, noiseless, tender and thoughtful in her manners, perfect mistress of her feelings, healthy, able to bear tigue, and at least twenty-two years of age. Neither the crinoline nor the silk dress must enter into her wardrobe; the former is too cumbrous, while the latter by its rustling is sure to fret the patient and disturb his sleep. Whispering and walking in on tiptoe, as has been truly observed by Florence Nightingale, are an abomination in the sick chamber. Finally, a good nurse never fails to anticipate all, or nearly all, the more important wants of the sufferer.

Among other things to be specially attended to in nursing, is *ventilation*. Persons visiting the sick must at once be struck with the difference of pure air in those chambers where a proper ventilation exists and those where the reverse is the case. To insure this the fresh air should always be admitted from a window not open directly on the bed, or causing the patient to be in a draught. Even in winter it is highly proper that fresh air should be admitted some time during the day when there is a good fire and the patient well protected by covering.

The pillows, bedding and bed-clothes should be well aired and often changed, as also the flannel, under-garments, and night-dress. To facilitate this, it is well, when the patient is very ill and unable to help himself, to have the shirt open all the way down in front, and buttoned up. The patient often escapes great suffering and annoyance by this simple method. Where there is a discharge from the sores, or when water-dressings are applied to a limb, it is advisable to place the latter upon a folded sheet with a thin, soft oil-cloth underneath. Great tenderness and cleanliness should be used in dressing wounds or sores. Old linen, muslin and lint should always be had in readiness for this purpose. A great prejudice exists against the use of muslin, the preference being generally given to linen; but the former is really quite as good as the other, if it is soft and old.

In regard to the *cleanliness* of a sick-room, it is advisable to use a mop occasionally for the removal of flue from under the bed; when, however, the patient is in too critical a situation for dampness, a few tea-leaves scattered over the apartment will absorb the dust, and can be quietly taken up with a hand-brush. A frequent change of bed linen is very beneficial when practicable, and the clothes must always be folded smoothly under the patient. Great cleanliness should be observed in all the surroundings of the sick-room, and particular attention must be paid to the glasses in which medicine is given, in order to render the doses as palatable as possible. The patient should be washed whenever able, and his teeth and hair well attended to. The body seems infused with new vigor after such ablutions.

A frequent change of *posture* is immensely conducive to the comfort and well-being of a sick person, if performed with a careful eye to his particular condition. Severe pain, loss of sleep, excessive constitutional irritation, and dreadful bed-sores are sure to follow, in all low states of the system, if this precaution be not duly heeded. No patient must have his head suddenly raised, or be permitted to lie high, when he is exhausted from shock, hemorrhage, or sickness. Many lives have been lost by this indiscretion.

The apartment must be free from noise, the light should neither be too freely admitted nor too much excluded, except in head and eye affections, and the temperature must be regulated by the thermometer, from 65° to 68° of Fahrenheit being a proper average.

As the patient acquires strength, he may gradually sit up in bed, propped up at first by pillows, and afterward by a bed-chair.

His food and drink, and also, at times, his medicine, must be given from a feeding-cup during the height of his disease, and a good general rule is to administer them with great regularity, provided this does not interfere too much with his repose. If he is very weak, and sleeps very long, it will be necessary to wake him in order to give him nourishment; but, in general, sleep is more refreshing than food, and more beneficial than medicine. The bed-pan and urinal of course find their appropriate sphere under such circumstances.

As the appetite and strength increase, the patient is permitted to resume, though very gradually, his accustomed diet, and to exercise about the room, if not in the open air. After severe accidents and protracted sickness, a wise man will not bestir himself too soon or too much, but court the fickle goddess of health with becoming caution.

Dying patients should be carefully screened from their neighbors, placed in the easiest posture, have free access of air, and be not disturbed by noise, loud talking, or the presence of persons not needed for their comfort. As soon as the mortal struggle is over, the body must be removed.

The *excretions* should be removed as speedily as possible from the apartment, and the vessels in which they are received immediately well scalded, the air being at the same time perfectly purified by ventilation, or ventilation and disinfectants.

Finally, the nurse must take care of herself. She must have rest, or she will soon break down. If she is obliged to be up all night, she should be spared in the day.

CHAPTER V.

WOUNDS AND OTHER INJURIES.

The injuries inflicted in war are, in every respect, similar to those received in civil life. The most common and important are fractures, dislocations, bruises, sprains, burns, and the different kinds of wounds, as the incised, punctured, lacerated, and gunshot. With the nature, diagnosis and mode of treatment of these lesions, every army surgeon must, of course, be supposed to be familiar; and I shall therefore limit myself, in the remarks which I am about to offer upon these subjects, to a few practical hints respecting their management on the field of battle and in the ambulance.

Most of the cases of *fractures* occurring on the field of battle are the result of gunshot injury, and are frequently, if not generally, attended by such an amount of injury to the soft parts and also to the bone, as to demand amputation. The bone is often dreadfully comminuted, and consequently utterly unfit for preservation. The more simple fractures, on the contrary, readily admit of the retention of the limb, without risk to life.

In transporting persons affected with fractures, whether simple or complicated, the utmost care should be used to render them as comfortable as possible, by placing the injured limb in an easy position, and applying, if need be, on account of the distance to which they have to be carried, or the mode of conveyance, short side splints of binders' board, thin wood, as a shingle, or junks of straw, gently confined by a roller. For want of due precaution, the danger to limb and life may be materially augmented. Permanent dressings should be applied at the earliest moment after the patient reaches the hospital. If the fracture be attended with splintering of the bone, all loose or detached pieces should at once be extracted; a proceeding which always wonderfully simplifies the case, inasmuch as it prevents, in a great measure, the frightful irritation and suppuration which are sure to follow their retention. When this point has been properly attended to, the parts should be neatly brought together by suture, and covered with a compress wet with blood. As soon as inflammation arises—not before—water-dressings are employed. A suitable opening, or bracket, should be made in the apparatus to facilitate drainage and dressing.

Dislocations, accidents by no means common in military operations, are treated according to the general rules of practice; they should be speedily reduced, without the aid of chloroform, if the patient is faint or exhausted; with chloroform, if he is strong or reaction has been fully established. The operation may generally be successfully performed by simple manipulation; if, however, the case is obstinate, pulleys may be necessary, or extension and counter-extension made by judicious assistants.

Bruises, or contusions, unless attended with pulpification, disorganization, or destruction of the tissues, are best treated, at first, until the pain subsides, with tepid water impregnated with laudanum and sugar of lead, or some tepid spirituous lotion, and afterward, especially if the patient be strong and robust, with cold water, or cold astringent fluids. If the injury be deep seated, extensive, and attended with lesion of very important structures, the case will be a serious one, liable to be followed by the worst consequences, requiring, perhaps, amputation.

Sprains are often accompanied with excessive pain, and even severe constitutional symptoms. They should be treated with the free use of anodynes and with warm water-dressings medicated with laudanum, or laudanum and lead. The joint must be elevated and kept at rest in an easy position. Leeches may be applied, if they can be obtained; otherwise, if plethora exist, blood may be taken from the arm.

By-and-by sorbefacient liniments and friction come in play. Passive motion should not be instituted too soon.

Among the accidents of war are *burns*, and, occasionally, also scalds. The former may be produced by ordinary fire or by the explosion of gunpowder, either casual or from the blowing up of redoubts, bridges, houses, or arsenals, and vary from the trivial to the most serious lesions, involving a great extent of surface or of tissue, and liable to be followed by the worst consequences. Such injuries always require prompt attention; for, apart from the excessive pain and collapse which so often accompany them, the longer they remain uncared for the more likely will they be to end badly.

Various remedies have been proposed for these injuries. I have myself always found white-lead paint, such as that employed in the arts, mixed with linseed oil to the consistence of very thick cream, and applied so as to form a complete coating, the most soothing and efficient means. The dressing is finished by enveloping the parts in wadding, confined by a moderately tight roller. It should not be removed, unless there is much discharge or swelling, for several days. If vesicles exist, they should previously be opened with a needle or the point of a bistoury. A liniment or ointment of glycerin, lard or simple cerate, and subnitrate of bismuth, as suggested by my friend, Professor T. G. Richardson, of New Orleans, is also an excellent remedy, and may be used in the same manner as the white lead paint. In the milder cases, carded cotton, cold water, and alcohol, water and laudanum, generally afford prompt relief. Amputation will be necessary when there is extensive destruction of the muscles, bones or joints. Reaction must be promoted by the cautious use of stimulants; while pain is allayed by morphia or laudanum given with more than ordinary circumspection, lest it induce fatal oppression of the brain.

In burns from the explosion of *gunpowder*, particles of this substance are often buried in the skin, where, if it be not removed, they leave disfiguring marks. The best way to get

2

rid of them is to pick out grain after grain with the point of
a narrow-bladed bistoury or cataract needle.

The subject of *wounds* is a most important one in regard to
field practice, as these lesions are not only of frequent occurrence, but present themselves in every variety of form and
extent. Their gravity is influenced by numerous circumstances which our space does not permit us to specify, but
which the intelligent reader can readily appreciate. In many
cases death is instantaneous, owing to shock, or shock and
hemorrhage; in others it occurs gradually, with or without
reaction, at a period of several hours, or, it may be, not under
several days. Sometimes men are destroyed by shock, by
apparently, the most insignificant wound or injury, owing, not
to want of courage, but to some idiosyncrasy.

The indications presented in all wounds, of whatever nature, are—1st, to relieve shock; 2dly, to arrest hemorrhage;
3dly, to remove foreign matter; 4thly, to approximate and
retain the parts; and, 5thly, to limit the resulting inflammation.

1. It is not necessary to describe minutely the symptoms of
shock, as the nature of the case is sufficiently obvious at first
sight, from the excessive pallor of the countenance, the weakened or absent pulse, the confused state of the mind, the
nausea, or nausea and vomiting, and the excessive bodily
prostration. The case must be treated promptly: by free
access of fresh air and the use of the fan, by loosening the
dress or the removal of all sources of constriction, by dashing
cold water into the face and upon the chest, by recumbency of
the head, and by draught of cold water, or water and spirits,
wine or hartshorn, if the patient can swallow; aided, if the
case be urgent, by sinapisms to the region of the heart, the
inside of thighs and the spine, and stimulating injections, as
brandy, turpentine, mustard, or ammonia, in a few ounces of
water. No fluid must be put into the mouth so long as the
power of deglutition is gone, lest some of it should enter the
windpipe, and so occasion suffocation. Whatever the cause of

the shock may have been, let the medical attendant not fail to
encourage the sufferer by a kind and soothing expression,
which is often of more value in recalling animation than the
best cordials.

During an actual engagement, the medical officers, as well
as their servants, should carry in their pockets such articles as
the wounded will be most likely to need on the field of battle,
as brandy, aromatic spirits of hartshorn, and morphia, put up
in suitable doses.

2. The *hemorrhage* may be arterial or venous, or both arterial and venous, slight or profuse, primary or secondary,
external or internal. The scarlet color and saltatory jet will
inform us when it is arterial; the purple hue and steady flow,
when it is venous. When the wound is severe, or involving
a large artery or vein, or even middle-sized vessels, the bleeding may prove fatal in a few minutes, unless immediate assistance is rendered. Hundreds of persons die on the field of
battle from this cause. They allow their life current to run
out, as water pours from a hydrant, without an attempt to
stop it by thrusting the finger in the wound, or compressing
the main artery of the injured limb. They perish simply
from their ignorance, because the regimental surgeon has
failed to give the proper instruction. It is not necessary that
the common soldier should carry a Petit's tourniquet, but
every one may put into his pocket a stick of wood, six inches
long, and a handkerchief or piece of roller, with a thick compress, and be advised how, where, and when they are to be
used. By casting the handkerchief round the limb, and placing the compress over its main artery, he can, by means of
the stick, produce such an amount of compression as to put at
once an effectual stop to the hemorrhage. This simple contri-
vance, which has been instrumental in saving thousands of
lives, constitutes what is called the *field tourniquet*. A fife,
drum-stick, knife or ramrod may be used, if no special piece
of wood is at hand.

The most reliable means for arresting hemorrhage permanently is the *ligature*, of strong, delicate, well-waxed silk, well applied, with one end cut off close to the knot. Acupressure is hardly a proper expedient upon the battle-field, or in the ambulance, especially when the number of wounded is considerable. The rule invariably is to tie a wounded artery both above and below the seat of injury, lest recurrent bleeding should arise. Another equally obligatory precept is to ligature the vessels, if practicable, at the place whence the blood issues, by enlarging, if need be, the original wound. The main trunk of the artery should be secured only when it cannot be taken up at the point just mentioned. Lastly, it is hardly requisite to add that the operation should be performed, with the aid of the tourniquet, as early as possible, before the supervention of inflammation and swelling, which must necessarily obscure the parts and increase the surgeon's embarrassment, as well as the patient's pain and risk.

Venous hemorrhage usually stops spontaneously, or readily yields to compression, even when a large vein is implicated. The ligature should be employed only in the event of absolute necessity, for fear of inducing undue inflammation.

Torsion is unworthy of confidence in field practice, and the same is true of *styptics*, except when the hemorrhage is capillary, or the blood oozes from numerous points. The most approved articles of this kind are Monsel's salt, or the persulphate of iron and the perchloride of iron; the latter deserving the preference, on account of the superiority of its hemostatic properties. Alum and lead are inferior styptics.

Temporary *compression* may be made with the tourniquet, or a compress and a roller. It may be direct, as when the compress is applied to the orifice of the bleeding vessel, or indirect, as when it is applied to the trunk of the vessel, at some distance from the wound.

Constitutional treatment in hemorrhage is of paramount importance. It comprises perfect tranquility of mind and body, cooling drinks, a mild, concentrated nourishing diet, especially when there has been excessive loss of blood, anodynes to allay pain, induce sleep, and allay the heart's inordinate action, fresh air, and a properly regulated light.

Internal hemorrhage is more dangerous than external, because it is generally inaccessible. The chief remedies are copious venesection, elevated position, opium and acetate of lead, cool air, and cool drinks.

Exhaustion from hemorrhage should be treated according to the principles which guide the practitioner in cases of severe shock. Opium should be given freely as soon as reaction begins to quiet the tremulous movements of the heart and tranquilize the mind. When the bleeding is internal, the reaction should be brought about gradually, not hurriedly, lest we thus become instrumental in promoting or re-exciting the hemorrhage. *

Secondary hemorrhage comes on at a variable period, from a few hours to a number of days; it may depend upon imperfect ligation of the arteries, ulceration, softening or gangrene of the coats of these vessels, or upon undue constriction of the tissues by tight bandages. In some cases it is venous, and may then be owing to inadequate support of the parts. Whatever the cause may be, it should be promptly searched out, and removed.

3. The third indication is to remove all *foreign matter*. This should be done at once and effectually; with sponge and water, pressed upon the parts, with finger, or finger and forceps. Not a particle of matter, not a hair, or the smallest clot of blood must be left behind, otherwise it will be sure to produce and keep up irritation.

4. As soon as the bleeding has been checked and the extraneous matter cleared away, the edges of the *wound* are gently and evenly approximated and permanently retained by suture, and adhesive plaster, aided, if necessary, by the bandage. The best suture, because the least irritating, is that made of silver wire; but if this material is not at hand, strong, thin, well-waxed silk is used. The adhesive strips are applied in such a manner as to admit of free drainage. The

bandage is required chiefly in injuries extending deeply
among the muscles; when this is the case, its use should be
aided by compresses arranged so as to force together the deep
parts of the wound.

5. When the wound is dressed, the next duty of the surgeon is to moderate the resulting *inflammation*. For this
purpose the ordinary antiphlogastic means are employed. In
general, very little medicine will be required, except a full
anodyne, as half a grain of morphia, immediately after the
patient has sufficiently recovered from the effects of his shock,
and perhaps a mild aperient the ensuing morning, especially
if there be constipation with a tendency to excessive reaction.
The drinks must be cooling, and the diet light and nutritious,
or otherwise, according to the amount of depression and loss
of blood. In the latter event, a rich diet and milk-punch may
be required from the beginning. A diaphoretic draught will
be needed if the skin is hot and arid, aided by frequent sponging of the surface with cool or tepid water. General bleeding
will rarely, if ever, be required; certainly not if the injury is
at all severe, or if there has already been any considerable
waste of blood and nervous power.

Much trouble is, at times, experienced both in civil and
military practice, especially in very hot weather, in preventing
the access of flies to our dressing. The larvæ which they
deposit are rapidly developed into immense *maggots*, which
creeping over the wounds and sores of the patient, and gnaw-
ing the parts, cause the most horrible distress. The soldiers
in Syria, under Larrey, were greatly annoyed by these insects,
and our wounded in Mexico also suffered not a little from
them. The best prevention is bran, or light saw-dust, with
which the injured parts should be carefully covered. The use
of cotton must be avoided, inasmuch as it soon becomes hot
and wet; two circumstances highly favorable to incubation.

The best local applications are the water-dressings, either
tepid, cool, or cold, according to the temperament of the patient, the tolerance of the parts, and the season of the year.

Union by the first intention is, in all the more simple cases, the thing aimed at and steadily kept in view, and hence the less the parts are encumbered, moved or fretted, the more likely shall we be to attain the object.

The medical attendant should have a constant eye to the condition of the *bladder* after all severe injuries, of whatever character, as retention of urine is an extremely common occurrence, and should always be promptly remedied. Attention to this point is the more necessary, because the poor patient, in his comatose or insensible condition, is frequently unable to make known his wants.

Such, in a few words, are the general principles of treatment to be followed in all wounds; but there are some wounds which are characterized by peculiarities, and these peculiarities are of such practical importance as to require separate consideration. Of this nature are punctured, lacerated, and gunshot wounds.

Punctured wounds are inflicted by various kinds of weapons, as the lance, sabre, sword or bayonet. In civil practice, they are most generally met with as the result of injuries inflicted by nails, needles, splinters, fragments of bone. They often extend into the visceral cavities, joints, vessels, and nerves; and are liable to be followed by excessive pain, erysipelas, and tetanus; seldom heal by adhesive action; and often cause death by shock or hemorrhage. When the vulnerating body is broken off and buried, it may be difficult to find and extract it, especially when small and deep seated. When this is the case, the wound must be freely dilated, an eye being had to the situation of the more important vessels and nerves. In other respects, the general principles of treatment are similar to those of incised wounds. Opium should be administered largely; and, if much tension supervene, or matter form, free, incisions will be necessary.

In *lacerated wounds*, the edges should be tacked together very gently, and large interspaces left for drainage. A small portion will probably unite by the first intention; the remain-

der by the granulating process. Such wounds nearly always
suppurate more or less profusely, and some of the torn or
bruised tissues not unfrequently perish. The same bad consequences are apt to follow them as in punctured wounds. Warm
water constitutes the best dressing, either alone or with the
addition of a little spirits of camphor. Opium should be used
freely internally, and the diet must be supporting.

Gunshot wounds, in their general character, partake of the
nature of lacerated and contused wounds. They are, of course,
the most common and dangerous lesions met with in military
practice; often killing instantly, or, at all events, so mutilating the patient as to destroy him within a few hours or days
after their receipt. The most formidable wounds of the kind
are made by the conical rifle and musket balls and by cannon
balls, the latter often carrying away the greater portion of a
limb, or mashing and pulpifying the muscles and viscera in
the most frightful and destructive manner; while the former
commit terrible ravages among the bones, breaking them into
numerous fragments, each of which may, in its turn, tear up
the soft tissues, in a way perhaps not less mischievous than the
ball itself. The old round ball is a much less fatal weapon
than the conical, which seldom becomes flattened, and which
has been known to pass through the body of two men and
lodge in that of a third some distance off.

When a ball lodges, it makes generally only one orifice; but
it should be remembered that it may make two, three, and
even four, and at last bury itself more or less deeply. Should
the missile escape, there will necessarily be two openings; or,
if it meet a sharp bone and be thereby divided or cut in pieces,
as sometimes happen, there may be even three. The orifice
of entrance and the orifice of exit differ in their appearances.
The first is small, round, and often a little discolored from the
explosion of the powder; the other, on the contrary, is comparatively large, slit-like, everted, and free from color. These
differences, however, are frequently very trifling, particularly
if the ball be projected with great velocity and it do not en-

counter any bone. The opening of entrance made by the round ball is often a little depressed or inverted, but such an appearance is extremely uncommon in wounds made by the conical ball.

It is often a matter of great importance to determine, when two openings exist in a limb, whether they have been made by one ball, which has passed out, or by two balls, which are retained. The question is of grave importance, both in a practical and in a medico-legal point of view; but its solution is, unfortunately, not always possible. Sometimes the openings of entrance and exit are materially modified by the introduction but non-escape of a foreign body, as a piece of breastplate, belt, or buckle, along with the ball, which alone passes out, or by the flattening of a ball against a bone, or its division by a bone into several fragments, each of which may afterward produce a separate orifice. Generally speaking, the missile, at the place of entrance, carries away a piece of skin, and rends the skin where it escapes, the former being often found in the wound.

Bullets sometimes glance, bruising the skin, but not penetrating it; at other times they effect an entrance, but, instead of passing on in a straight line, are deflected, coursing, perhaps, partially round the head, chest, or abdomen, or round a limb. Such results are most commonly caused by a partially spent bullet coming in contact with bones, aponeuroses, and tendons; and the round is more frequently served in this way than the conical.

Gunshot wounds bleed profusely only when a tolerably large artery has been injured, and in this event they may speedily prove fatal. During the Crimean war, however, many cases occurred in which there was no immediate hemorrhage, imperiling life, notwithstanding the limbs, lower as well as upper, were left hanging merely by the integuments. Under such circumstances, *intermediary* hemorrhage, as it is termed, is apt to show itself as soon as reaction takes place; generally within a few hours after the accident.

The pain is of a dull, burning, smarting, or aching character, and the patient is pale, weak, tremulous, nauseated, and despondent, often in a degree far beyond what might be expected from the apparent violence of the injury, and that, too, perhaps, when the individual is of the most undaunted courage and self-possession in the heat of battle. At other times, a man may have a limb torn off, or be injured in some vital organ, and yet hardly experience any shock whatever; nay, perhaps be scarcely conscious that he is seriously hurt. The pain and prostration are always greater, other things being equal, when a bone has been crushed or a large joint laid open, than when there is a mere flesh wound.

The gravity of gunshot wounds of the *joints* has been recognized by all practitioners, both military and civil, from time immemorial. The principal circumstances of the prognosis are the size and complexity of the articulation, the extent of the injury, and the state of the system. A gunshot wound of a ginglymoid joint is, in general, a more dangerous affair than a similar one of a ball-and-socket joint. The structures around the articulation often suffer severely, thus adding greatly to the risk of limb and life. Of 65 cases of gunshot wounds of different joints, related by Alcock, 33 recovered; but of these 21 lost the limb. Of the 32 that died no operation was performed upon 18.

Gunshot wounds of the smaller joints, even those of the ankle, often do very well, although they always require long and careful treatment. Lesions of this kind, involving the shoulder, are frequently amenable to ordinary means. If the ball lodges in the head of the humerus, it must be extracted without delay, its retention being sure to excite violent inflammation in the soft parts, and caries or necrosis in the bone, ultimately necessitating amputation, if not causing death.

Gunshot wounds of the *knee-joint* are among the most dangerous of accidents, and no attempt should be made to save the limb when the injury is at all extensive, especially if it involves fracture of the head of the tibia or condyles of the

femur. Even extensive laceration of the ligament of the pa-
tella should, I think, as a general rule, be regarded as a sufficient cause for amputation. In 1854, Macleod saw upwards
of forty cases of gunshot wounds of the knee in the French
hospitals in the Crimea, and all, except one, in which an attempt
was made to save the limb, proved fatal. Of nine cases which
occurred in India, not one was saved. Guthrie never saw a
patient recover from a gunshot wound of the knee-joint; and
Esmarch, who served in the Schleswig-Holstein wars, expressly
declares that all lesions of this kind demand immediate amputation of the thigh.

When, in bad cases of these articular injuries, an attempt
is made to save the limb, the patient often perishes within the
first three or four days, from the conjoined effects of shock,
hemorrhage, and traumatic fever. If he survives for any
length of time, large abscesses are apt to form in and around
the joint, the matter burrowing extensively among the muscles, and causing detachment of the periosteum with caries
and necrosis of the bones.

Muscles, badly injured by bullets, generally suppurate, and
are very apt to become permanently useless. Special pains
should, therefore, be taken to counteract this tendency during
the cure. Large shot and other foreign bodies sometimes lodge
among these structures, where their presence may remain for a
long time unsuspected.

Cannon balls often do immense mischief by striking the
surface of the body obliquely, pulpifying the soft structures,
crushing the bones, lacerating the large vessels and nerves, and
tearing open the joints, without, perhaps, materially injuring
the skin.

A very terrible form of *contusion* is often inflicted upon the
upper extremity of artillerymen by the premature explosion of
the gun, while in the act of loading, causing excessive commo-
tion of the entire limb, laceration of the soft parts, and most
extensive infiltration of blood, accompanied, in many cases, by
comminuted fracture, and penetration of the wrist and elbow

joints. The constitutional shock is frequently great. If an attempt be made to save the parts, diffusive suppuration, and more or less gangrene, will be sure to follow, bringing life into imminent jeopardy. An attempt in such a case to save the limb would be worse than useless, if, indeed, not criminal; amputation must be promptly performed, and that at a considerable distance above the apparent seat of the injury, otherwise mortification might seize upon the stump.

In the *treatment* of this class of injuries, the first thing to be done, after arresting the hemorrhage and relieving shock, is to extract the ball and any other foreign substance that may have entered along with it, the next being to guard against inflammation and other bad consequences.

In order to ascertain where the ball is, the limb should be placed as nearly as possible in the position it was supposed to have been at the moment of the accident. A long, stout, flexible, blunt-pointed probe, or a straight silver catheter, is then passed along the track and gently moved along until it strikes the ball. In many cases the best probe is the surgeon's finger. Valuable information may often be obtained by the process of pinching or digital compression, the ends of the fingers being firmly and regularly pressed against the wounded structures, bones as well as muscles, tendons, and aponeuroses. Occasionally, again, as when a ball is lodged in an extremity, its presence is easily detected by the patient, who may make such an examination as he lies in bed.

The situation of the foreign body having been ascertained, the bullet-forceps take the place of the probe, the blades, which should be long and slender, being closed until they come in contact with the ball, when they are expanded so as to grasp it, care being taken not to include any of the soft tissues. If there be any loose or detached splinters of bone, wadding, or other foreign material, it should now also be removed; it being constantly borne in mind that, while a ball may occasionally become encysted, and is at all times, if smooth, a comparatively harmless tenant, such substances always keep up irritation, and should, therefore, if possible, be got rid of without delay.

Although preference is commonly given to the bullet-forceps, properly so called, as an extractor, the polypus and dressing-forceps, generally answer quite as well, especially the former, the latter being adapted only to cases where the foreign body is situated a short distance below the surface, or where the wound is of unusual dimensions, admitting of the free play of the instrument.

During the extraction, the parts should be properly supported, and if the wound is not large enough for the expansion of the instrument, it must be suitably enlarged. When the ball is lodged a short distance from the skin, it may often be readily reached by a counter-opening.

When a bullet is embedded in a bone, as in the head of the tibia, or in the condyles of the femur, and the parts are not so much injured as to demand amputation, extraction may be effected with the aid of the trephine and elevator. Sometimes a bullet-worm, as it is termed, an instrument similar to that used in drawing a ball from a gun, will be very convenient for its removal.

The operation being completed, the parts are placed in an easy, elevated position, and enveloped in tepid, cool or cold water-dressings, as may be most agreeable to them and to the system. The best plan, almost always, is to leave the opening or openings, made by the ball, free, to favor drainage and prevent pain and tension. If the track be very narrow, it may heal by the first intention, but in general it will suppurate, and portions of tissue may even mortify. Erysipelas, pyemia, and secondary hemorrhage are some of the bad consequences after gunshot injuries, the latter usually coming on between the fifth and ninth day, the period of the separation of the sloughs.

CHAPTER VI.

AMPUTATIONS AND RESECTIONS.

In endeavoring to decide so important a question as the loss of a limb, various circumstances are to be considered, as the age, habits and previous health of the patient, the kinds of injury, and the number, nature, and importance of the tissues involved. In military practice, amputation must often be performed in cases where in civil practice it might be avoided.

It may be assumed, as a rule, that young adults bear up under severe accidents and operations, other things being equal, much better than children and elderly subjects; the strong than the feeble; the temperate than the intemperate; the residents of the country than the inhabitants of the crowded city.

The following circumstances may be enumerated as justifying, if not imperatively demanding, amputation in cases of wounds, whatever may be their nature:

1st. When a limb has been struck by a cannon ball or run over by a railroad car, fracturing the bones, and tearing open the soft parts, amputation should, as a general rule, be performed, even when the injury done to the skin and vessels is apparently very slight, experience having shown that such accidents seldom do well, if an attempt is made to save the limb, the patient soon dying of gangrene, pyemia, or typhoid irritation. The danger of an unfavorable termination in such a case is always greater when the lesion affects the lower extremity than when it involves the superior.

2d. No attempt should be made to save a limb when, in addition to serious injury done to the integuments, muscles or bones, its principal artery, vein or nerve has been extensively lacerated, or violently contused, as the result will be likely to be gangrene, followed by death.

3d. A lacerated or gunshot wound penetrating a large joint, as that of the knee or ankle, and accompanied by comminuted fracture, or extensive laceration of the ligaments of the articulation, will, if left to itself, be very prone to terminate in mortification, and is therefore a proper case for early amputation.

4th. Gunshot wounds attended with severe comminution of the bones, the fragments being sent widely around among the soft parts, lacerating and bruising them severely, generally require amputation, especially in naval and military practice.

5th. Extensive laceration, contusion, and stripping off of the integuments, conjoined with fracture, dislocation, or compression and pulpification of the muscles, will, in general, be a proper cause for the removal of a limb.*.

Amputation is not to be performed, in any case, until sufficient reaction has taken place to enable the patient to bear the additional shock and loss of blood. As long as he is deadly pale, the pulse small and thready, the surface cold, and the thirst, restlessness, and jactitation excessive, it is obvious that recourse to the knife must be wholly out of the question. The proper treatment is recumbency, with mild stimulants, sinapisms to the extremities, and other means calculated to re-excite the action of the heart and brain. Power being restored, the operation, if deemed necessary, is proceeded with, due regard being had to the prevention of shock and hemorrhage, the two things now mainly to be dreaded. .

One of the great obstacles about immediate amputation is the difficulty which the surgeon so often experiences in respect to the cases demanding the operation, and the uncertainty that none of the internal organs have sustained fatal injury; a circumstance which would, of course, contra-indicate the propriety of such interference.

---

* Gross' Surgery, vol. i. p. 395.

Cases occur, although rarely, where, notwithstanding the most violent injury, or perhaps, even the loss of a limb, there is hardly any appreciable shock, and, in such an event, the operation should be performed on the spot.

The results of the military surgery in the Crimea show that the success of amputations was very fair when performed early, but most unfortunate when they were put off any length of time. This was the case, it would seem, both in the English and French armies.

Should amputation ever be performed in spreading gangrene? The answer to this question must depend upon circumstances. We may give our sanction when the disease, although rapid, is still limited, and when the patient, comparatively stout and robust, has a good pulse, with no serious lesion of a vital organ and no despair of his recovery, but a cheerful, buoyant mind, hopeful of a favorable issue. No operation is to be done when the reverse is the case; if it be, the patient will either perish on the table, from shock and hemorrhage, or from a recurrence of mortification in the stump.

Lacerated, contused and gunshot wounds are often of so frightful a nature as to render it perfectly certain, even at a glance, that the limb will be obliged to be sacrificed in order that a better chance may be afforded for preserving the patient's life. At other times, the injury, although severe, may yet, apparently, not be so desperate as to preclude, in the opinion of the practitioner, the possibility of saving the parts, or, at all events, the propriety of making an attempt to that effect. The cases which may reasonably require and those which may not require interference with the knife, are not always so clearly and distinctly defined as not to give rise, in very many instances, to the most serious and unpleasant apprehension, lest we should be guilty, on the one hand, of the sin of commission, and, on the other, of that of omission; or, in other, and more comprehensive terms, that while the surgeon endeavors to avoid Scylla, he may not unwittingly run into Charybdis, mutilating a limb that might have been saved, and endangering life by the retention of one that should have been promptly amputated. It is not every man, however large his skill and experience, that is always able to satisfy himself, even after the most profound deliberation, what line of conduct should be pursued in these trying circumstances; hence the safest plan for him generally is to procure the best counsel that the emergencies of the case may admit of. But in doing this, he must be careful to guard against procrastination: the case must be met promptly and courageously; delay even of a few hours may be fatal, or at all events, place limb and life in imminent jeopardy. Above all, let proper caution be used if the patient is obliged to be transported to some hospital, or to a distant home, that he may not be subjected to unnecessary pain, exposed to loss of blood, or carried in a position incompatible with his exhausted condition. Vast injury is often done in this way, by ignorant persons having charge of the case, and occasionally, even by practitioners whose education and common sense should be a sufficient guarantee against such conduct.

Little need be said here about the *methods* of amputation. In cases of emergency, where time is precious, and the number of surgeons inadequate, the flap operation deserves, in my opinion, a decided preference over the circular, and, in fact, every other. The rapidity with which it may be executed, the abundant covering which it affords for the bone, and the facility with which the parts unite, are qualities which strongly recommend it to the judgment of the military surgeon. The flaps should be long and well shaped, and care taken to cut off the larger nerves on a level with the bone, in order to guard against the occurrence of neuralgia after the wound is healed. Whatever method be adopted, a long stump should be aimed at, that it may afford a good leverage for the artificial substitute. No blood should be lost during or after the operation, and hence the main artery of the limb should always be thoroughly compressed by a tourniquet, not by the fingers of assistants, who are seldom, if ever, trustworthy on such occasions.

Anæsthetics should be given only in the event of thorough reaction; so long as the vital powers are depressed and the mind is bewildered by shock, or loss of blood, their administration will hardly be safe, unless the greatest vigilance be employed, and this is not always possible on the field of battle, or even in the hospital. Moreover, it is astonishing what little suffering the patient generally experiences, when in this condition, even from a severe wound or operation.

In the war in the Crimea, the British used chloroform almost universally in their operations; the French also exhibited it very extensively, and Baudens, one of their leading military surgical authorities, declares that they did not meet with one fatal accident from it, although it was given by them, during the Eastern campaign, thirty thousand times at least. The administration of chloroform is stated by Macleod to have contributed immensely to the success of primary amputations.

The *dressings* should be applied according to the principles laid down under the head of wounds. The sutures, made with silver wire or fine silk, should not be too numerous, and the adhesive strips must be so arranged as to admit of thorough drainage. A bandage should be applied from above downward, to control muscular action and afford support to the vessels; the stump rest upon a pillow covered with oil-cloth, and the water-dressing be used if there is danger of overaction. Pain and spasm are allayed by anodynes; traumatic fever, by mild diaphoretics. Copious purging is avoided; the drink is cooling; and the diet must be in strict conformity with the condition of the patient's system. The first dressings are removed about the end of the third day; after that once or even twice a day, according to the nature and quantity of the discharges, accumulation and bagging being faithfully guarded against.

The following statistics of amputations, both in the continuity of the limbs and of the articulations, possess peculiar interest for the military surgeon. They are derived chiefly from a review which I published of Mr. Macleod's "Notes of the Surgery in the Crimea," in the North American Medico-Chirurgical Review for January, 1860.

The number of cases given by Macleod is 732, with a mortality of 201. Of these, 654 were primary, with 165 deaths, or 26·22 per cent.; and 78 secondary, with 36 deaths, or in the ratio of 46 1. The mortality of the greater amputations —as those of the shoulder, arm and forearm, and the hip, thigh, knee and leg—was 39·8 per cent. for the primary operations, and 60 per cent. for the secondary.

The increase of mortality from amputations as we approach the trunk, has long been familiar to surgeons, and the results in the Crimea have not changed our previous knowledge. Thus the ratio of mortality of amputations of the fingers was 0·5; of the forearm and wrist, 1·8; of the arm, 22·9; of the shoulder, 27·2; of the tarsus, 14·2; of the ankle-joint, 22·2; of the leg, 30·3; of the knee-joint, 50·0; of the thigh, in its lower third, 50 0, at its middle, 55 3, at the upper part, 86 8, and at the hip, 100·0. The limb was removed at the latter joint in 10 cases, all of which rapidly proved fatal. The French had 13 cases, primary and secondary, with no better luck.

Legouest has published a table of most of the recorded cases of amputation at the *hip-joint*, for gunshot wounds. Of these 30 were primary and all ended fatally; of 11 intermediate, or early secondary, 3 recovered; and of 3 remote, 1 recovered. "Thus," says Macleod, "if we sum up the whole, we have 4 recoveries in 44 cases, or a mortality of 90 9 per cent." Some of the primary cases died on the table; and all the rest, except two, before the tenth day. In the Schleswig-Holstein war, amputation at the hip joint was performed seven times, with one cure. Mr. Sands Cox, recording the experience of civil and military hospitals up to 1846, gives 84 cases, most of them for injury, with 26 recoveries. Dr. Stephen Smith, of New York, has published tables of 98 cases showing a ratio of mortality of one in 2 2-3. In 62 of these cases, the operation was performed in 30 for injury, with a mortality of 60 per cent.

Amputation in the upper third of the *thigh* was performed 39 times, with a fatal result in 34. Of these cases only one was secondary, and that perished. Amputation of the middle third of the limb was performed in 65 cases, of which 38 died. Of these cases 56 were primary, with 31 deaths, giving thus a mortality of 53·3 per cent.; 9 cases were operated upon at a later period, and of these, 7 died, or 77·7 per cent. Amputation of the lower third of the thigh was performed 60 times, 46 being primary, with a mortality of 50 per cent., and 14 secondary, with a mortality of 71·4 per cent,

Amputation at the *knee* was performed primarily in 6 cases, of which 3 died, and once secondarily, with a fatal result. Chelius refers to 37 cases of amputation of the knee, collected by Jæger, of which 22 were favorable; and of 18 cases recorded by Dr. Markoe, of New York, as having occurred in the practice of American surgeons, 13 got well. These cases added together, afford an aggregate of 61, with a mortality of 21, or 34.4 per cent.

The *leg* was amputated 101 times, with 36 deaths, or a mortality of 35·6 per cent. Of these cases 89 were primary, with 28 deaths, and 12 secondary, with 8 deaths.

Amputation at the *ankle-joint* was performed in 12 cases, death following in 2. Of these cases 3 were secondary, and all favorable.

The arm was removed at the *shoulder-joint* in 39 cases, with a fatal issue in 13, or 33·3 per cent., 33 being primary, with 9 deaths, and 6 secondary, with a fatal issue in 4. If we couple these cases with 21 that occurred during the previous period of the war, we shall have an aggregate of 60 cases, with 19 deaths, or a mortality of 31·6 per cent. The advantage of a primary over secondary amputation of the shoulder has long been known to military surgeons. Thus, of 19 primary cases mentioned by Mr. Guthrie as having occurred between June and September, 1813, 18 recovered, while of 19 secondary cases 15 died. The experience of the late Dr. Thomson, in Belgium, is equally decisive.

Amputation of the upper *arm* was performed 102 times, with death in 25 cases, or mortality of 24·5; 96 of the cases being primary. Of the secondary cases one-half proved fatal.

The *forearm* was amputated primarily 52 times, and the hand at the wrist once, with only one death; while of 7 secondary operations, upon the same parts, 2 died.

Resection is one of the aids of conservative surgery, and military practice affords numerous occasions for its employment. The operation, however, is not equally applicable to all the articulations. Resection of the *shoulder-joint* has hitherto afforded the most flattering results. It is more especially applicable in cases of gunshot injuries, unattended by serious lesion of the vessels and nerves of the limb, or severe laceration of the muscles and integuments. A portion of the humerus, embracing, if necessary, from four to five inches in length, together with a part or even the whole of the glenoid cavity of the scapula, may be safely and expeditiously removed under such circumstances, and yet the patient have an excellent use of his arm.

Williams mentions 19 cases of gunshot wounds of the shoulder-joint in which resection was performed, and of which 3 proved fatal. Baudens saved 13 out of 14 cases, and the British surgeons, in the Crimea, lost 2 patients out of 27.

Resection of the *elbow* has of late engaged much attention among military men, and although the results are less flattering than in the operation upon the shoulder, they are, nevertheless, highly encouraging. Of 82 cases which occurred in the Schleswig-Holstein and in the Crimean campaigns, only 16 died, or 1 in about 5.

The *wrist-joint* has seldom been the subject of excision; doubtless, cases not unfrequently occur in which it might be resorted to with advantage.

Dr. George Williams has collected the history of 11 cases of excision of the *hip-joint* for gunshot injury, 6 of which occurred in the Crimea. Of this number 10 died. Of 23 amputations at the hip-joint by the English and French surgeons in the East, all died.

Excision of the *knee-joint* for gunshot injury holds out no prospect of advantage, experience having shown that, when the articulating extremities of the femur and tibia are fractured by a ball, the proper remedy is amputation.

The *ankle-joint* has been resected in a few instances only for gunshot injuries, and the results have thus far been by no means flattering. When the joint is seriously implicated, amputation will undoubtedly be the more judicious procedure.

Resection of the bones in their continuity is seldom practiced in this class of injuries, and experience has offered nothing in its favor. The operation was performed several times in the Crimea, but proved invariably fatal.

The *after-treatment* in resection must be conducted upon the same principles as in amputation. The measures must, for the most part, be of a corroborating nature. The limb must be placed in an easy position, and be well supported by a splint or fracture-box, to prevent motion. The operation is liable to be followed by the same bad effects as amputations.

CHAPTER VII.

ILL CONSEQUENCES OF WOUNDS AND OPERATIONS.

The bad consequences to be apprehended after wounds, amputations, and other operations, are traumatic fever, hemorrhage, excessive suppuration, spasms, erysipelas, gangrene, pyemia, and tetanus.

a. Traumatic fever usually sets within the first few hours after the injury, or soon after reaction has been fairly established. In camp practice its tendency generally is to assume a low, typhoid character, especially if there is much crowding of the sick, with imperfect ventilation and want of cleanliness. Not unfrequently it displays an endemic or epidemic disposition.

The treatment must be exceedingly mild; the patient will not bear depletion, but will, notwithstanding this fever, probably require stimulants and tonics, with nutritious food and drink from the very commencement. A gentle anodyne and diaphoretic mixture, as morphia and antimony in camphor-water, may be needful, in the early stage, to quell the fictitious excitement or attempt at overaction.

b. The likelihood of *secondary hemorrhage* must be steadily kept in view in these cases; much may be done to prevent it by the proper use of the ligature at the time of the operation or dressing, but it is often unavoidable, especially in gunshot wounds, owing to the injury sustained by the coats of the vessels by the grazing of the ball. However induced, it should receive the most prompt attention, inasmuch as the loss even of a few ounces of blood may prove destructive to the already exhausted system.

c. Spasm of the muscles is not peculiar to amputations; it often exists in a most severe degree in cases of fractures and gunshot wounds. Anodynes in full doses, with a little antimony, the use of a moderately-tight bandage, and warm water-dressing, medicated with laudanum and acetate of lead, are the most appropriate measures.

d. Profuse suppuration may be looked for in nearly all bad wounds, whatever their character, and also in many of the amputations performed on the field of battle. The exhausting effects must be counteracted by supporting remedies, as quinine, iron, cod-liver oil, and brandy, with frequent change of dressing, cleanliness, and ventilation. Bagging is prevented by counter-openings and careful bandaging.

e. Erysipelas usually manifests itself within the first thirty-six hours after the injury or operation; often assumes an endemic or epidemic character; is easily distinguished by the peculiar reddish blush rapidly spreading over the surface, together with the stinging or smarting pain and increased swelling; and should be treated with dilute tincture of iodine, or anodyne and saturnine lotions, quinine and tincture of iron, with nutritious food and drinks.

f. *Gangrene* is sufficiently common after severe lesions on the battle-field, especially that variety of it denominated hospital gangrene. During the Crimean war, this form of gangrene raged with extraordinary virulence and fatality among the French in the hospitals on the Bosphorus. It also prevailed about the same period within some of the hospitals in the south of France, and it is asserted that the "Euphrate," a transport ship, in her voyage to the Mediterranean was obliged, from this cause alone, to throw sixty of her men overboard within thirty-six hours! After the taking of the Quarries and the assault upon the Redan, during the heat of summer, in 1855, the English surgeons lost a number of their cases of amputation of the thigh from moist gangrene of a most rapid character, the system having been literally overwhelmed by the poison. When hospital gangrene is endemic, it attacks not only open wounds and sores, but also the slightest scratches, cicatrices, and stumps. Persons laboring under diarrhœa, dysentery, and scurvy are most obnoxious to it.

The proper remedies are sequestration of the patients, the free use of the nitric acid lotion, iodine to the inflamed skin, charcoal, port wine, or yeast cataplasms, and frequent ablutions with disinfecting fluids, aided by opium, quinine, tincture of iron, lemon-juice, and other supporting means. Mopping the affected surface freely with strong nitric acid often answers an excellent purpose. The favorite remedy of Pouteau was the actual cautery.

g. *Pyemia*, the purulent infection of the French writers, is one of the chief dangers after severe wounds and operations.

It was the great source of the mortality after amputations, especially secondary, during the war in the Crimea. It usually comes on within from three to eight days after the injury, and is nearly always fatal. Its characteristic symptoms are rigors, followed by copious sweats, rapid failure of the vital powers, delirium, and a withered appearance of the countenance, frequently conjoined with an icterode tinge of the eye and skin. On dissection, the large veins leading from the stump or wound are found filled with pus, with redness of the lining membrane; and abscesses, usually small and filled with unhealthy fluid, are seen scattered through the lungs, muscles, and cellular substance, matter also occasionally existing in the joints. The treatment is essentially the same as in erysipelas.

h. Traumatic tetanus is not very common in military practice. It is most liable to show itself in tropical countries, in hot, damp weather, and in persons of a nervous, irritable temperament, occasionally supervening upon the most insignificant injuries, as, for example, a mere scratch. In India the disease is often provoked by unextracted balls, and both in that country and on the continent of Europe the operation which was most frequently followed by it during the recent wars, was amputation at the shoulder-joint.

The effects of sudden vicissitudes of temperature in developing tetanus, are well known. They are most striking in tropical regions, when the change is from hot to cold, or from dry to wet. Larrey had repeated opportunities of observing the development of the disease under such circumstances, both in Egypt and Germany. After the battle of Bautzen, the exposure of the wounded to the cold night air produced over a hundred cases of tetanus, and a large number suffered from a similar cause after the battle of Dresden. Like effects were witnessed at Ferozepore and Chillianwallah. Baudens, in his treatise on gunshot wounds, states that the influence of cold and moisture in developing the disease, during the French campaigns in Africa, was most striking. Of forty slightly

3

wounded men, placed in a gallery on the ground floor, during the prevalence of a northeasterly wind, fifteen were speedily attacked with tetanus. Similar effects have several times been noticed in this country. Thus, after the battle of Ticonderoga, in 1758, nine of the wounded who were exposed the whole night after the action, in open boats upon Lake George, died of lock-jaw; and during our war with Great Britain, most of those who suffered on board the Amazon, in the engagement before Charleston, were attacked with this disease a fortnight after, in consequence of a very sudden change of weather, the wind blowing cold and wet.

The extremes of heat and cold both favor the production of tetanus. In the East and West Indies, the slightest prick of the finger or toe is often sufficient to induce the disease, and the inhabitants of the Arctic regions not unfrequently suffer in a similar manner. Dr. Kane, in his memorable expedition, lost two of his men from this affection, and he adds that all his dogs perished from a like cause.

The *mortality* from traumatic tetanus is notorious. Hardly one recovers. Nearly all perish in two or three days from the attack.

The most reliable remedies are opium, in the form of morphia or acetated tincture, in large doses, in union with camphor and antimony. The effects of Indian hemp are uncertain. Chloroform will mitigate pain and spasms. Amputation, except, perhaps, when the wound affects a finger or toe, will be worse than useless, as will also be counter-irritation along the spine. To prevent the disease should be our business; and to do this no wounded person should ever be exposed to the cold night air, or to currents of air at any time. *After all amputations, however trifling, special directions should be given upon this point.*

CHAPTER VIII.

INJURIES OF THE HEAD, CHEST, AND ABDOMEN.

* The immediate effects of *concussion* of the brain are those of fainting or collapse, and must be treated accordingly; by recumbency, access of cold air, the use of the fan, dashing of cold water upon the face and chest, and sinapisms to the precordial region, thighs, feet, and spine, aided, in the more severe cases, by stimulating injections. If the patient can swallow, he may take a little wine or brandy. A smelling-bottle may be held near, not to, the nose. Reaction is not promoted too rapidly, for fear of secondary consequences.

The period of danger from collapse being over, the patient is sedulously watched, that overaction may not occur, the risk now being from inflammation; or, the stage of excitement being happily passed, from the remote effects of the injury. If the concussion was at all severe, all bodily and mental excitement must be for a long time avoided.

Compression of the brain arises, surgically speaking, from two causes only: effusion of blood and depressed bone. In the former case, the characteristic symptoms—insensibility and coma, dilated and fixed pupil, stertorous breathing, and paralysis—frequently do not come until some time after the receipt of the injury. The first symptoms will probably be those of concussion, or exhaustion. By-and-by the patient regains his strength, gets up, talks, or walks, and then suddenly drops down, as if he had been shot, in a state of utter unconsciousness. The effusion of blood, kept in abeyance during the collapse, has had full play, filling empty places, and causing unmistakeable effects. Such an occurrence will be most apt to happen when there has been extensive separation of the dura mater, or rupture of the middle meningeal artery.

If, on the other hand, the compression is due to depression of the skull, the symptoms are nearly always immediate.

When the case is one of sanguineous compression, it must be treated very much as one of ordinary apoplexy; at first, by efforts at *gradual* reaction, and afterward by purgatives, bleeding, and means to favor cerebral accommodation and prevent inflammation. The trephine is not thought of unless the unconsciousness obstinately persists, and there is reason to believe, from the nature of the phenomena, especially the existence of a wound or contusion on the head, that the blood may be reached by the instrument.

Gunshot injuries of the skull, with or without lodgment of the ball, may be productive merely of concussion of the brain, or of concussion and compression. When the missile penetrates the bone, and tears up the cerebral tissues and membranes, death usually occurs instantly, or within a short time after the receipt of the accident, without, perhaps, any attempt at reaction. Nevertheless, a number of cases of injury of this nature, in which the patient either partially or completely recovered, have been recorded by military surgeons. In some instances the ball merely penetrates the skull, with no apparent depression, and in this event the treatment should evidently be very simple, being limited, in a great degree, after the occurrence of reaction, to the prevention of inflammation of the brain. A similar course should be adopted when the bone is broken and only slightly depressed, especially if there be no urgent or obstinate symptoms of compression. When, on the contrary, the bone is badly fractured, comminuted, or forced greatly beyond the natural level, the proper plan is to trephine whether there be any external wound or evidences of compression or not. If the operation be neglected, loss of life from inflammation will be sure to arise within the first six or ten days after the receipt of the injury. In the punctured fracture, as it is named, the trephine is invariably employed at the earliest moment, however flattering, apparently, the head symptoms may be. If the instrument be withheld, fatal cerebritis or arachinitis will be no less certain than when the bone is shattered and driven down upon the brain.

Fracture of the skull by *contre-coup*, so common in civil practice, is seldom met with on the field of battle; doubtless for the reason that the injury is hardly ever inflicted upon the top or the base of the cranium, as it is when a person is struck upon the vertex or falls upon his nates. The most frequent fracture among soldiers is the punctured. A ball has been known to break the internal table of the skull without the external.

The skull is sometimes frightfully injured without any serious lesion of the scalp. Macleod refers to a case, which occurred at the Alma, where it was completely destroyed by a glancing shot, without any material implication of the soft parts. A round shot ("en ricochet") struck the scale from an officer's shoulder, and merely grazed his head as it ascended. The result was instant death. The skull was so completely mashed that its fragments rattled under its scalp as if loose in a bag. The condition of the brain was, unfortunately, not ascertained.

In the more simple forms of fractures of the skull, however induced, the practice of trephining is now much less common than formerly, and there is no doubt that the patient often makes a good recovery, though it is by no means certain that such a person may not suffer seriously, at a more or less remote period, from epileptic and other affections. I am convinced from my own observation that this happens not unfrequently. Dr. Stromeyer, surgeon-in-chief in the Schleswig-Holstein campaign in 1849, expresses strong opposition to the use of the trephine in gunshot and other fractures of the skull, even with depression, on the ground that, independently of the mischief inflicted in the operation upon the tissues, admission of air to the contused portion of the brain greatly augments the danger of inflammation. Of 41 cases of gunshot fractures of the skull with depression, reported by him, 34 were cured, and of these 1 only had been trephined.

When operative interference is deemed improper, the most simple treatment should be enforced. Any probing that may be necessary should, if practicable, be performed with the finger, and the wound should not be enlarged, except when we are compelled to elevate depressed or remove loose bone.

When trephining is required, it should be done as early as possible, and without chloroform or ether, unless the patient is very unruly, as the anæsthetic might tend to provoke inflammation of the brain. Every particle of depressed bone should be elevated, and such portions as are loose, detached, or driven into the brain, and easily accessible, removed. All bleeding vessels are tied, the edges of the wound are *gently* approximated with silver sutures, and the head, well shaved and raised, wrapped in warm or cold water-dressing, as may be most grateful to part and system. The great danger after all severe injuries and operations upon the skull is inflammation of the brain and of its membranes, and to the prevention of this, therefore, the surgeon should direct his most zealous efforts. The patient must be frequently visited, and every untoward symptom promptly met by appropriate measures, of which active purgation, loss of blood by venesection, leeching or cupping, a restricted diet, and exclusion of light and noise from the apartment, with perfect rest, are the most reliable.

Wounds of the *brain* must be managed upon general principles; all foreign matter is at once removed, and the parts being restored as nearly as may be to their normal relations, the surgeon endeavors to keep the resulting inflammation within proper limits. Most of such lesions prove fatal within the first week from their receipt. If the patient survive for any length of time, death will generally come at last from exhaustion, cerebritis, or fungus.

Portions of the *skull*, sliced off by the sabre or sword, should be replaced and secured by wire sutures, even if they are attached merely by small shreds of the scalp.

Scalp wounds of every description, but in particular the contused, lacerated, punctured, and gunshot, are extremely prone to be followed by erysipelas; death may also occur from cerebritis, arachnitis, and pyemia. The slightest lesion, then, of this region of the body should be zealously watched.

Wounds of the *face* must be treated with an eye to the avoidance of disfiguring scars, by wire sutures and cold water-dressing. When a large portion of the lower jaw is shot away, the tongue will be apt to fall back upon the glottis, causing suffocation. The organ should be drawn forward with the finger or tenaculum, and the patient observe the prone position until the tendency is lost.

One of the great sources of annoyance and danger, in gunshot wounds of the face, is secondary hemorrhage. It frequently appears soon after the accident, and, although it often ceases spontaneously, it is sometimes controlled with much difficulty. Paralysis, partial or complete, is not uncommon, owing to injury of the branches of the facial nerve.

In the management of wounds about the mouth, throat, and face, great care must be taken not to allow the offensive mucous and salivery secretions to pass into the stomach. The neglect of this precaution is apt to be followed by a low typhoid state of the system, very similar to what occurs in pyemia, or blood poisoning. I have repeatedly witnessed these effects after operations upon the jaws, mouth, and even the nose.

In fractures of the bones of the face from gunshot an exception should be made to the general rule of removing fragments which are nearly detached, observation having shown, says Mr. Macleod, that the large supply of blood in this region will enable them to resume their connection with the other tissues, in a way that would be fatal to similarly placed portions in other situations.

Gunshot and other wounds of the *chest* are, as stated elsewhere, extremely fatal; death, if the lesion be at all severe, being usually speedily caused by shock, hemorrhage, or asphyxia; or, at a more or less remote period, by inflammation and effusion. When the lungs are wounded, the characteristic symptoms will be hemoptysis, with suffocative cough, great prostration, and excessive alarm. A copious flow of blood may take place in the thoracic cavity from a wound of one of the intercostal arteries.

Any foreign matter that is easily accessible, is at once removed, but officious probing is out of the question. The wound, if small and unaccompanied by serious hemorrhage, is closed in the usual manner, the chest being firmly encircled by a broad bandage, to compel diaphragmatic respiration. Under opposite circumstances, it is kept open, the patient lying upon the affected side to favor the escape of blood with as much elevation of the head as the case may admit of. The main reliance for arresting pulmonary bleeding is upon venesection, copious, and frequently repeated, unless the exhaustion amounts to absolute collapse. Sugar of lead, opium, and veratrum viride are frequently exhibited, sinapisms are applied to the extremities, and, in short, everything is done to control cardiac action. Inflammatory symptoms are counteracted in the usual manner, and effused fluids, causing oppression, and resisting ordinary measures, are, unhesitatingly, evacuated by puncture, as the only chance of escape.

Wounds of the *heart* and *aorta*, of whatever nature, are usually fatal; now and then, however, an astonishing exception occurs.

Wounds of the *abdomen*, merely penetrating its walls, but not its contents, are brought together by sutures, extending down nearly to the peritoneum, otherwise they will be followed by hernia. When they involve the intestine, and are incised, they are sewed up with a fine needle and silk thread, either interruptedly or continuously, the ends of the ligature being cut off close.

Contusions of the walls of the abdomen by round shot are among the most dangerous injuries to which the body is exposed, often rupturing both the hollow and solid viscera, and rapidly causing death, without much apparent sign of so severe an accident. The most important symptoms of these contusions are vomiting and pain in the abdomen; and the

great object of the treatment, in the event the patient survives their immediate effects, is the prevention of peritonitis,
which often comes on in the most stealthy manner. Laceration of an internal organ is nearly always promptly fatal.
Shell wounds of the walls of the abdomen are generally followed by extensive sloughing. Abscesses among the muscles
of the abdomen are not uncommon after gunshot injuries.

Balls often traverse the walls of the abdomen for a considerable distance without entering its cavity, or they pass in
without injuring any of the contained viscera.

"The fatality of penetrating wounds of the belly," ob-
serves Macleod, "will depend much on the point of their
infliction. Balls entering the liver, kidneys, or spleen, are
well known to be usually mortal, although exceptional cases
are not rare. Wounds of the great gut are also always recognized as much less formidable than those which implicate the
small. Thomson saw only two cases of wounds of the small
gut, after Waterloo, in the way of recovery; but Larrey re-
ports several. Gunshot wounds of the stomach are also
exceedingly fatal. Baudens records a remarkable case of recovery, although complicated with severe head injuries. The
syncope which followed the severe hemorrhage in this case
lasted for ten hours, and doubtless assisted, along with the
empty state of the stomach at the moment of injury, in preventing a fatal issue."

Gunshot wounds of the *bladder* occasionally occur; the
ball may penetrate the organ in any direction, and at the same
time commit extensive havoc in the neighboring parts, both
soft and osseous. Such lesions are generally fatal. Simple
gunshot wounds, on the contrary, are sometimes recovered
from, especially when they are treated by the retention of the
catheter, thus allowing the urine to flow off as fast as it de-
scends from the kidneys. The operation of laying open the
wounded viscus through the perineum, as originally proposed
by Dr. Walker, of Massachusetts, might be performed in such
a contingency. Such a procedure would be much more likely

to prevent urinary infiltration than the catheter, however carefully retained, during the detachment of the sloughs, as well as before the contiguous structures have been glazed with lymph.

Balls, pieces of cloth, fragments of bone, and other foreign bodies, if retained in the bladder, generally serve as nuclei calculi, and should, therefore, be as speedily extracted as possible, either through the perineum, or by means of the forceps or lithotriptor. Quite a number of cases, in which the operation of lithotomy was successfully performed for the purpose of effecting the riddance of balls and other extraneous substances, have been reported by different writers, as Morand, Larrey, Baudens, Langenbeck, Guthrie and Hutin.

CHAPTER IX.

DISEASES INCIDENT TO TROOPS.

The diseases which attend armies, or molest soldiers in camps, garrisons and hospitals, and which so often decimate their ranks, and even, at times, almost annihilate whole regiments, are the different kinds of fevers, especially typhus and typhoid, dysentery, diarrhœa, and scurvy. These are, emphatically, the enemies of military life, doing infinitely more execution than all the weapons of war, however adroitly or efficiently wielded, put together. Pneumonia, pleurisy, and hepatitis, of course, slay their thousands, and various epidemics, especially cholera, not unfrequently commit the most frightful ravages. " War," says Johnson, " has means of destruction more formidable than the cannon and the sword. Of the thousands and tens of thousands that have perished, how small a proportion ever felt the stroke of an enemy !" Frederick the Great used to say that fever cost him more men than seven pitched battles, and it has long been a matter of

history that more campaigns are decided by sickness than by
the sword. The great mortality which attended our armies
in Mexico was occasioned, not by wounds received in battle,
but by the diseases incident to men carrying on their military
operations in an inhospitable climate, badly fed, subjected to
fatiguing marches, and obliged to use unwholesome water.
Thousands perished, during their absence, from fever, dysentery and diarrhœa, and a still greater number from the effects
of these diseases, after the return of the troops to their native
soil. The latter affection, in particular, pursued many, like a
relentless foe, to their graves long after they had been cheered
by the sight of their homes and friends.

In the war in the Crimea disease destroyed incomparably
more soldiers than the sword, the musket, and the cannon.
Typhus and typhoid fever, dysentery, diarrhœa, scurvy, and,
lastly, malignant cholera, annihilated vast numbers, both in
the British, French and Russian ranks. According to Dr.
Macleod, whose "Notes on the Surgery of the War in the
Crimea," are so well known to the profession, the proportion
of those lost among the British by sickness to those lost by
gunshot and other injuries, was, during the entire campaign,
as 16,211 to 1761, exclusive of those killed in action. The
difference he supposed to have been still greater among the
French and Russian forces. In December, 1854, and in January, 1855, not less than 14,000 French soldiers were
admitted into the Crimean ambulances on account of disease,
whereas, during the same period, only 1500 were admitted on
account of wounds. Of the whole number nearly 2000 died.
During the last six months of the campaign, in which the city
was stormed and taken, the French had 21,957 wounded as an
offset against 101,128 cases of disease.* At Walcheren, in
1809, the British lost one-third of their troops by disease,
and only 16 per cent. by wounds. In the Peninsular war,
from January, 1811, to May, 1814, out of an effective force

---

* Macleod, op. cit., p. 67.

of 61,500 men, only 42.4 per 1000, says Macleod, were lost
by wounds, while 118.6 were lost by disease.

The number of sick that may be expected to be constantly
on hand during any given campaign is estimated, on an average, at 10 per cent.; but this proportion must necessarily be
exceeded, especially in an invading army, with raw, undisci-
plined and unacclimated troops. This was eminently true
even in the Crimea, in a climate comparatively healthy, within
a few miles of the sea. We may well imagine what would
be the effects of the climate of the South upon the Northern
troops, if they were to pass far, during the hot season, beyond Mason and Dixon's line. Disease, in its worst form,
would be sure to invade and thin their ranks at every step.
Fever—typhoid, typhus, remittent, intermittent, and yellow—
dysentery, diarrhœa, scurvy, pneumonia, and inflammation
of the liver, would accomplish more, infinitely more, for the
Southern cause than all the weapons of war that could be
placed in the hands of the Southern people. Typhoid, typhus
and yellow fever, dysentery, diarrhœa and scurvy would, in
all human probability, soon become epidemic, and occasion a
mortality truly appalling. The Southern soldier, on the contrary, thoroughly acclimated as he is, would suffer comparatively little. The British in the Crimean war lost 5,910 men
from diarrhœa and dysentery, the whole number of cases
having been 52,442, affording thus a mortality of 11.26 per
cent. Cholera, of which there were 7,575 cases altogether,
destroyed 4,513, or in the ratio of 59·57 per cent. Typhus
fever killed 285 out of 828 cases; fever not typhus, 3,161,
out of 30,376. The French and Russian troops suffered in
still larger numbers from these diseases. Macleod asserts that
the former lost their men by typhus fever by thousands, and
the latter by tens of thousands. The British suffered but
little from intermittent fever, whereas this disease did great
mischief among the French, causing serious mortality, either
directly or indirectly, besides disqualifying large numbers for
service.

Scurvy was another dreadful enemy which the British and French troops were compelled to encounter in the Crimea. It prevailed more or less extensively for a long time, and served to impart its livery to the other diseases of the soldiery, masking their character, and remarkably augmenting their virulency.

Considering, then, the frequency of the occurrence of these diseases, and their excessive fatality, it behooves the military surgeon to use every means in his power to guard, in the first place, against their outbreak, by the employment of proper hygienic or sanitary measures; and in the next, to treat them with all possible diligence and judgment when their development is unavoidable. It is, of course, impossible, in a work of this description, to enter into any details upon the subject; but there are several points which cannot, I conceive, be too forcibly impressed upon the mind of the military practitioner. I refer to the great, the paramount importance of—1st, proper isolation of the sick, or, what is the same thing, the importance of not crowding them together; 2dly, free ventilation; 3dly, bodily cleanliness; 4thly, little medicine; 5thly, a good supply of fresh vegetables and fruits, especially oranges and lemons; 6thly, careful and tender nursing.

Painful experience has shown in all parts of the world, that the crowding together of the sick and wounded is one of the worst calamities that can befall them. For want of this precaution, diseases, otherwise easily manageable, often assume an epidemic character, or, in the absence of this character, often baffle the best directed efforts for their relief. When the wounded are crowded together they frequently become the victims of erysipelas, hospital gangrene, pyemia, and phlebitis; occurrences which, under better regulations, might in many cases be entirely prevented.

Of the propriety of constant and thorough *ventilation*, it is unnecessary to speak. If pure air is so essential in health, it is easy enough to see how important it must be in sickness. *Cleanliness* of body should be regarded as a religious duty;

it may be effected with the sponge and tepid, cool or cold water, according to the exigencies of the case, and cannot be performed too frequently or too thoroughly, care being, of course, taken not to worry or fatigue the patient. In some instances the water may be medicated with common salt, potassa, vinegar, or Labarraque's solution. Nothing is generally more grateful to the sufferer, in the different kinds of fevers, than frequent sponging of the surface with cool or tepid water.

The use of heroic *medicines*, or of any medicines in large doses, in these diseases, and also in cases of severe wounds, cannot be too severely reprobated. More men, there is reason to believe, have been killed in this manner in the armies and navies of the world than by the sword and the cannon. Let medicines, then, be administered sparingly. Let the secretions be well seen to; but purge little, and use depressants with all possible wariness. Give iced water, but not too freely, and lumps of ice when there is much thirst with gastric irritability and excessive restlessness. Mild diaphoretics and anodynes, will, as a general rule, be highly efficacious, but the latter should be exhibited with great caution when there is cerebral oppression. Lemon-juice and potassa are indispensable in scurvy, or where there is a marked tendency to scorbutic disease. Quinine is one of the great remedies in most, if not in all, of these diseases, especially when, as is so often the case, they are associated with a malarious origin. The good average dose is from two to five grains, repeated from three to five times in the twenty-four hours. When marked debility prevails, the best stimulants are brandy, in the form of milk-punch or toddy, and Madeira, Port, or Sherry wine.

Immense suffering and loss of life are often occasioned for the want of fresh vegetables and fruits in military operations, as well as in the garrison and the hospital. A daily supply of these articles should, therefore, be provided at almost any hazard and expense. In all low states of the system, however induced, the strength can never be rapidly brought up without a diet which partakes more or less of this character.

There is a form of *dysentery*, very common in India, which is exceedingly apt, when large masses of troops are habitually congregated together, to assume an epidemic character; and it is for this reason that it has often been supposed to be contagious. For such an opinion, however, there does not seem to be any valid reason. Ballingall, who witnessed at least 2,000 cases of this disease, asserts that he never once met with a circumstance tending to create such a suspicion; and the views advanced by this eminent surgeon are those now pretty generally, if not universally, entertained by the British practitioners in India.

"The remote causes of dysentery in India are conceived to be heat, particularly when combined with moisture; the immediate and indiscriminate use of fruits; the abuse of spirituous liquors, and exposure to currents of wind and to noxious night-dews." Troops recently arrived from Europe are particularly prone to the disease.

Tropical dysentery presents itself in two varieties of form, the *acute* and the chronic. The first, which is an extremely fatal disease, is seated in the rectum and colon, the latter being often involved through nearly its entire extent, and it frequently commits very serious, if not irreparable, mischief in these structures before the patient and the attendant are aware of its true character, owing to the absence of urgent pain and pyrexia. In general the attack is ushered in by the ordinary symptoms of diarrhœa, such as griping pain in the bowels, and frequent calls to stool with excessive straining, the evacuations being, at first, thin and copious, but without fetor and but little streaked with blood. The tongue-skin and pulse are nearly, perhaps entirely, normal. Gradually the pain becomes more violent, as well as more fixed, and is felt in both iliac regions, or even along the whole track of the colon; the discharges consist chiefly of blood and mucus, or of a fluid resembling water in which fresh beef has been macerated; the tongue is covered with a white coat; the skin is either hot and dry, or bathed with clammy perspiration; and the straining is so excessive as to occasion prolapsus of the rectum. The pulse is, even at this stage, often but little affected, being, perhaps, only somewhat increased in quickness. Sometimes, however, it is very full, bounding, and vibratory, without much velocity, and when this is the case it always, according to Ballingall, forebodes evil. Toward the close of the attack, the passages are frequently involuntary and intolerably fetid, gangrenous portions of the mucus coat of the bowels are sometimes extruded, and the surface of the body emits a peculiar, cadaverous smell. The average period at which death occurs is about one week, but many cases linger on much longer.

The remedies upon which the India practitioners mainly rely in the treatment of this horrible form of disentery are venesection, mercury and opium; leeches, purgatives, diaphoretics, warm bathing, blisters and enemata being employed as auxiliaries. Venesection is always practiced early, and, even when the patient is not very robust, boldly, it being, apparently, regarded as the sheet-anchor of the physician's hope. Calomel is administered in doses of from ten to twenty grains, along with two or three grains of opium, twice or thrice in the twenty-four hours; and, while profuse salivation is discountenanced, production of slight ptyalism is generally aimed at.

Such treatment as this seems altogether frightful to the modern American practitioner; it strikes him as unnecessarily harsh, and as well calculated to augment the mortality of the disease. We might, in this country, perhaps bleed, and that pretty freely, at the very commencement of an attack of dysentery; at all events, leech very copiously, but we would certainly draw blood sparingly if the attack had already made serious constitutional inroads, or if it was of an epidemic character; and, as to giving mercury with a view to ptyalism, however slight, few men would, I presume, be so fool-hardy. The India practitioners do not, it appears, employ quinine in the treatment of this form of dysentery; a remedy so extremely needful in many cases of this disease as it prevails in this country, especially in our Southern latitudes, where it is not unfrequently of a malarious origin.

The *chronic* form of India dysentery, termed hepatic flux, more frequently attacks persons who have been for some time inured to the climate of that country, and is always associated with biliary derangement. "This flux, like the other, often assumes at its commencement the appearance of a common diarrhœa, and becomes afterwards characterized by frequent and severe fits of griping, resembling colic pains, particularly urgent about the umbilical region. Each attack of griping is generally succeeded by a call to stool, and the evacuations are always unnatural in color and consistence, free from any admixture of blood, but generally of a yeasty or frothy appearance, and accompanied with large discharges of flatus; while in passing they are attended with a sense of scalding about the anus. The patient, after each evacuation, feels considerably relieved, and hopes to enjoy an interval of ease; but the recurrence of the griping, accompanied with a sensation of air passing through the bowels, and succeeded again by a call to stool, gives him little respite. From the commencement of the attack, the patient complains of nausea, want of relish for his food, and preternatural thirst, attended often with a disagreeable taste in the mouth. The tongue is furred or loaded, and not unfrequently covered with a yellow bilious coat. The pulse is quickened and the skin parched.*

Cholera morbus must, necessarily, in this country, especially in our Southern latitudes, and during the hot summer months, be a more or less frequent attendant upon camp life, although much may be done, by a proper observance of hygienic laws, to prevent it. When the disease breaks out it

* Ballingall's Military Surgery, p. 511, 1844.

cannot be arrested too speedily. The most appropriate remedies, particularly in its earlier stages, are perfect quietude,
abstinence from drink, sinapisms to the epigastrium, and an
efficient dose of morphia and camphor, or even morphia alone.
If torpor of the liver exists, blue mass or a few grains of
calomel may be advantageously combined with the anodyne.
The swallowing of small lumps of ice will greatly assist in
allaying the gastric irritability. A mustard and salt emetic
will be indicated if the stomach is loaded with ingesta. The
bowels are quieted with an anodyne enema; and to relieve
thirst, and reduce heat of skin, the surface is frequently
sponged with cool or tepid water. A combination of carbonate of potassa and acetated tincture of opium, with fresh
lemon-juice, in peppermint or camphor-water, will often act
like a charm in relieving the gastric and intestinal irritability,
the cramps, and other distressing symptoms.

The exposure of the soldier, both in the tent and on the
field, renders him extremely prone to *rheumatism*, frequently
attended with high inflammatory excitement and severe pain.
Such an attack is often effectually put to flight if, at its in-
ception, it be treated with a large anodyne and diaphoretic
mixture, as fifteen grains of Dover's powder, a third to half a
grain of sulphate of morphi, with a fourth of a grain of tartar
emetic, or, what is perhaps still better, a drachm of the wine
of colchicum in union with a full dose of morphia or black
drop. When the disease has already made some progress,
an active purgative should precede the exhibition of these
medicines.

Sore throat, tonsilitis, and catarrhal affections, or what, in
common language, are called *colds*, are very common among
soldiers, especially the raw troops just mustered into service,
ill clothed, inexperienced, and unaccustomed to camp life.
The moment such disease sets in, no matter how light it may
be, the person should be compelled to report himself at the
surgeon's quarters, in order that he may receive the necessary
attention and advice. Generally, an attack of this kind will

promptly yield to a trifling prescription, as a little hot drink, a mild aperient, or, better still, a quarter of a grain of morphia, a grain of opium, or a large dose of Dover's powder.

In an army not under strict discipline, or where proper care is not observed in enlisting, *mania a potu* is very apt to show itself, much to the annoyance of the nurses and the physicians. If, in such a case, the patient be not well secured, he may, in his perverted military ardor, do serious mischief to himself and to his attendants. A moderately active mercurial purge at the outset of the disease will often go far in quieting the system and in abridging the attack. After the medicine has operated, a mild opiate and sedative treatment will generally be the most soothing. Alcoholic stimulants are, in general, to be withheld.

Nostalgia is another complaint liable to assail the soldier, even the hardiest, especially if he is a person of strong domestic attachments, or engaged in an "affaire du cœur." It is more apt to show itself in soldiers enlisting for the foreign service, or in those who are forcibly expatriated, and is often attended with great suffering, terminating in confirmed melancholy. It is characterized by a love of solitude, a vacant, stultified expression of the countenance, a morose, peevish disposition, absence of mind, pallor of the cheeks, and progressive emaciation. Many of Bonaparte's troops, during the campaign in Egypt, suffered from this complaint; some in a very distressing degree. In this country, nostalgia will not be likely to occur, at least not to any extent, as our people are essentially of a roving habit, and of an eminently social disposition. The treatment is rather moral than medical; agreeable amusements, kindness, gentle but incessant occupation, and the promise of an early return to home and friends, constituting the most important means of relief.

It is impossible, even under the most rigid discipline, to prevent *gonorrhœa* among soldiers. They will expose themselves, in spite of all that can be done to prevent it, and they often pay a heavy penalty for their indulgence, not only from the suffering entailed by the primary disease, but its different complications, especially chordee, cystitis, and orchitis. The symptoms of gonorrhœa are too well understood to require enumeration here. The treatment should, from the start, be rigidly antiphlogistic; by rest, low diet, active purgation, and the antimonial and saline mixture, with the addition of a small quantity of copaiba. The penis and scrotum are well supported, and covered with warm water-dressing, the former organ being bathed in tepid salt water, at least thrice daily, for twenty minutes at a time. When the discharge is greatly lessened, but not till then, recourse is had to injections of lead, sulphate of zinc, or nitrate of silver, at first very mild and gradually increased in strength, repeated every six, eight or twelve hours. The treatment is continued, in a modified form, for about five days after all the specific symptoms have vanished.

Chordee is best relieved by a full anodyne, as half a grain of morphia, in union with the fourth of a grain of tartar emetic, given towards bedtime, or by a large enema of laudanum; with warm water-dressings to the genitals.

For the relief of *cystitis*, the most appropriate remedies are anodyne diaphoretics, in the form of Dover's powder, or a solution of morphia and tartar emetic, aided by the free use of bicarbonate of soda and moderate quantities of diluents.

Orchitis is treated by suspension of the affected organ, with strong lead and anodyne lotions, and the judicious exhibition of antimony, in union with morphia or black drop.

Chancres must be thoroughly cauterized at the beginning, either with nitrate of silver, nitric acid, or acid nitrate of mercury; and, subsequently, or after the disease has made some progress, like any common sore, with mild measures; mercury being studiously withheld, except in the hard form of the disease, but not even then while there is much inflammation or inordinate constitutional excitement. In a word, all harsh measures must be avoided. The patient will generally do a thousand times better without than with mercury. The greatest possible attention must be paid to cleanliness, and for this purpose the parts should be frequently bathed in tepid salt water, aided by the syringe if there be a tight prepuce. The best local application is the warm water-dressing, covering in the entire genitals; if much swelling and pain are present, it may be advantageously medicated with lead and opium. As the inflammation subsides, the sore may be dressed with some gently stimulating lotion, as two grains of tannin, the eighth of a grain of sulphate of copper, and half a drachm of laudanum to the ounce of water, a weak mixture of sherry and water, or a solution of nitrate of silver, zinc or iodide of iron. If the ulcer is disposed to spread, or presents a sloughy or unhealthy aspect, it will be proper to touch it lightly twice a day with the solid nitrate of silver, or a solution of one part of acid nitrate of mercury to four parts of water.

The *constitutional* treatment is rigidly antiphlogistic, or tonic and supporting, according to the particular nature of the case. The bowels should receive early attention; the skin be kept moist; and pain be allayed by anodynes. Perfect recumbency should be observed until the parts are nearly healed. If mercury be required, the best forms will be calomel and blue mass, in small doses, twice a day, with a vigilant eye to their effects, ptyalism being studiously avoided in every case.

If *bubo* supervene, the treatment must be prompt and efficient, with a view to the prevention of further mischief. Recumbency, the topical use of iodine with warm water-dressing, medicated with lead and opium, light diet, and the antimonial and saline mixture, constitute the most appropriate measures. If matter form, an early and free incision is made, and the part afterward treated as a common sore, the granulating process being promoted by mild means. Mercury is carefully withheld, at all events in the early stage of the disease.

The army is no place for soldiers laboring under secondary or tertiary syphilis; the sooner they are dismissed from the service the better, especially if they are volunteers.

Ophthalmia is one of the annoyances of the soldier's life. Liable to be caused by cold, it is capable of assuming several varieties of form, and sometimes prevails extensively as an epidemic. The granular and purulent, in particular, are to be feared, as they frequently destroy the sight, and even the eye, in a few days, occasioning intense suffering. To ascertain the condition of the parts, the lids must always be gently everted with a probe or the finger. The greatest cleanliness should be observed in these affections; the patient should, if possible, be sequestered, at all events not be permitted to use the same basins and towels; the light should be excluded from the apartment; and the general and local treatment should either be strictly antiphlogistic or of a mixed character, partly antiphlogistic and partly stimulant. The applications should be of the mildest description, especially those intended for the inflamed surface. The syringe is frequently used to wash away the secretions. Strong collyria generally do immense harm in all forms and stages of ophthalmia. Blood may be taken from the arm, or by cups or leeches from the temples, if the symptoms are unusually urgent, and the patient plethoric. In rheumatic inflammation of the eye, colchicum and morphia, given freely at bed time, will be of immense service.

When *foreign matter* gets into the eye, or becomes imbedded in the cornea, speedy removal must be effected, and the parts afterwards treated with rest, cold or tepid bathing, gentle aperients, and seclusion from light. Particles of steel and other sharp bodies are picked out with the point of a delicate bistoury or cataract needle. The effects of lime and other alkalies are neutralized by syringing the eye freely with a weak solution of vinegar; those of nitrate of silver, with a weak solution of common salt, a thorough coating of olive oil being afterward applied.

Carbuncles, boils, and abscesses, which are of frequent

occurrence in army practice, demand prompt attention, both on account of the suffering they induce and the disqualification they may entail for temporary duty. They should be opened early and freely, and no time be lost in amending the general health by gentle mercurial and other purgatives, alterants, and tonics, particularly quinine and iron. The most appropriate remedies are tincture of iodine and warm water-dressings.

In carbuncles the affected structures, after free division, will generally require the thorough application of some escharotic or detergent stimulant, as Vienna paste, nitric acid, nitrate of silver, or acid nitrate of mercury.

Frost-bite is extremely common among soldiers during the cold wet weather of winter. Thousands of the French troops perished from this cause in Russia, during Napoleon's retreat from Moscow. Frost-bite was very prevalent among the English during their first winter in the Crimea, and the French suffered in still greater numbers, as well as more severely. The habit which the men had of sleeping in their wet boots, at one time almost universal, contributed greatly to its production, wet and cold combined diminishing the circulation and vitality of the feet and toes. On the 21st of January, 1855, when the thermometer stood at 5°, not less than 2500 cases of frost-bite were admitted into the French ambulance, and of these 800 died, death in many having no doubt been expedited by the effects of erysipelas, pyemia, and hospital gangrene. Weak and intemperate persons are most apt to have frost-bite and to perish from its effects.

In the treatment, in incipent cases, cloths, wrung out of cold water impregnated with a little spirits of camphor or alcohol, should be applied, or the parts be covered for a few minutes with snow, or immersed in cold water. On no account must they be exposed to warmth, either moist or dry. Excessive reaction is controlled by lead and laudanum lotions, or dilute tincture of iodine. If gangrene occurs, the ordinary measures, local and general, are indicated. All rude manipulation in dressing the injured part greatly aggravates the disease. In general, spontaneous amputation is waited for, experience having shown that operative interference, even when the part is perfectly black, and attached only by a few living shreds, is extremely prone to be productive of excessive pain and constitutional irritation, often proceeding to an alarming extent.

Among the great evils, both of civil and military practice, are *bed-sores*, which, unless the greatest possible precaution be used, are sure to arise during the progress of acute diseases and of severe accidents, necessitating protracted recumbency. The hips and sacral region are their most common sites, with the heel in cases of fractures of the leg. The earlier symptoms are a sense of prickling, as if the part were rubbed with coarse salt, or a burning, itching or smarting pain, with a brownish or livid discoloration of the skin, and slight swelling. Then gangrene ensues, followed by horrible suffering.

To prevent these sores, which often prove destructive to life, when there is already much exhaustion from previous suffering, the posterior surface of the body should be frequently examined, particularly if the patient is in a state of mental torpor, and pains taken to ward off pressure by the use of air cushions and other means. The parts should be sponged several times a day with some alcoholic lotion containing alum, or painted with a weak solution of iodine. If gangrene or ulceration occurs, a yeast or port wine poultice is used, the separation of the slough is aided with the knife, while the granulating process is promoted by the usual remedies.

Ulcers of the leg are causes of disqualification in enlisting, but they sometimes occur after the soldier has entered the service, from fatigue, injury, or undue constriction of the limb. However induced, they should be managed as any other forms of inflammation, recumbency with elevation of the affected parts, tepid water-dressings, a restricted diet, and cooling purgatives constituting the most important elements of the treatment. When the healing process has fairly commenced, the leg should be supported with the roller or adhesive strips.

As preventive of ulcers of the legs, the limbs should be daily washed in cold water with Castile soap, and no soldier should be permitted to wear garters.

CHAPTER X.

MILITARY HYGIENE.

Much disease and suffering may be prevented, and many lives saved, by a careful observance of hygienic regulations. There is no question whatever that immense numbers of soldiers everywhere fall victims to their recklessness and the indulgence of their appetites and passions. We would not advocate too much restraint; men are but men everywhere, and soldiers form no exception to the general law. They, like civilians, must have their amusements and recreations. The bow cannot last long, if kept too constantly and too tightly on the stretch. Occasional relaxation is indispensable to health.

Indolence, however, should never be countenanced in any army. Its demoralizing effects, and its influence upon the health of the soldier, have been noticed and commented upon in all ages. "The efficacy," says an eminent military surgeon, in speaking on this subject, "of due attention to the occupation of the mind must never be lost sight of. Many illustrations of its powerful influence, whether for good or evil, whether in resisting or accelerating the inroads of disease, may be found both in ancient and in modern times, from the retreat of the ten thousand Greeks under Xenophon down to the present day. It may be observed, that disease goes hand in hand with indolence and inactivity, whether of body

4

or of mind; and that, on the contrary, where the minds of
soldiers are agreeably occupied, and their bodies energetically
employed, as in the attainment or pursuit of victory, disease
is kept in abeyance." It was the observation of another experienced authority in military medical affairs, Mr. Alcock;
that, "the period of the smallest loss to an army is a victorious and vigorously prosecuted campaign, with frequent battles and much marching;" an assertion corroborative of the
facts, long since so painfully realized, that sickness, however
induced, destroys incomparably more soldiers than the sword
and the musket.

No intemperance, either in eating or drinking, should be
tolerated in an army; both are demoralizing, and both predis-
pose to, if not actually provoke, disease. Alcoholic liquors
should not be permitted to be used except as medicine, and
then only under the immediate direction of the medical officer.
The ordinary drink and food should be selected with special
reference to their healthful properties. The use of bad water,
even for a short time, is invariably productive of mischief.
The tea and coffee should be of good quality, and well prepared, to preserve their agreeable flavor and their soothing
and refreshing effects. Lager beer, ale, and porter, if sound,
are both nourishing and wholesome, if consumed within judicious limits.

The practice of allowing soldiers spirituous liquors, as a
portion of their daily rations, has, I believe, been pretty
generally, if not entirely, abandoned in the European service.
Its injurious effects upon the health and morals of troops have
long been deprecated. In the British army in India, the use
of alcoholic liquors was, at one time, universal, on the suppo-
sition that it had a tendency to counteract the depressing
influences of a tropical climate; the men took their spirits
regularly before breakfast, and not unfrequently several times
during the day, especially if on active duty; but it was soon
found that it produced quite a contrary impression, causing
instead of preventing debility, and affording a temptation to

general drunkenness, which was followed by insubordination and crime. The result was, that the government abolished the alcoholic ration system altogether, substituting coffee and tea, which are now regularly served once, and often twice a day.

The condition of the 13th Regiment of Light Infantry, stationed at Jellalabad, during the late insurrection in India, affords a happy illustration of the salutary effects of abstinence from spirituous liquors. While the siege was progressing, the men, during a period of five months, were entirely debarred from drinking, and yet their health and courage were most excellent. As soon, however, as the garrison was relieved, and they began to indulge in spirits, many of them in a short time became sick and riotous. The experience of Major-General Wylie, of the Bombay army, was precisely similar. When the soldiers under his command were quartered in districts where no liquor could be obtained, their health, discipline and morals were all that could be desired; whereas, under opposite circumstances, insubordination and disease prevailed to a frightful extent.

During the Crimean war, coffee and tea were found to be eminently wholesome and invigorating, enabling the troops to sustain fatigue and resist disease. When the men were in the trenches, and could not obtain their usual supply of these articles, they became languid, and suffered from dysentery and diarrhœa. To produce their peculiar sustaining and exhilarating effects, coffee and tea should be taken hot and moderately strong, with sugar, if not also with cream.

Fresh meats are always preferable to salt, though good ham and smoked beef may be taken once a day with advantage as an agreeable change. Fresh fish are always acceptable. Pickled pork and beef are far from being good articles as a portion of the daily rations. The frequent use of fresh vegetables is indispensable to the health of the soldiery. Ripe fruits are nearly equally so. Without a proper admixture of this kind, dyspepsia, bowel complaints, and scurvy will,

sooner or later, inevitably ensue; and woe to the man that is
assailed by them! The acids and other properties contained
in these substances are indispensable to the healthy condition
of the blood and solids, and the importance of such a diet
cannot be too deeply or too frequently impressed upon the
attention of every commissariat. Potatoes, rice, hominy,
beans, peas, beets, spinach, lettuce, asparagus, radishes, horse-
radish, water-cresses, dried peaches and apples, and the different kinds of fruits as they come into season, should be constantly on hand. Soups, both animal and vegetable, are
generally grateful to the palate, as well as useful to the system, and should be used whenever the occasion is favorable
for their preparation.

Eggs, butter, milk and butter-milk should be freely in-
dulged in whenever they can be procured. Serious disease
is often engendered by bad bread and biscuit, and it should
therefore be made a part of the duty of every medical officer
to see that no articles of this kind are brought into camp.

When in the camp or barracks, the soldier should take his
meals with the same regularity as the ordinary citizen at his
home. Neglect of this precaution must necessarily lead to
great bodily inconvenience, and, if long persisted in, may
ultimately lead to serious disease, especially dyspepsia and
other disorders of the digestive apparatus. He should not dis-
regard regularity even with respect to his alvine evacuations;
for there are few things more conducive to the preservation of
the health.

The soldier's *dress* should be in strict conformity with the
season of the year and the vicissitudes of the weather. He
should at no time, be either too hot or too cold, but always
comfortable, changing his apparel with the alterations of the
temperature. Flannel should be worn next the surface both
winter and summer. The shoes must be thick and warm,
with broad soles; and woolen stockings will be more comfortable, especially when the troops are marching, than cotton.
A thin woolen cap-cover, found so useful in India, will pro-

tect the neck from the hot sun, and an oil-silk cap-cover, from the rain. In very wet weather the shoulders might be defended with a cape of oil-cloth.

Frequent *ablutions* will largely contribute to the comfort of the soldier and the preservation of his health. They should be performed at least once a day, the best time being late in the afternoon or in the evening just before retiring. The feet, in particular, should be often washed, especially in marching, for reasons which need not be dwelt upon here. The under-shirt should be changed every night, and frequently washed, to promote the healthy state of the skin.

Exposure to the hot sun, to cold and wet, must alike be avoided. Sojourning in malarious regions will be certain to be punished by an attack of neuralgia or intermittent fever.

All *offals* should be promptly removed from the camp, and carried to a distance of several miles, or be well buried.

The privies should be in the most favorable location as it respects ventilation, and be closed at least every three or four days; or, what is worthy of consideration, every man should be compelled to bury his alvine excretions, as was the custom, in time of war, among the ancient Hebrews, each man being obliged to carry a paddle for that purpose. The emanations from these sources cannot receive too much attention, especially when large masses of men are crowded together, as they are then extremely prone to induce disease.

Finally the medical officer should make it his special duty to see that every recruit is *vaccinated*, or, if the operation was performed prior to his enlistment, at a distant period, matter should again be inserted, experience having shown that the effects of the virus are, in time, in many instances, totally eradicated from the system. In most of the European armies re-vaccination is extensively practiced; and it is asserted by Stromeyer that during the Schleswig-Holstein war, on an average, 38 operations out of 1,000 were successful.

It is impossible to bestow too much care and attention upon the selection of the camp ground, and the arrangement of the tents, as a vast deal of the comfort and health of the soldiers must necessarily depend upon them. The following judicious remarks upon this subject are from the pen of an eminent military surgeon, the late Dr. Ballingall, who served in various campaigns, and who was for many years, as stated elsewhere, Professor of Military Surgery in the University of Edinburgh.

" A camp," says Ballingall, " is most advantageously situated on a gentle declivity, on a dry soil, and in the vicinity of a running stream. In order to ascertain the state of the ground it may sometimes be necessary to dig into it to some extent; for, although apparently dry on the surface, it may be found sufficiently wet at the depth of a few feet; and if so, ought, if possible, to be changed, particularly if an encampment is to be stationary. A camp should never be formed on ground recently occupied, nor on a field of battle where much carnage has recently occurred. Many favorable spots are to be found on banks of rivers, which, perhaps, upon the whole, afford the most eligible sites. We must yet bear in mind that, when the banks of the rivers are low, or the country subject to periodical rains or sudden inundations from the melting of snow on contiguous mountains, there may be a very serious danger from this cause. Against the danger of such a position, we are cautioned in Mezerey's ' Medecine d'Armee,' which states a case in which the Austrian army lost 500 men and 200 horses from a sudden inundation of this kind."

When damp ground or a low situation is unavoidable, it should be abandoned as soon as possible, for a better, and, in the meantime the greatest care should be taken to protect the soldiers from damp or wet with straw or other suitable means.

An army has been known to suffer severely from disease contracted in a malarious region. Against such a calamity useful information may often be elicited from the people of the neighborhood, especially physicians conversant with insalubrious sites.

When an army is obliged to remain for a long time stationary, an occasional change of camp will be greatly conducive
to health, although such change should involve a good deal of
labor and temporary inconvenience. A camp under such circumstances should, at all events, be frequently ventilated, and
kept constantly clean, a pure atmosphere being of paramount
importance to health and comfort. It may often be difficult
to do this, but it must, nevertheless, be done; the welfare of
the service absolutely demands it, and no medical officer honestly performs his duty unless he interests himself personally
in these matters "The most obvious and perfect way," says
Ballingall, "of thoroughly airing the tents is by shifting
them occasionally, and exposing the straw, blankets and soldier's clothing to the open air; the necessity of frequently
changing the straw, and enforcing cleanliness in camp, in
every possible way, are circumstances too obvious to require
any effort of reasoning to enforce. With this view the slaugh-
tering of cattle, and everything likely to create noxious or
putrid effluvia, ought to be conducted without the camp, and
on the side of it opposite to that from which the wind generally blows." The demoralizing influence of a camp life is
well known, and I am convinced that there is nothing so well
calculated to counteract this influence as rigid discipline,
reasonable activity of mind and body, strict temperance, both
in eating and drinking, and frequent religious worship. Every
regiment should have its chaplains, not less than its medical officers, not only with a view of restraining vice and promoting morality, but of affording to the poor soldier, away
from home and friends, in the hour of his mortal extremity,
those consolations which the minister of the gospel alone
knows how to impart. The mitigation of the horrors and
miseries of war, not less than the tendencies of the age in
which we live, absolutely demand such a provision.

CHAPTER XI.

DISQUALIFYING DISEASES.

Troops, whether regulars or volunteers, should include no men that are not perfectly qualified, both physically and mentally, for the hardships of the public service. They should, in a word, be perfectly sound, or, what is the same thing, free from all defects, congenital or acquired. It is for this reason that they are always subjected to a most thorough examination by the recruiting or regimental surgeon. This examination is, as a general rule, a great deal more rigid in the regular than in the volunteer service. In the former, the regulations are such that, if the recruit is not found to be sound after he has been inspected by the regular army surgeon, the expense incident to his enlistment and transportation falls upon the medical officer who committed the oversight.

An examination of the kind here mentioned demands both time, patience and skill. In order to make it thorough, the candidate must be completely stripped, so that if any disease or defect in the exterior of the body exist, it may be at once rendered apparent. The examination, however, must not be limited to the exterior; it must embrace also the interior. The disqualifying affections may be arranged according to the organs and regions in which they are seated, under separate heads :—

1. The eye and ear. 2. The brain, as the seat of intellect. 3. The lungs and heart. 4. The stomach, bowels, anus, liver and spleen. 5. The kidneys, bladder and urethra. 6. The testicles. 7. The exterior of the abdomen. 8. The limbs, including the joints.

The diseases which unfit a man for military service are defects of sight, of hearing, and of speech; weakness of intellect; paralysis; epilepsy; hernia; hydrocele; varicocele; imperfect development or absence of the testes; hemorrhoids,

anal fistule, and fissure of the anus; unusual protuberance of
the abdomen; organic lesion of the internal organs; large
tumors; aneurism; varix of the extremities; ulcers, or large
scars indicative of their former existence; bad corns, bunions;
overlapping toes; flatfootedness; deformity of the hands and
fingers; contractions from burns or other causes; badly united
fractures; unreduced dislocations; diseased joints; loss of
the incisor and canine teeth; serious disfigurement of the features; spinal curvature; ill-formed shoulders; habits of intemperance; diminutive stature or excessive overgrowth.

In the regular army no man is enlisted under the age of
eighteen or over that of forty-five. In the volunteer service,
similar regulations obtain, although they are not so rigidly
enforced.

Recruiting surgeons, after having examined a candidate for
enlistment, are obliged to certify, on honor, that they consider
him, in their opinion, to be free from all bodily defects and
mental infirmity, which would, in any way, disqualify him for
performing the duties of a soldier.

When men become disqualified for service, in consequence
of disease or accident, a surgeon's certificate is also required,
in order to aid them afterward in procuring a pension and ex-
emption from ordinary military duties. The affections which
may justify a soldier in applying for a release from further
service, are organic visceral lesions, deafness, blindness, mental imbecility, lameness, large herniæ, and such mutilations as
interfere with the proper handling of the sword and musket.

CHAPTER XII.

FEIGNED DISEASES.

Soldiers, influenced by a desire to quit the service, to re-
visit their homes, or evade active duty, will not hesitate, at
times, to play the part of impostors, feigning diseases, or even

inflicting upon themselves more or less serious injuries, with the hope of accomplishing their designs. This deception, technically called malingering, would be of comparatively little consequence if it were always, or even generally, confined to a few members of a regiment; but when it is remembered that it is liable to become epidemic, spreading from individual to individual; it assumes a deep importance, well calculated to arouse the attention both of the medical officer and of the military commander. Its effects, then, become eminently demoralizing to the service, which, if proper care be not employed to detect and punish it, might seriously suffer, especially when such an outbreak occurs on the eve of a battle. Great ingenuity is often displayed by malingerers, requiring no little vigilance and skill on the part of the surgeon for its successful exposure, and yet it is not less necessary for his own credit than for the honor of the service that he should not permit himself to be deceived.

The number of diseases imitated by this class of dissemblers, is surprisingly great, and there is also quite a list of self-inflicted injuries. Among the former are various mental diseases, as mania and imbecility; deafness; amaurosis; epilepsy; paralysis; hæmatemesis; hæmoptysis; gastritis; dysentery and diarrhœa; affections of the heart; rheumatism; lumbago; wry-neck; contractions of the joints; incontinence of urine; bloody urine; and stone in the bladder: among the latter, opthalmia, opacity of the cornea, œdema of the limbs, wounds, and amputations of the fingers.

Space will not permit me to enter into any details respecting this important subject. I shall, therefore, content myself with a presentation of such facts as may be supposed to be of special practical interest.

First of all, the medical officer should weigh well in his own mind the nature of the disease for which a soldier applies for a certificate of discharge, or inability to perform duty. If the case is one of recent standing, it will be well not to come to too hasty a conclusion as to its diagnosis; it should be ex-

amined and re-examined before any definite opinion is given.
Day by day facts may be developed revealing the true character of the affection. If the patient is really sick, or affected
with some serious chronic disorder, his general appearance
will hardly fail to afford some evidence of its existence. The
pallor of the countenance, the functional disturbance of the
suffering organ, the bodily prostration, the want of appetite,
and the gradual emaciation, will almost unerringly point to
the nature and seat of the disease. When, on the other
hand, the malady is simulated, all, or nearly all, the usual
phenomena of disease will be absent. Impostors, moreover,
are generally very zealous in talking about their disorders, or
in obtruding them upon the notice of their surgeons; whereas those who are really sick and suffering make comparatively
little complaint. A malingerer may often be detected by
carefully watching his movements, coming suddenly upon him
when he is asleep, or when his attention is directed to some
one else, tickling his foot when he feigns paralysis, or pricking his back when he pretends to be laboring under lumbago.
Sometimes a determined threat will promptly restore him to a
sense of his duty, as the application of the actual cautery in
incontinence of urine, rheumatism of the joints, or mental
imbecility. Now and then the exhibition, in rapidly repeated
doses, of a nauseous draught, answers the purpose. Whatever expedients be employed, the surgeon cannot exercise too
much address, otherwise he will be almost sure to be baffled.

Mental alienation, or *mania*, unless the result of inebria-
tion and of acute disease, generally comes on gradually, being
preceded by a marked change in the moral character of the
individual, loss of appetite and sleep, and other evidences of
general disorder.

Genuine *deafness* is also gradual in its approaches, and,
when fully established, is invariably attended by a peculiar
listless state of the countenance with more or less change of
the voice. Before a final decision is given, a careful inspec-
tion of the ears should be made, to ascertain whether there is

any obstruction or appearance of matter. The unexpected discharge of a pistol, in a case of feigned deafness, might suddenly decide the diagnosis.

Amaurosis may be simulated by the internal use of belladonna, or by the direct application of this article to the eye, causing dilatation and immobility of the pupil. These effects are often accompanied by unnatural vascularity of the conjunctiva, and they generally disappear spontaneously in a few days. In genuine amaurosis, too, there is always a dilated condition of the vessels of the eye.

Feigned *epilepsy* differs from the real in the absence of lividity of the countenance, the want of froth at the mouth, and the partial character of the convulsions. The pupil does not contract, as in the genuine disease, the general sensibility is unimpaired, the tongue is not injured, the nails are not discolored, the hand, if opened, is again firmly shut, and the individual often watches with his eye the impression the attack is making upon the by-standers. The application of a heated case-knife, or of a cloth wrung out of hot water, often speedily reveals the imposition.

Paralysis is frequently imitated, but is generally easily detected, simply by watching the patient, tickling his feet when he is asleep, or threatening him with the hot iron. The disease, when it attacks the lower extremity, is nearly always caused by apoplexy, and is then generally associated with mental weakness and difficulty of articulation. Partial paralysis of the upper extremity is frequently induced by lying upon the arm, by suppression of the cutaneous perspiration, and disease of the spinal cord.

Hæmet-mesis may be simulated by swallowing blood, or an infusion of logwood, and ejecting the fluid afterward by vomiting. It should be recollected that the real disease is almost invariably connected with serious organic lesion, as ulceration of the stomach, induration and enlargement of the liver, or visceral obstruction, and that the patient, consequently, will exhibit all the characteristics of a sick person.

Soldiers sometimes counterfeit *hæmoptysis*, by cutting the gums, or chewing substances impregnated with coloring matter. A case is related by Guthrie, in which a man, for this purpose, swallowed a piece of cork full of pins. The immediate effect was hæmoptysis, and the remote one death, by wounding the carotid artery.

Gastritis may be simulated by spontaneous vomiting, a faculty possessed by some persons, and by pretended pain in the epigastric region. The attack in general speedily yields to a large sinapism and a brisk emetic.

Dysentery and *diarrhœa* are occasionally feigned by exciting, artificially, irritation of the rectum, by mixing blood with the alvine evacuations, or by borrowing the discharges of persons actually affected with these diseases. In genuine dysentery and diarrhœa there are always well-marked constitutional phenomena, which are of course absent in the spurious. Careful watching of the patient, and compelling him to use a close stool, will soon remove any doubt that may exist respecting the nature of the case.

Disease of the *heart*, in the form of palpitation, may, it is said, be produced by the use of hellebore. Mr. Hutchinson, of England, refers to an epidemic of this kind among the members of the Marine Artillery. Organic cardiac disease could easily be detected with the stethoscope.

Rheumatism being a very common disease among soldiers, is often counterfeited; but the cheat is of easy detection when it is recollected that the real affection, especially the acute form, is attended with more or less swelling and constitutional disturbance.

When *lumbago* is made the subject of deception, the attack seldom long withstands the application of rash remedies, or the threatened use, if speedy relief do not arise, of the hot iron.

Contraction of the *joints*, a not unfrequent source of imposition, is easily detected by the use of anæsthetics, or simply by pricking the parts suddenly with a needle, when the patient is off his guard.

When *wry-neck* is simulated, both the sterno-cleido-mastoid muscles are rendered rigid by the effort at deception; whereas in the real disease the contraction is confined to one side.

Incontinence of urine, bloody urine, and stone in the bladder, have all been simulated by designing soldiers. The former is said to be at times epidemic, and then its detection is of course easy, as the ordinary disease never assumes such a character. Harsh remedies are the best means of relief. Ballingall states that fictitious cases of incontinence have been successfully treated by the cold bath, by prescribing a few lashes on the loins, with the avowed object of strengthening the parts. In the Austrian army the imposter is obliged to do duty with a urinal.

Bloody urine has been provoked by injecting blood into the bladder, and by scarifying the urethra.

Calculus is almost unknown among soldiers; it is sometimes attempted to be counterfeited by scraping the walls and throwing the lime into the urinal. When stone actually exists, the sound will generally promptly detect it.

Self-inflicted *injuries* of various kinds are resorted to for the purpose of deception. Thus malingerers often provoke inflammation of the eye and temporary opacity of the cornea by means of corrosive sublimate, lime, tobacco, nitrate of silver, and other irritants. A great number of men have been known to suffer from this cause at the same time, as if the disease was an epidemic. Ulcers of the legs are produced by pricking the skin with pins or needles, frictions with sand, or caustic applications. Œdema of the limbs may be excited by tight ligatures; disease of the scrotum and testicle, by inflation of the parts with air. All such tricks are usually readily detected by the medical officer and his assistants.

Self-mutilation sometimes amounts to the destruction of an eye, an entire finger, or even the greater portion of the hand.

Occasionally it is limited to slight wounds, and the imposition may then be practiced on an extensive scale, as was the case in the French army at the battles of Lutzen and Bautzen, in which nearly 3000 soldiers were slightly injured in the hand, causing the belief that the wounds had been voluntarily inflicted.

CHAPTER XIII.

MEDICAL, SURGICAL AND DIETETIC FORMULÆ.

Under this head I propose to notice such formulæ, or medical, surgical, and dietetic preparations, as have been found serviceable in my own practice, or in the practice of others.

1.—*General Remedies.*

Among the more simple *purgatives* may be mentioned the following: all drastic articles should, if possible, be excluded from the prescriptions of the military surgeon:—

　　R.—Massæ ex Hydrargy. gr. x;
　　　　Pulv. Ipecac. gr. i.
　　M. ft. pil. ii.

A mild laxative in dyspepsia and disorders of the stomach and liver.

　　R.—Extr. Colocynth. c;
　　　　Massæ ex Hydrargy.
　　　　Pulv. Rhei. v. Jalapæ, aa gr. x;
　　　　Ant. et. Potassæ Tart. gr. $\frac{1}{16}$.
　　M. ft. pil v.

An active, antibilious purgative, from three to five being an ordinary dose. Calomel may be substituted for the blue mass, if there is much disorder of the liver and secretions.

The safest *emetics* are ipecacuanha, infusion of eupatorium perfoliatum, and mustard and common salt, an even tablespoonful of each to half a pint of tepid water, one-half to be taken at once, the remainder, if necessary, in fifteen minutes. Sulphate of copper or zinc will afford the most prompt emetic effect in case of great urgency, as in poisoning.

The following formula will be found very serviceable in the earlier stages of most inflammatory affections, especially the cutaneous, articular, and traumatic, unaccompanied by disease of the alimentary canal:

R.—Ant et Potass. Tart. gr. iss;
    Magnesiæ Sulph. ℥i;
    Morphiæ Sulph. gr. ss;
    Sacch. Albi. ℨii.
    Aquæ Destil. ℥vi. M.

This is the antimonial and saline mixture, of which repeated mention occurs in the preceding pages, and which I am in the daily habit of prescribing in my surgical as well as medical practice. It may be rendered depressant by the addition, to each dose,—which is half an ounce, repeated every two or three hours,—of from three to eight drops of the tincture of veratrum viride; anodyne, or diaphoretic, by laudanum, or morphia; anti-periodic, by quinine; anti-gonorrhœal, by copaiba, gum-arabic being used, in the latter case, as one of the ingredients; and anti-rheumatic, by colchicum. If quinine be used, the addition of aromatic sulphuric acid will be required, which is also an excellent solvent of the salts.

R.—Vini Colchici Sem. ℨi;
    Morphiæ Sulph. gr. ss;
    Potassæ Carbon. gr. x;
    Aquæ Destil. ℥ss. M.

In rheumatic and gouty affections, taken at bedtime, and followed by a mild aperient next morning.

The following will be found to be pleasant and efficient *diaphoretics* :—

R.—Spirit. Mindereri, ℥iv;
    Sp. Æther, Nitrici. ℨii;
    Morphiæ Acet. gr. i. M. S.

Tablespoonful every two or three hours. If there be much
heat of surface, we may. add to each dose the eighth, twelfth
or fifteenth of a grain of tartar emetic.

  R.—Potassæ Carbon. ʒi ;
    Morphiæ Sulph. gr. i ;
    Sacch. Albi. ʒii ;
    Suc. Limonis recent. ℥ii ;
    Aquæ Menth. v. Destil. ℥iiiss.
    Sp. Æther. Nitrici. ℥ss. M. S.

Tablespoonful every hour or two.

 The effervescing draught, so valuable in irritability of the
stomach, is composed as follows :—

  R.—Suc. Limonis recent. ℥ji ;
    Sacch. Albi. ʒjiss;
    Aquæ Destil. ℥ij. M.
  R.—Potassæ Carbon. ʒi ;
    Aquæ Destil. ℥ij. M.

Put two tablespoonfuls of the lemonade with one of the alka-
line solution, and let the mixture be drunk while effervescing,
repeating the dose at pleasure.

 As *antiperiodics* quinine and arsenic are the main reliance
of the modern practitioner. The former may be given by
itself, in pill or solution, in doses varying from two to ten
grains, according to the urgency of the case or the state of
the system. My usual dose is ten grains every eight, ten, or
twelve hours, until the paroxysm is arrested. If the symptoms are unusually violent, we need not hesitate to administer
fifteen or even twenty grains at a dose, being of course careful
to watch the effects, which will generally be more pleasant if
a little morphia be combined with the quinine.

 In chronic, or frequently recurring intermittent and neu-
ralgic affections, arsenic forms a valuable, and, indeed, in
many cases, an indispensable addition ; also iron, if there be
evidences of anæmia. I prefer myself the arsenious acid to
Fowler's solution, convinced that it is much more efficacious

and at the same time less apt to cause nausea and anasarca. The following formula will be found advantageous :

R.—Acid. Arseniosi, gr. iss ;
 Quiniæ Sulph.
 Ferri Sulph aa ʒi ;
 Morphiæ Sulph. gr. i ;
 Extr. Nucis Vomicæ, Ɖi.
 M. ft pil. xxx
 S. One every five, six or eight hours.

Quinine is also one of the best *tonics*, and it may always be beneficially combined with other articles, as iron, gentian, quassia, nux vomica, and capsicum. The fluid extracts and aromatic tinctures of bark and gentian will also be found useful. One of the best chalybeate preparations is the tincture of the chloride of iron, in doses of from twenty to twenty-five drops three or four times daily.

Expectorants constitute a large class of remedial agents, but they nearly all derive their active principles from the admixture of tartar emetic, ipecacuanha, or squills. They may generally be usefully combined with potassa and anodynes, being rendered palatable by syrup or sugar.

Nurses should be familiar with the manner of administering *enemata* or injections, as frequent occasions arise for their employment. They may be cathartic, as when they are designed to empty the lower bowel, or to promote the action of other remedies; stimulant, as in case of excessive exhaustion; nutritive, as when food cannot be taken by the mouth; anodyne, when it is wished to allay pain and induce sleep.

A *cathartic* effect may readily be induced by an injection of a pint and a half of cold water, or water in which a little ground mustard or common salt has been stirred, a mixture of warm water and castor oil, or an infusion of senna, or senna and Epsom salts. Turpentine is particularly indicated when the bowels are distended with flatus.

Stimulating injections may be made of brandy, alcohol, mustard, salt, or spirits of camphor or turpentine, mixed with more or less water; and they are often extremely serviceable in promoting reaction.

Nutritive enemata may be necessary in the low stages of fever, and in gunshot and other injuries attended with lesion of the gullet. The best ingredients are essence of beef, strong beef-tea, brandy, or brandy and milk, introduced in small quantity, so as not to oppress and irritate the rectum.

Anodyne injections may consist of laudanum, black drop, morphia, hyoscyamus, or belladonna, either alone, or variously combined, and administered with about two ounces of tepid water, or some demulcent fluid.

The best *syringe* now in use is the gutta-percha, which is not liable to be deranged, and which has the additional advantage of durability. It should be of various capacities, from eight to sixteen ounces, according to the intention to be fulfilled by it. The nozzle must be well oiled previously to its introduction, and care taken that no air be pushed into the bowel.

2.—*Topical Remedies.*

R.—Tinct. Iodinæ,
     Sp. Vini Rectific. aa ℥j. M.
To be applied with a large camel-hair pencil, or cloth mop. I hardly ever use the pure tincture of iodine for local purposes.

R.—Plumbi Subacet. ℥j;
     Pulv. Opii, ʒi. M.
To be put in half a gallon of *hot* water, and the solution to be used warm or cold, as may be deemed best. Laudanum may be substituted for the opium.

R.—Pulv. Ammoniæ Hydrochlor. ℥j;
     " Potassæ Nitrat. ʒij;
     " Opii, ʒj. M.
To be used as the preceding; being particularly valuable in inflammation of the joints, on unbroken surfaces.

The *warm water-dressing* consists of warm water, simple or

medicated with laudanum, acetate of lead, or any other ingredient that may be desired, applied upon flannel or muslin cloths, properly folded, and covered with oiled silk, to confine heat and moisture.

The *cold water-dressing* is composed of cold water, also simple or medicated, applied with cloths, the parts being constantly exposed to the air to prevent evaporation. The cloths are to be wet whenever they become heated or dryish, the water being pressed upon them from a sponge.

Water-dressings, if long continued, will occasionally cause irritation, itching, and pustulation of the skin, rendering it necessary to replace them with cataplasms, or other soothing remedies.

Among *poultices* decidedly the best, for ordinary purposes, are the flaxseed and slippery elm. The former is made by mixing a suitable quantity of linseed meal with hot, or, what is still better, boiling water, and rapidly stirring it into a thick mush-like consistence. The mixture is then spread upon a fold of cloth, in a layer a third of an inch thick, when it is covered with bobinet or gauze to prevent it from adhering to the parts. A piece of oiled silk, larger than the poultice, is placed upon its outer surface, to retain heat and moisture.

The elm, and, in fact, all other cataplasms, are prepared and used upon the same principles as the linseed. Like water-dressings, poultices may be simple or medicated, according to the object proposed. They should be changed at least twice, or, in warm weather, even three or four times in the twenty-four hours.

Adhesive plaster is cut, in the direction of its length, into strips of suitable length and breadth, warmed by holding the backs against a smooth vessel, as a pitcher or tin case, and applied in such a manner as to bring the middle of each piece over the wound, the edges of which are, meanwhile, carefully supported by an assistant. A suitable space is left between the strips for drainage. If things progress favorably, substitution need not be made under three or four days. If the wound be large, only a few of the strips are taken off at a time, lest, all support being lost, the edges should be forcibly separated.

Before the soiled dressings are removed, everything intended for the new should be prepared, or put in its proper place. The strips of plaster must be removed with great gentleness.

If the injured parts are covered with hair, the surface must always be shaved before the application of the dressings.

Proper material for *sutures* should always be kept on hand, ready for use. The silver wire is the best, as it is less irritating than any other. Silk, however, answers exceedingly well; the thread should be rather thin, and be well waxed. Saddler's silk is the article used for the ligation of large arteries.

Among the more common and useful *unguents* for dressing wounds, burns, abraded surfaces, or fissures, are the following :

   R.—Pulv. Opii, $\mathfrak{z}$ss ;
    Pulv. Rhei, $\ni$i ;
    Ung. Cetacei, $\mathfrak{z}$i. M.

To these ingredients may advantageously be added, in many cases of healing sores, or eruptions, requiring a mild stimulus, a drachm of the ointment of the nitrate of mercury, a few drops of nitric acid, two drachms of ointment of acetate of lead, a small quantity of myrrh, or of balsam of Peru, or from six to eight grains of sulphate of quinine.

   R.—Ung. Cetacei, $\mathfrak{z}$j ;
    Bismuth. Subnitr. $\mathfrak{z}$ij. M.

Extremely soothing and valuable in superficial excoriations, slight burns, and eczematous affections. Turner's cerate may be employed for similar purposes, but should always be considerably diluted.

The best *disinfectants* are the chloride of soda, chloride of lime, Labarraque's solution and the hypermanganate of potassa, of which an abundant supply should always be on hand in every hospital, free use of it being made, by sprinkling and otherwise, upon the dressings, as well as upon the bedding and the rooms.

The *sponges* about a hospital should be of the softest kind, perfectly clean, and always ready for use. The same articles should never be employed upon different persons, especially where there are foul or specific sores, as contagion might thus be communicated by direct inoculation, as has, for example, so often happened during the prevalence of hospital gangrene.

3.—*Dietetic Preparations.*

The diet of the sick-room has slain its thousands and tens of thousands. Broths, and slops, and jellies, and custards, and ptisans are usually as disgusting as they are pernicious. Men worn out by disease and injury must have nutritious and concentrated food. The ordinary preparations for the sick are, in general, not only nutritious, but insipid and flatulent. Nitrogenous food is what is needed, even if the quantity taken be very small. Animal soups are among the most efficient supporters of the exhausted system, and every medical man should know how to give directions for their preparation. The life of a man is his food. Solid articles are, of course, withheld in acute diseases, in their earlier stages, but when the patient begins to convalesce they are frequently borne with impunity, and greatly promote recovery. All animal soups should be made of lean meat; and their nutritious properties, as well as their flavor, may be much increased by the addition of some vegetable substance, as rice or barley. If the stomach is very weak, they may be diluted, or seasoned with pepper.

Essence of beef, so frequently given in the low stages of fever, and in the exhaustion consequent upon severe injuries and operations, is prepared by cutting from a quarter to half a pound of lean beef into thin pieces, and putting it into a wide-mouthed porter bottle, corked tightly, and placed in a kettle of cold water, which is then heated till it boils. After

it has been digested in this way for a
decanted, and seasoned with salt and

Beef tea, much less nourishing t
by putting a quarter of a pound o
half of water, and boiling it for
of mace being added during th
skimmed.

To make *chicken broth* requ
quart of cold water, with a t
whole being slowly boiled
proper skimming.

Chicken jelly is prepared
all the bones broken, in a
tained in boiling water for t
is then strained, and season

Vegetable soup is compo
and a piece of bread, witl
pint in a closely-covered v
introduced near the close
are added at pleasure.

To form *rice jelly* a
twice that quantity of
water, until the whole
jelly is strained off and

Sago jelly is compo
quart of water, juice a
to render it agreeable.
hour, it is boiled until
the mass being constant

Oatmeal gruel is cor
meal and a half pint o
water, and allowed to
strained through a hai
a similar manner.

Arrow-root pap cr
substance made into a

of boiling water, and kept on the fire
nourishing properties of arrow-root
by using milk instead of water in its

relished by the sick; and there is
valids made of a thinly sliced and
iled in a quart of water until it
n it should be strained upon a

various dietetic preparations
increased by the addition of
When salt, or salt and pepper
should be consulted. Great
g these compounds that they
a double boiler should be

when a stimulant is re-
, is made by mixing good
proportion of about one
f the latter. Sugar and
xture palatable.
ered of great service to
to a pint of fresh milk,
as much good Madeira
ixture is then strained

leira, Port and Sherry.
ne sometimes produces
h as well as the system

te and yolk of which
f cold water with a
with two tablespoon-

s: Now printing from the

CPSIA information can be obtained
at www.ICGtesting.com
Printed in the USA
LVHW081910060323
741056LV00004B/60